D1598246

❧ *Emerson and the Climates of History*

Emerson and the Climates of History

%& Eduardo Cadava

Stanford University Press, Stanford, California 1997

Stanford University Press, Stanford, California
© 1997 by the Board of Trustees of
the Leland Stanford Junior University

Printed in the United States of America

CIP data appear at the end of the book

Stanford University Press publications are distributed exclusively
by Stanford University Press within the United States,
Canada, Mexico, and Central America; they are distributed
exclusively by Cambridge University Press
throughout the rest of the world.

For my mother and father

✆ Acknowledgments

As Emerson tells us in the early pages of his first book, we are never solitary while we read and write, even when we are alone. Suggesting that the solitude that characterizes our work is always composed of several voices—not the least of which are all the voices of the friends, colleagues, and books that countersign our thoughts and work—he reminds us that the same responsibility that binds us to others also asks that we reveal the traces of our appropriations. These appropriations can be registered most easily when it is a matter of explicit citation, when we let an other speak in the text "with more or less visible quotation marks," but they are also legible when, without even knowing it, without knowing where we are going when we speak, we repeat or let an other speak. The incalculability of all the influences that make us who we are, that give our language its signature, names the climate within which we exist, think, and write.

Like the writings of Antiphanes, which he compared to "a city where the words froze in the air as soon as they were pronounced and the next summer, when they were warmed and melted by the sun, people heard what had been spoken in the winter," this book is a palimpsestic record of the several atmospheres within which it was written. As such, it bears the traces of a community of friends and colleagues whose readings and comments at various stages of this project have been indispensable to my thinking about Emerson and the politics of his linguistic and meteorological reflections. I have benefited especially from discussions with Lauren Berlant, Mitchell Breitwieser, Homer O. Brown, Eric Cheyfitz, Peter Connor, Karin Cope,

Kelly Dennis, Ed Dryden, Emory Elliott, Diana Fuss, Chris Fynsk, Bill Gleason, Anke Gleber, Stathis Gourgouris, Jerrold Hogle, Walter Hughes, George Kateb, Joseph Kronick, Kathryne Lindberg, David Lloyd, Jim McMichael, Elissa Marder, Donald Pease, Guy Pollio, Arnold Rampersad, Dan Rogers, Avital Ronell, Charles Sherry, Timothy Sweet, Harvey Teres, Jane Tompkins, Cornel West, Patricia Williams, Barbara Wuest, and Laura Zakarin.

I would like to give special thanks to John Carlos Rowe, who has perhaps seen these pages transform more than anyone else and whose generous energy will be readable by everyone who has been fortunate enough to benefit from his rigor and gifts as a teacher and scholar. His own Emerson has been the provocation and challenge without which mine would never have been invented. I would also like to express my gratitude to Eugenio Donato and Joseph Riddel, whose untimely deaths prevented them from seeing this project through to its end. Always letting me go wherever I felt obliged to go, Eugenio Donato was one of those rare teachers who wish not to teach his students how to read and think like him, but instead, like him, to read and think. I thank him for his love of thought. Joseph Riddel's encouragement and friendship often moved me to intellectual sites I never thought I would visit. He supported this project from its inception and his own example as an "American Scholar" led me to believe that questions of history could never be approached away from a thinking of language.

I wish to thank the University of California, the National Endowment for the Humanities, the Ford Foundation, and Princeton University for the fellowship and research support without which this book could never have been finished. I would also like to thank the staffs at the Boston Public Library, the Houghton Library at Harvard University, and Firestone Library at Princeton University for all of their assistance throughout this project.

Portions of this book have appeared in earlier versions in *Arizona Quarterly* (autumn 1993) and *boundary 2* (summer 1994). I am grateful to the editors for their permission to reprint this material.

I want to thank Helen Tartar for everything that she is: a fabulous editor, a thoughtful, perceptive, and warm human being. Her enthusiasm and support for this work have been breathtaking, and her patience, openness, and generosity throughout the project have been exemplary. I thank her for her willing and scrupulous attention to the manuscript. I thank her for her wonderful ear. I thank her for her friendship.

Emerson once said, "There are some purposes we delay long to execute simply because we have them more at heart than others." I refer here to my wish to thank those people whose love and support has been the strongest reason for finishing this book. I want to thank my mother and father, whose faith in me is a blessing I will never take for granted. This book is for them, with my profound gratitude for everything that they have given me; my son, Gerry, whose love and patience during times when he must have wondered why I was spending more time with Ralph Waldo than with him are a source of joy for me; and Liana, whose love and friendship helped me finish a project that never wanted to end. Her being has touched every one of these pages. It is through her that I have begun to understand how to conduct my life. I mention these debts here, but I know that, being the greatest of all, they must be answered in other places, in other ways.

Contents

❧ Abbreviations

The following abbreviations have been used for frequently cited works. Citations are given by volume number (where relevant) and page.

Works by Emerson:

AS   *Emerson's Antislavery Writings*. Ed. Len Gougeon and Joel Myerson. New Haven: Yale University Press, 1995.

EL   *The Early Lectures of Ralph Waldo Emerson*. Ed. Stephen E. Whicher, Robert E. Spiller, and Wallace E. Williams. 3 vols. Cambridge: Harvard University Press, 1961.

J   *The Journals and Miscellaneous Notebooks of Ralph Waldo Emerson*. Ed. William H. Gilman, et al. 16 vols. to date. Cambridge: Harvard University Press, 1960–.

L   *The Letters of Ralph Waldo Emerson*. Ed. Ralph L. Rusk. 6 vols. New York: Columbia University Press, 1939.

W   *The Complete Works of Ralph Waldo Emerson*. Ed. Edward Waldo Emerson. 12 vols. Centenary Edition. Boston: Houghton Mifflin, 1903–4.

Works by other writers:

AR   Thomas Paine. *The Age of Reason*. Ed. Philip S. Foner. Secaucus, N.J.: Citadel Press, 1974.

To confront American culture is to feel oneself encircled by a thin but strong presence: a mist, a cloud, a climate. I call it Emersonian, an imprecise term but one that directs us to a dominant spirit in the national experience. Hoping to engage that spirit, I am not sure that anyone can even grasp it. How grasp the very air we breathe?

—Irving Howe, *The American Newness*

🎐 "We Cannot Write the Order of the Variable Winds"

> This book may need more than one preface, and in the end there would still remain room for doubt whether anyone who had never lived through similar experiences could be brought closer to the *experience* of this book by means of prefaces. It seems to be written in the language of the wind that thaws ice and snow: high spirits, unrest, contradiction, and April weather are present in it, and one is instantly reminded no less of the proximity of winter than of the triumph over the winter that is coming, must come, and perhaps has already come.
>
> —Nietzsche, *The Gay Science* (1887)

There is no sentence in Emerson that is not touched by the weather. This is not to say that every sentence in Emerson mentions the weather explicitly, but rather to suggest that each of his sentences is touched by the successive changes in direction, the shifting and transitory movement, that we associate with the signature of the weather. Like the weather, Emerson's writing moves and happens according to the rhythms and crises of its own atmospheres, storms, and pressure zones. Like the weather, whose variable and unpredictable nature makes it difficult to circumscribe, the gestures of his writing—the diverse and contradictory mobility of their analytical incursions, the excesses and intuitions of their diagnoses—resist, from the very beginning, all our efforts to bring together or stabilize whatever we might call his "thought." To say this is to suggest that Emerson's recourse to climatic and meteorological imagery is always more than a mere motif or theme in his writing. If his writing can never avoid its meteorological figures—from the sun and wind and snow that close his first book, *Nature*, to the summer that opens his "Divinity School Address," from the snow puddle on which he becomes a transparent eyeball to the snow and clouds and rain that shower the end of "The Poet," from "the impressions of the actual world" that fall on us "like summer rain" to the winds and thunder and lightning, the mists and snowstorms that trace the movement of our "Illusions"— it is because this has been his way of telling us what it is. Emerson's writings are themselves a kind of weather. We could even say that they come to us in the form of the weather.

This focus on the weather may help us account for Emerson's obsession throughout his writings with the relation between the permanent and the transitory. Like the weather, whose cyclical and repetitive character is joined always to its unpredictability and constant alteration, his language works to trace the permanency of the infinite variability that makes nature nature. As he explains in his essay "History," "Nature is a mutable cloud which is always and never the same," "an endless combination and repetition of a very few laws" (*W*, 2: 13, 15). If his writings oscillate between the values of eternity and those of transformation, it is because what is at stake for him is the possibility of registering a movement whose persistent return belongs to the movement of transition, metamorphosis, and fugacity that names the always-shifting conditions of our historical existence. "We are the changing inhabitants of a changing world," he writes in a journal entry from 1827. "The night & the day, the ebbing and flowing of the tide, the round of the seasons, the waxing & waning moon, the flux & reflux of the arts & of the civilization of nations & the swift and sad succession of human generations, these are the monitors among which we live" (*J*, 3: 72–73). "The things we now esteem fixed," he says elsewhere, "shall, one by one, detach themselves, like ripe fruit, from our experience, and fall. The wind shall blow them none knows whither. The landscape, the figures, Boston, London, are facts as fugitive as any institution past, or any whiff of mist or smoke, and so is society, and so is the world" (*W*, 2: 274). The transitoriness of both nature and history can be said to be inscribed within the movement of Emerson's own language. What characterizes this language is the way in which its figures are always "in transit, always passing into something else," always emerging only in order to disappear (*W*, 8: 4). The shifting movement, the rapid transitions that we have always associated with Emerson's language, can be read in terms of his wish to remain faithful to something that is always about to vanish, his desire to practice what he called "the art of perpetual retreating and reference" (*W*, 3: 46).

This transit between the evanescence of nature and that of language can be read everywhere in Emerson, but he makes the link between what he calls "the method of nature" and the possibility of his writing in general when he suggests that we are to "study the mind in nature, because we cannot steadily gaze on it in mind; as we explore the face of the sun in a pool, when our eyes cannot brook his direct splendors." "It seems to me," he goes on to say, that if we should "celebrate this hour by exploring the *method of nature*," we should "see *that*, as nearly as we can, and try how far it is transferable to the literary life" (*W*, 1: 197). Emerson's entire corpus can be read as both an effort to realize this transfer and a means of registering the consequences of such a transfer—one of which is the difficulty of our being able to bring nature and writing together within a particular configuration or thought. By the term "configuration" I refer to the systematic organization of a work or corpus around a particular meaning, purpose, or feature. If Emerson suggests that we explore the method of nature, it is not in order to encourage us to understand it within one thought, but rather to ask us to respect its irreducible and singular multiplicity. As he explains in "The Method of Nature":

The method of nature: who could ever analyze it? That rushing stream will not stop to be observed. We can never surprise nature in a corner; never find the end of a thread; never tell where to set the first stone. . . . The wholeness we admire in the order of the world, is the result of infinite distribution. Its smoothness is the smoothness of the pitch of the cataract. Its permanence is a perpetual inchoation. Every natural fact is an emanation, and that from which it emanates is an emanation also, and from every emanation is a new emanation. If anything could stand still, it would be crushed and dissipated by the torrent it resisted, and if it were a mind, would be crazed; as insane persons are those who hold fast to one thought, and do not flow with the course of nature. (*W*, 1: 199)

What is said here of the method of nature can be said of every word or sentence in Emerson's corpus—and not only because, as he tells us in "Poetry and Imagination," "all things in Nature" have "a mysterious relation to his thoughts and life," or because the "world is an immense picture-book of every passage in human life," but also because "natural objects" are "like words in a sentence" (*W*, 8: 8–9). Nature is in fact always another name for writing in Emerson. "Nature will be reported," he explains, "all things are engaged in writing their history. The planet, the pebble, goes attended by its shadow. The rolling rock leaves its scratches on the mountain; the river, its channel in the soil. . . . Not a foot steps into the snow, or along the ground, but prints, in character more or less lasting, a map of its march. . . . In nature, this self-registration is incessant" (*W*, 4: 261– 62). If the method of nature belongs to the movement of Emerson's words, however, it is also because of their shared capacity to mark a certain limit. Both indicate the limit of thinking in general—not a limit fixed by external boundaries or assigned to it, not one imposed from elsewhere, but the limit that thinking encounters within itself. This limit already is inscribed within the movement of the weather. Like the movement of Emerson's writing, the tendency of nature to incline or drift away from understanding can be read in the word *climate*. Derived from the ancient Greek word *klima*, it refers not only to a latitudinal zone of the earth but also to an inclination or slope. Climate therefore refers to both what falls from the sky and what falls away from understanding. Referring to whatever is incalculable and uncontrollable, it is at times another word for chance and time.

If nature is a form of writing that registers what passes, that carries the past within its movement, this is because, as Emerson suggests, every natural fact is an emanation that bears not only the past and the present but also the future. A palimpsest of several figural levels from several different moments, nature becomes an apt description of Emerson's language, which always can be shown to be composed of other language. Like each natural fact, which transforms, even as it emerges from, the one before it, his language works to move itself beyond itself to other places. His figures are evoked only to be transformed by their relation to different figures. This entanglement among past, present, and future is what enables language to give way to singular events. It confirms that language always refers to something other than itself, to language as something other. Belonging to the principle of transformation, which takes its point of departure from what it seeks to overcome, it tells us that both nature and writing are born out of the past. "*Panta rei*: all things are in flux," Emerson writes, citing Heraclitus, "It is inevitable that you are indebted to the past":

You are fed and formed by it. The old forest is decomposed for the composition of the new forest. The old animals have given their bodies to the earth to furnish through chemistry the forming race, and every individual is only a momentary fixation of what was yesterday another's, is today his and will belong to a third to-morrow. So it is in thought. Our knowledge is the amassed thought and experience of innumerable minds: our language, our science, our religion, our opinions, our fancies we inherited. Our country, customs, laws, our ambitions, and our notions of fit and fair,—all these we never made, we found them ready-made; we but quote them. Goethe frankly said, "What would remain to me if this art of appropriation were derogatory to genius? Every one of my writings has been furnished to me by a thousand different persons, a thousand things. . . . My work is an aggregate of beings taken from the whole of Nature; it bears the name of Goethe." (*W*, 8: 200)

That the transitive character of nature and thought belongs to the transit between the past and the present within which something new is produced means that we must always pass through our inheritance in order to invent our future. In other words, the new can only be new, really new, if it is produced through memory and repetition— but a memory and repetition which at the same time introduce a new element. This is why, when Emerson tells us that "our debt to tradition through reading and conversation is so massive . . . that, in a large sense, one would say there is no pure originality" (*W*, 8: 178), he wishes to suggest the difficulty we encounter in trying to overcome inherited representations, the fact that there can be no transformation that does not involve an "art of appropriation" that displaces other language. "We cannot overstate our debt to the Past," he explains, "but the moment has the supreme claim. The Past is for us; but the sole terms on which it can become ours are its subordination to the Present. Only an inventor knows how to borrow" (*W*, 8: 204).

    If we can take these statements as the beginning articulations of a protocol for reading Emerson—he does claim in "The American Scholar" that "there is a right way of reading" (*W*, 1: 91)—we might suggest that what is at stake in reading him is the possibility of our being able to trace the way in which he mobilizes terms from one shifting context to another. It is in this mobilization that we can perhaps begin to measure his engagement with changing historical and political relations, with a process of transformation, wherein his language works to change further the shifting domains of history and politics, and wherein the traces of the historical and the political are inscribed within the movement of this language. If his language seeks to transform language, then, it does so in order to transform the relations within which we live.

The possibility of such transformation, however, involves a risk: the risk we all take when we borrow the language of structures we wish to overcome—the risk of having our critical position toward any particular form of cultural authority be appropriated and neutralized by the dominant culture we set out to question. This appropriation can happen because repetition belongs to the conditions of what is not yet thought, to the conditions, that is, of all possible futures. If this risk cannot be avoided, it is because it inhabits the possibility of transformation in general. To put it another way, if we are to lessen the chances that we will simply repeat the structures of authority we seek to change, we must try to understand the genealogy of the language we use—we must try to understand the history that is sealed within this language and which, if not taken into account, may align us without our knowing it with positions we oppose. This is not to say that, in order for this transformation to be effective, for something new to be produced, we must have a certain form of historical understanding (that, for example, of a certain kind of knowledge of American history), but according to Emerson, such understanding increases the chances that we will not merely repeat the past. This is why, in accordance with his experience of writing, he suggests that a writer must be concerned with the past, that of literature, history, philosophy, culture, and nature in general (*W*, 1: 93). It is only by measuring the extent to which he is inscribed within a particular genealogy that he can consider himself a responsible heir of the past. It is only by giving an account of the past, of the past as it survives in the present, that he can begin to provide for a future.

This may help to explain Emerson's voracious reading—which ranged in all directions. He read new and old books. He read horticultural journals, political speeches, literary and philosophical writings, books on history and religion, on geology and all aspects of the earth sciences, on anatomy and racial science, on astronomy and science in general. We could say that the library in his head contained a miniaturized history of the America in which he lived and of the world in general. And from almost everything he read, Robert Richardson notes, "he culled phrases, details, facts, metaphors, anecdotes, witticisms, aphorisms, and ideas. He kept this energetic reading and excerpting up for over forty years; the vast system of his personal notebooks and indexes—including indexes to indexes—eventually reached over 230 volumes. . . . The notebooks were in part his storehouse of original writing and in part a filing system, designed to store and give him access to the accumulating fruits of this reading on every topic that ever interested him throughout his life." [1] These notebooks also help to account for a method of composition that consists largely in the recirculation of passages drawn from their pages. This recirculation belongs to Emerson's effort to produce something new, to give a new direction and purpose to fragments of the past. "Every word we speak," he says, "is million-faced or convertible to an indefinite number of applications. If it were not so we could read no book. Your remark would only fit your case, not mine" (*J*, 8: 157). It is because, as he puts it elsewhere, "each age must write its own books" that there must be "creative reading as well as creative writing" (*W*, 1: 88, 93). If the effort to transform history requires an act of reading and writing that works to revise past texts to meet present needs, [2] we can begin to trace Emerson's engagement with history and politics in terms of the changes he effects on the language he inherits. That is to say, the performativity at work within his language calls for the same responsibility in his readers. It requires a work of reading that is also a labor of invention.

In what follows, I have tried to remain faithful to this obligation. In order to begin to read Emerson's relation to history and politics, I have tried to remain as close as possible to the movements of his language. I have wanted to trace the ways in which, in their movement, his words and sentences not only open onto the history inscribed within them but also work to engage already-changing historical and political relations. In the process, I have tried to take seriously three of Emerson's claims: first, that "in good writing every word means something" (*J*, 3: 271); second, that words and sentences do not have any worth by themselves but only in relation to other words and sentences (*J*, 13: 352); and third, that when we read creatively—that is, rightly—the meaning of any given sentence can become "as broad as the world" (*W*, 1: 93). In order to measure the ways in which Emerson's language works to revise the language he inherits, I have put his language in relation to other language—his own as well as that of others. In this way, I have tried to draw out the world of which his works are an important articulation—a world which bore witness to vast capitalist development, to the rise of various secondary institutions (such as schools, asylums, factories, and plantations), rapid urbanization and industrialization, and a growing inequality in the distribution of wealth—a world in which debates over the nature of war, revolution, race, slavery, liberty, democracy, and representation were of crucial importance to America's effort to invent its national and cultural identity. I have tried to read the features of this world in the traces it left in Emerson's language. Wishing to follow these traces as closely as possible, I have organized each of my three chapters around a relatively small fragment of his corpus: in the first chapter, a sentence drawn from his war journals in which he associates the domains of history and politics with that of nature; in the second chapter, the first paragraph of his first book, *Nature*; and in the third chapter, two poems written during the war, "Boston Hymn" and "Voluntaries." In each instance—whether I am reading a sentence, a paragraph, or a poem—I try to reconstitute, at times against the grain of traditional histories, what we could call the historical element in this writing.

Although I do not claim to have read or proposed a general reading of all of Emerson's works, I have tried to write a text which, in the face of the event of his writing, tries to respond in my own idiom to what I believe makes this writing singular. This is of course what, according to Emerson, every reading does. "What can we see, read, acquire, but ourselves?," he asks, "Cousin is a thousand books to a thousand persons. Take the book, my friend, and read your eyes out; you will never find what I find" (*J*, 3: 327). As he already knows, however, there can be no pure singularity—every reading must reveal the traces of its appropriations, the traces of its relations to others. "It is as difficult to appropriate the thoughts of others, as it is to invent," he tells us in "Quotation and Originality." "Always some steep transition, some sudden alteration of temperature, or of point of view, betrays the foreign interpolation" (*W*, 8: 183). It is in this transition or alteration, I would argue, that we can read the movement whereby his texts open onto history. His emphasis on the various refractions, exchanges, and allusions that help to constitute this movement is related therefore to the values his texts produce in the act of reading and writing. For him, the more a book is quoted or alluded to by other texts, the more this book quotes, alludes to, or appropriates other texts or contexts, the better it is. In a world where everything begins in the past, use rather than "originality" determines value. Emerson's strategy for using language involves his consistent effort to refer to history, but to a history that—no longer a history that establishes its truth by evoking the authority of so-called facts, that finds its conditions in the past, present, or promised presence of meaning and truth—comes in the form of writing. If his writing seeks to expose us to another history, to another history of history, this other history is one in which "permanence is but a word of degrees," in which everything is "medial," in which "all things unfix, dispart, flee" (*J*, 7: 364 and 362). This means that history is something to which we can never be present. It is a process in which, during the moment of its occurrence, "everything is in flight" (*W*, 8: 5). To write history—which, for Emerson, means to make history—is therefore not to represent a past or present presence. It is to trace the transitive movement that, belonging to what we call the past or the present, prevents either one from ever being present to itself: since it is always unsettled, since it always flees from itself. In other words, to write history is to write in a manner that remains faithful to the way in which language—without which there could be no past or present—moves away from itself. It is, in the wording of Emerson, "to explore the double meaning, or . . . the quadruple, or the centuple, or much more manifold meaning, of every sensuous fact" (*W*, 3: 4).

If I have chosen to sacrifice what some might consider a more comprehensive reading of Emerson's corpus in order to pay closer attention to a few lines, it is not only because of a necessary modesty but also because I have wanted to delineate a model for reading Emerson. I have wanted to suggest that there can be no reading of his language that does not trace the movement of his figures and tropes as they become something else. He warns us against a literalism that refuses to recognize the figural and metaphoric elements of all language in his essay "Culture." There, in a passage that can be read proleptically as an attack on the literalism that often attends a certain Californian version of new historicism, he writes: "There are people who can never understand a trope, or any second or expanded sense given to your words, or any humor; but remain literalists, after hearing the music, and poetry, and rhetoric, and wit, of seventy or eighty years. They are past the help of surgeon and clergy. But even these can understand pitchforks and the cry of fire! and I have noticed in some of this class a marked dislike of earthquakes" (*W*, 6: 140). This is why, in order to read him, we must remain as vigilant as possible to a language that performs its historical and political work through the mobilization of figures whose movement and multiple significations refer to both the linguistic past sealed within them and the unpredictability of a future that could alter, and thereby create, the meaning of our historical existence.

In my attempt to demonstrate that Emerson's language is traversed by his preoccupation with the central political and social issues of his time, I wish to contribute to the ongoing reevaluation of Emerson's relation to the domains of history and politics. This reevaluation—led by critics such as Len Gougeon, Sacvan Bercovitch, Michael Lopez, Carolyn Porter, Lawrence Buell, Barbara Packer, and David Robinson—marks a significant critical turn in American literary historiography, which works to revise what critics like F. O. Matthiessen, Charles Feidelson, R. W. B. Lewis, Richard Chase, and Harold Bloom have understood to be the major theme of the Emersonian tradition: ahistoricism. Until recently, even those critics who would grant that Emerson does indeed, at certain times and under pressing circumstances, address the contemporary issues of his day suggest that his various protests against existing forms of political authority are in the long run weakened, if not compromised, by his insistence on the idealist and spiritual basis of such authority. Although we might attribute some of the reasons for this conservative image of Emerson to the fact that many of his antislavery materials only now have become generally available, I would suggest that this image of his relation to reform is also due to the reluctance of his readers to find his politics, to measure his relation to history, in what I would call a textual model of history—a model of history in which everything is submitted to interpretation.

In what follows, then, I historicize Emerson by trying to clarify the important thematic and rhetorical connections between his writings and some of the central literary, theological, and political texts or movements of his period. I suggest, first, the extent to which his writings may be read as both symptomatic and critical of the governing cultural rhetorics through which Americans of his day thought about the most important issues of their particular historical moment and, second, that what often has been understood as his retreat from the arena of the political into the domain of the spiritual is in fact an effort on his part to re-treat or rethink the nature of the political in terms of questions of representation. This act of rethinking coincides with an obligation that, for Emerson, has everything to do with the meaning of America, insofar as America was itself conceived in terms of a rethinking of the nature and concept of representation. Once Emerson is situated in terms of his particular historical and social moment, the questions he raises and his means of addressing them begin to take on their distinct social weight. Although this reading has certain relays with the work of those critics now involved in reassessing Emerson's relation to history, it differs, I believe, in its attempt to think through the way in which the figures of his rhetoric—figures (like frost, snow, the auroras, and nature in general) which often seem to have nothing to do with either history or politics—are themselves traversed by the conflictual histories of slavery, race, destiny, revolution, and the meaning of America.

My first chapter, "The Climates of History," is a reading of the relationship between Emerson's analysis of the political climate of the 1840s, 1850s, and early 1860s and his earlier, more "philosophical" writings. Focusing primarily on his war journals, his addresses on the emancipation of the British West Indies and the Fugitive Slave Law, and essays such as *Nature*, I argue that nature for Emerson is a principle of articulation among politics, history, and language. In the chapter, I emphasize Emerson's tendency to render political and historical issues in climatological and meteorological terms. Giving an account of the role of the weather in the discourses of war, race, and slavery within and against which Emerson writes, I try to suggest what is for him the ambidexterity of the ideologeme of nature—its capacity, for example, to be thematized and used within both arguments for slavery and arguments against it. Within the context of such ambidexterity, I also suggest that the force of his analogies between nature and history or politics belongs to the incalculability that structures each of their terms. For him, whether we are forecasting the weather or speculating on the future of history or politics, we are dealing with something "uncalculated and uncalculable" (*W*, 3: 69). I try to demonstrate that this obsession with the climate is always linked to his understanding of the unknown effects produced by poli-

tics, history, rhetoric, or nature. In its relation to the possibility of a
future, the weather becomes an important barometer—or what he
elsewhere calls a "differential thermometer" (*W*, 3: 178)—of what
generally has been read as Emerson's optative mood, a mood that is
itself subject to the variable winds attending the "social storms" and
"revolutions" that beset America during his day (*W*, 6: 102).

My second chapter, "Nature's Archives," is a reading of some of
the political, religious, and literary backgrounds to *Nature*. Focusing
on Emerson's relation to such figures as Thomas Paine and Daniel
Webster as well as to certain theological and economic issues of the
period, I again emphasize the relationship among history, politics,
and language. In so doing, I suggest that *Nature*—which generally
has been read as Emerson's plea that the American writer shed the
burden of history in order to begin to write a literature that would be
peculiarly "American"—inaugurates Emerson's revolutionary politics. Demonstrating that the opening of the essay alludes to Webster's
1825 speech at the groundbreaking ceremony for the Bunker Hill
Monument, to Paine's *Rights of Man* and *The Age of Reason*, and to
chapter 11 of Luke, I suggest the necessity of looking for Emerson's
sources in places other than literary or philosophical ones and the
way in which we can begin to read Emerson's politics in terms of the
transformations he effects on the texts to which he alludes. For example, his opening two sentences, "Our age is retrospective. It builds
the sepulchres of the fathers," revise Webster's claim in his Bunker
Hill speech that "we are among the sepulchres of our fathers." More
particularly, his substitution of the phrase "the fathers" for Webster's
"our fathers" works as an indictment of Webster's cultural provincialism as well as of his effort to establish an American tradition
grounded in patriarchy—an effort that, for Emerson, goes against
the promise of the American Revolution, insofar as the revolution
was a revolution against patriarchy. In this chapter, then, I argue that
Emerson's invocation of the rhetoric of Webster, Paine, and the Bible
opens his essay onto questions of history, politics, religion, and language. The opening lines of *Nature* can be said to commemorate a
discontinuous sequence of events. They form a kind of sepulchre that
entombs and releases a series of values, all of which are associated
with the meaning of America. What may at first seem to us a complicated strategy of allusion and displacement becomes less so when we

recall that Webster's "Bunker Hill" speech was well known during Emerson's day, that Paine's republican rhetoric had been a pervasive cultural resource in America since the mid-1770s, and that the Bible had been a reference point for American oratory since the Puritan settlement in the early seventeenth century.

My final chapter, "The Rhetoric of Slavery and War," returns to Emerson's later writings in order to suggest again the relays between the rhetorico-political strategies of his early writings and those of his later works. Focusing on two poems, "Boston Hymn" (written to celebrate the Emancipation Proclamation) and "Voluntaries" (written to celebrate the heroism of the 54th regiment, the first black troop organized for the Union Army), I trace Emerson's appropriation and mobilization of the discourses of religion and abolition within his prowar and antislavery arguments. In the process, I give an account of the crises of representation over which the war was fought, which are linked to the acts of representation that rendered, and sometimes justified, the suffering and death brought on by the war. I link these crises to Emerson's analysis of the Puritan rhetoric of mission and errand that often helped to justify westward expansion, slavery, racism, and the marginalization of cultural diversity in general. If he wishes to revise this rhetoric—and thereby to revise the consequences of this Puritan legacy—he does so by aligning the revolutionary forces of emancipation with the transformative capacity of nature. Suggesting that this recourse to a rhetoric of nature corresponds to his appeal to the virtues of liberty and justice, I argue that these two poems work to transform Emerson's linguistic inheritance in order to renew the power and promise of what for him is still America's legacy. Including a condensed history of the contradictions at the heart of American nationalist ideology, they mobilize the relation between the weather and history at work throughout Emerson's writings in order to provoke a reconsideration of this legacy and to offer a national genealogy that, asking us to confront the possibility that the past may live on in the present, demands that we become answerable for our future.

If this book hopes to contribute to the ongoing revision of our understanding of the relation between Emerson's writings and the socio-political issues of his day, it also seeks to provide a kind of model for considering the complicated relations between literature and history in general. Like Emerson, I believe that texts are worldly. They are events, and whether or not they try to deny it, they are a part of the historical moment in which they are found and read. If Emerson can complain of his "experience of the feeble influence of thought on life"—it is "a ray as pale & ineffectual as that of the sun in our cold and bleak spring," he says—if he can claim that "the actual life, & the intellectual intervals" seem to lie in "parallel lines & never meet" (*J*, 5: 489), he nevertheless asserts in "Experience" that "one day, [he] shall know the value and law of this discrepance." If he adds that he has "not found that much was gained by manipular attempts to realize the world of thought," he reminds us that there can be no action that is not at the same time an action of thought. This is why, he claims, "polemically, or in reply to the inquiry, why not realize your world," that "the true romance which the world exists to realize, will be the transformation of genius into practical power" (*W*, 3: 84–86). I want to suggest that this transformation can only happen with the transformation of the language within which and with which we encounter the world and everything in it. It can only occur, that is, through a task of thinking that is also a labor of reading and writing. Today, this task and labor must take place within the climates of a history whose ambidextrous ideologemes have not ceased to be an urgent social and political problem. We are far from having put wars, racisms, forms of slavery, and debates over the nature of liberty, freedom, and democracy behind us. This is why nothing is more necessary than to analyze, with the greatest vigilance, all of these elements in all of their various manifestations. In what follows, I suggest that this ambidexterity perhaps can be studied best in Emerson with regard to the shifting subject of nature. It is the ideologeme that he uses most pervasively, the one that explicitly or implicitly accompanies his entire career. For him, there can be no deconstruction of American ideologies that does not position nature at the problematic center of its investigations. As he tells us in "The American Scholar":

The first in time and the first in importance of the influences upon the mind is that of nature. Every day, the sun: and, after sunset, night and her stars. Even the winds blow; even the grass grows. Every day, men and women, conversing, beholding and beholden. The scholar is he of all men whom this spectacle most engages. He must settle its value in his mind. What is nature to him? There is never a beginning, there is never an end, to [its] inexplicable continuity . . . but always circular power returning to itself. Therein it resembles his own spirit, whose beginning, whose ending, he never can find, so entire, so boundless. (*W*, 1: 84–85)

To say that we begin and we end without beginning and ending is to say that we have no beginning or end that is ours. As Emerson explains elsewhere, "Our life is consentaneous and far-related. This knot of nature is so well tied that nobody was ever cunning enough to find the two ends. Nature is intricate, overlapped, interweaved and endless" (*W*, 6: 36). This is why this book may be in need of more than one preface—belonging to a process that has no ending, it can only refer to what is coming, must come, and perhaps has already come: another reading. It is also why the closer we come to "Emerson" the more we come to know that there is no such thing as the Emerson-text. Just as "we cannot write the order of the variable winds" (*W*, 6: 321), we can never write the order of the "endless passing of one element into new forms, the incessant metamorphosis" that characterizes his writing. "All thinking is analogizing, and it is the use of life to learn metonymy" (*W*, 8: 15), he tells us. In what follows, I have sought to trace the consequences of this lesson for a thought of history whose work of representation tries to represent something that is not representable—not only the climates of our history but history itself.

Chapter One

❦ The Climates of History

> A hard frost, a sudden thaw, a "hot spell," a "cold snap," a
> contrary wind, a long drought, a storm of sand,—all these
> things have had their part in deciding the destinies of dynas-
> ties, the fortunes of races, and the fate of nations. Leave the
> weather out of history, and it is as if night were left out of the
> day, and winter out of the year.
>
> —C. C. Hazewell, *Atlantic Monthly* (1862)

> *The apparent weather-makers of politics.*—Just as the people se-
> cretly assume that he who understands the weather and can
> forecast it a day ahead actually makes the weather, so, with a
> display of superstitious faith, even the learned and cultivated
> attribute to great statesmen all the important changes and
> turns of events that take place during their term of office as
> being their own work, provided it is apparent that they knew
> something about them before others did and calculated ac-
> cordingly: thus they too are taken for weather-makers—and
> this faith is not the least effective instrument of their power.
>
> —Nietzsche, *Human, All-Too Human* (1878)

"It is impossible to extricate oneself from the questions in which
your age is involved," Emerson writes in his war journal late in the
summer of 1863. "You can no more keep out of politics than you can
keep out of the frost" (*J*, 15: 28, 182). The analogy he draws between
the natural occurrence of frost and occurrences in the moral and
political world suggests that the course of human events is as inexorable and authoritative as the laws of nature. The political climate prevails upon everyone. It makes it impossible to avoid the
consequences and calamities of the war, the questions that destined
America to its civil crisis—questions that, for Emerson, exhibit the
nature of politics. In what follows, I wish to consider the implications
of this analogy between frost and politics within the specific context
of Emerson's analysis of the political climate of the 1850s and 1860s

as well as within the more general context of his writings as a whole. Touching on the pervasive and essential analogy in his works between natural and human history, that is to say, on history as he understands it, the analogy may help us think about what he means not only by "frost" and "politics," but also by "man," "history," and "nature." Moreover, occurring as it does in Emerson's war journals, within the context of a reference to "the questions" of his age, the analogy is situated within the history and politics of his day as well as within the specific context of the Civil War. It becomes a means to see the way in which Emerson addresses a contemporary event in terms of the history that both precedes and follows it. It therefore can serve as an important key to any evaluation of what we might wish to call his "political" strategy. To be more precise, as an analogy, it opens onto the questions of language and representation that are inseparable from the transformative, and hence political, power at the heart of all of Emerson's writings. What is at stake in our being able to read this sentence is perhaps nothing less than the possibility of reading any of his sentences.

While at first we might be tempted to say that what compels him to make this analogy is his wish to legitimize his own transcendental themes in a moment of political urgency—either by naturalizing the political in order to reassert more fundamentally his own right to speak, his own will to authority, or by marshaling his particular form of transcendentalism to the barricades in order to convince his countrymen of the war's importance—we should perhaps no longer rush to think that we know what these themes are. Or, better still, we should perhaps no longer presume that knowing what Emerson's themes are—Nature and Politics, to be sure, but also Spirit, History, the Over-Soul, Art, Self-Reliance, and America, to name only a few among many—is the same as understanding what any one of them might mean. It may even be the case that we will remain unable to trace the political or the natural in Emerson as long as we continue to remain certain about what is political or natural in his work and what is not. To say this is also to say that we can know the political or the natural in this work only if we begin to call into question the integrity of both of these domains.

This questioning is initiated by Emerson's analogy. The simplicity of the analogy in fact belies its powerful consequences for our understanding of either "politics" or "nature." The relation between politics and the natural phenomenon of frost is perhaps more than a simple affinity or analogy, all the more so since it would appear that politics and frost could have nothing to do with one another. Not only does politics belong to the being of man's social and cultural existence while frost belongs to the being of nature, but frost also implies a certain chill or coldness that is not usually associated with the heat and passion of the political domain. Yet Emerson seems to suggest the contrary, to exhibit the ineluctable relatedness between the two. This is not to say that this relatedness exists in a fixed manner between some particular politics and nature, for the latter can accommodate itself to political systems that are different from, and even opposed to, one another. When Emerson suggests that "the views of nature held by any people determine all their institutions," (*W*, 7: 49), he suggests that there is something within nature, something within what he means by nature, that addresses the question of institutional structures and the political stakes of interpretive conflicts. The question of nature does not raise the question of whether a politics is implied—since it always is—but rather the question of which particular politics is implied in this particular nature. Within the context of Emerson's analogy, the heat and coldness of the political domain are not derived from material properties but from a transference from the figural to the literal that stems from the ambivalent relation between politics, as a process whose inevitability lies in its being natural to the existence of man, and nature, as a process whose force, whose transformative power coincides with what is political within the world of human affairs. Governed by the laws of figural language that link together natural history and human history, the structure of this analogy works to efface any strict opposition between politics and nature: there can be neither a politics without nature nor a nature without politics.

What is at stake is the discovery of the specificity of such an entanglement, for the selection of the analogy is no more arbitrary than its power and significance. If the analogy imposes itself on Emerson, it is in part because certain of its motifs belong to a long and powerful sequence of writing, going back at least to Plato and Aristotle, that has insisted on the tie between climate and politics. When he writes, both here and elsewhere, of "the influences of climate and soil in political history" (*W*, 2: 98), he invokes various eighteenth-century Augustan and Enlightenment debates over the effects of climate on political systems—debates that he knows grow out of much earlier writings. Herodotus's catalogs of the governments of various peoples, for example, later served both Plato and Aristotle as they discussed the role of climate in determining forms of government. Pliny subsequently argues that political organization depends largely on the heat or cold of a region. Such theories are reinforced by the Bible as well as by sixteenth- and seventeenth-century writers, such as Robert Burton, Shakespeare, and Jean Bodin, but blossom most fully in eighteenth-century writers, such as John Arbuthnot, Edward of Clarendon, and Sir William Temple in England, and Georges Louis de Buffon, Jean Fontanelle, Rousseau, and, perhaps most importantly, Montesquieu in France.[1] The pertinence of such debates to the context of Emerson's claim becomes clearer when we remember that they are usually organized around the issues of race and nationality, issues that are, of course, central to the political and historical context of the Civil War.[2] Resituating the terms of his analogy within the specific network of relations and questions that attend America's present civil crisis, he mobilizes the history of these terms toward a rethinking of their respective meanings.

What do frost and politics mean if they are at least analogous to each other? Only if we remain attentive to the considerable ambivalences and contradictions that burden and motivate Emerson's thinking about this question may we begin to see how the risks of his history could get translated into practical terms. This is not to say that there would ever be a direct link between this thinking and whatever practical effects we might claim are its results. If history is a risk for Emerson, it is precisely because the effects of our actions and our thoughts are always unforeseeable. Any attempt to read the relations between Emerson's writings and their effects must take into account this incalculability—an incalculability that may in turn help us understand the ways in which his writings were appropriated and neutralized by various historical, social, and institutional forces in mid-nineteenth-century America and beyond, despite his efforts of resistance. At the same time, it also may account for why Emerson had such a profound influence on the rhetoric of abolitionism, women's rights, and labor, and why figures who perhaps strike us as more radical than Emerson—Margaret Fuller, Henry Thoreau, Walt Whitman, Wendell Phillips, Theodore Parker, and Frederick Douglass, to name only a few—relied on him as a source of oppositional authority. It is perhaps only within the context of this incalculability, within the obligation to consider the effects of certain of Emerson's "political" decisions, that we can trace his engagement with the issues of his day.

If I insist on tracing this analogy as it appears and reappears, in different contexts and even in different forms, it is not to suggest that there is a certain persistence or stubbornness in Emerson's use of the trope. Rather, it is to suggest the way in which his language means: not by the accumulation of multiple associations around a strongly held center, but through the mobilization of terms from one shifting context to another. This mobilization names an engagement with changing historical and political relations, an intensification of a transformation in progress, wherein language not only works to alter and set in motion the shifting domains of history and politics but wherein the historical and the political leave their traces in language. In other words, and in Emerson it is always a matter of words, if Emerson's language works to change language, it does so in order to change much more than language—it does so because it seeks to produce something new and singular. That language actively conditions the possibility of what we call history or politics requires that we begin to account for how language works historically to establish reference and meaning. This approach would, at the same time, need to remain open to a future whose unpredictability could transform the regimes of meaning previously thought to condition its past, though, according to Emerson, such transformations happen historically only by remaining faithful to the singularity of the linguistic past within which they take place.[3] Although this reading has certain relays with the work of other critics now involved in reassessing his relationship to history, it differs, I believe, in its attempt to account for the way in which the figures of his rhetoric—figures which, as I've suggested, often seem to have nothing to do with either history or politics—are themselves traversed by the conflictual histories of slavery, race, destiny, revolution, and the meaning of America.[4] This is why much of what follows will involve tracking the history inscribed within Emerson's analogy—for him, historical and political truths are already caught in the power of a language that lies beyond the movements of its own understanding. Only in this way may we begin to measure the extent to which his writings can be read as both symptomatic and critical of the governing cultural rhetorics through which Americans of his day thought about the most important issues of their particular historical moment.

In the long run, this approach may help us explain Emerson's tendency to render political and historical issues in climatological or meteorological terms. Emphasizing the analogy that exists "between man's life and the seasons" (*W*, 1: 28), time and time again he associates meteorological metaphors with the issues of politics, slavery, race, property, and speculation, both economic and philosophical. The force of these analogies comes in part from the incalculability that structures each of their terms. Indeed, one reason that an investigation into the weather provides such a good entry into what he means by the political may be that in both forecasting the weather and "speculating on the future in politics," we deal with what he calls "a fluxional protean incalculable element" (*J*, 15: 286). His obsession with the climate—perhaps no more evident than when, in a journal entry of 1837, he writes, "Climate touches not my work" (*J*, 5: 301)—figures the specifically protean and fluxional Spirit that wanders throughout his work, one that is always linked to the anticipation of unknown effects, whether these be of politics, nature, history, or rhetoric. Emerson links this Spirit with one of the variable phenomena of climate when, in his discussion of language in *Nature*, he claims that "*spirit* primarily means *wind*" (*W*, 1: 25).[5] Referring to *wind* as the etymological origin of the word *Spirit*, he returns the meaning of what he understands as a concept—the indeterminate generality of Spirit—to its metaphorical origin. Most of the historical process by which this transformation of *wind* to *Spirit* was effected has been "hidden from us," he explains, "in the remote time when language was framed" (*W*, 1: 26).[6] The determination of the truth of Spirit must pass therefore through the detour of a metaphorical system. This is why the weather in Emerson is in general a principle of articulation among nature, language, and history. In its relation to the possibility of a future, it is also a wonderful barometer of what generally has been read as his optative mood—a mood that is itself subject to the variable winds attending the social and political storms that beset America during his day. We eventually may have to ask why we have for so long considered Emerson to be one of the "patient naturalists" he so often condemned for freezing "their subject under the wintry light of the understanding" (*W*, 1: 74).

Storms of Civil Crisis

If it is impossible for Emerson to extricate himself from the questions of his age, we should perhaps begin by indicating briefly what some of these questions might be. As is so often the case in his writings, his tendency to recirculate passages—his own as well as those of others—can lead us to passages that may help to situate and gloss the one at hand. The line "It is impossible to extricate oneself from the questions in which your age is involved" in fact reappears a few months later in his address "Fortune of the Republic," first delivered on December 1, 1863.[7] There, he encourages his audience "to wake up and correct the country," to "combat the dangers and dragons that beset the United States at this time," by directing their energies toward the questions of their particular age: "We are in these days settling for ourselves and our descendents, questions which, as they shall be decided in one way or another, will make the peace and prosperity or the calamity of the next ages" (*W*, 11: 539, 516). Addressing the questions of war, slavery, abolition, government based on force, and the limits of the executive power, in each case, he suggests, we should measure the question under consideration in terms of its relation to questions of morality and liberty. It is therefore no surprise that the line with which we are concerned first appears in a journal entry of May 3, 1851, which refers to the event that for Emerson demanded a reconsideration of the relations among law, morality, and liberty: the passing of the Fugitive Slave Law. He writes: "it is not possible to extricate oneself from the questions in which your age is involved, the last year has forced us all into politics" (*J*, 14: 385). It also reappears in a notebook that Emerson kept in the mid-1850s and simply entitled "Liberty"—a notebook devoted to material about abolition, slavery, and human liberty, a notebook devoted, that is, to the question(s) of America—and is then soon recirculated, in a slightly altered form, in his 1856 speech "Kansas Relief Meeting": "I had been wiser to have stayed at home, unskilled as I am to address a political meeting, but it is impossible for the most recluse to extricate himself from the questions of the time" (*AS*, 111). The sentence with which we began therefore punctuates Emerson's writings from just after the passing of the Fugitive Slave Law on through the Civil War. We could even say that it bears the traces of an entire historical debate over the possibility of war and liberty, the extension of slavery and its relation to democracy, and in general the meaning of America in the 1850s and 1860s.

Emerson evokes these same questions in 1863, at a time when the North is beginning to experience its vulnerability. The battles at Bull Run, Shiloh, Antietam, and Fredericksburg had given evidence of the struggle's horror.[8] Although the abolitionists William Garrison, Wendell Phillips, and Charles Sumner were encouraged by Lincoln's decision to enforce an Emancipation Proclamation, the six months beginning January 1, 1863—the effective date of the Proclamation— were for most northerners a period of great despair and frustration. Fears of emancipated slaves either rising against their masters or competing for work with northern white labor increased dissatisfaction with the administration and the war.[9] Supporters of the war were faced with the difficult task of justifying the continuing bloodshed even as the patriotism and dedication to the Union that had followed the attack on Fort Sumter appeared to be diminishing.

Emerson's insistence on the overwhelming necessity of confronting the political issues of the time is, therefore, above all a call to responsibility, a call that requires, in response to the urgency and precariousness of the historical moment, a passionate and determined effort of reflection. One can no more escape this obligation to think than the obligation to act—especially since, as he writes to James Elliot Cabot in a letter dated August 4, 1861, less than four months after the outbreak of the war, "The war,—though from such despicable beginnings, has assumed such huge proportions that it threatens to engulf us all—no preoccupation can exclude it, and no hermitage hide us"(*L*, 5: 253).[10] Indeed, this thinking, however theoretical it might seem to be, is inseparable from the political experiences or passions within which it takes place. To say that all thinking is political, however, does not relieve us of the responsibility of specifying the effects of certain modes and forms of thought. On the contrary.

If Emerson calls for the necessity of a thought that is at the same time an act, he does so in the name of something that, for him, has not yet occurred: an urgent, but careful, reevaluation of the ways of thinking that led the American people into the war. Only through this act of reflection can one address and refer to the massively present reality of the war. For Emerson, the war itself—precisely because of the suffering, the killing, and the brutality in which it consists—comes in the form of both a tremendous imperative to think and a powerful means of persuasion. This may help to explain why, even though he continues during the years 1861–1865 to express a number of fears and uncertainties over the progress of the war, over the constancy of the public's support and the expenditure of the nation's energy, and even over the possibility that, after the war, political interests might still be "as sectional and (narrow) timorous as before" (*J*, 15: 77–78),[11] his journals and lectures of this same period are mostly filled with praise for the war and for what he sees as its powerful capacity to clear the way for moral and intellectual reform. "A benefit of War," he tells us, "is, that the appeal not being [any] longer to letter & form, but now to the roots of strength in the people, the moral aspect becomes important, & is urgently presented and debated" (*J*, 15: 351). In passage after passage, he claims that the war "sweeps away all the false issues on which it began, and arrives presently at real and lasting questions." It is "a realist" that "shatters everything flimsy and shifting . . . and breaks through all that is not real as itself"; it "comes crushing through party walls that have stood 50 or 60 years as if they were solid" and thereby reduces "the screaming of leaders, the votes by acclamation of conventions" to "idle wind." It is an educator "that goes on educating us . . . to see the bankruptcy of all narrow views," "an eye-opener" that will not only show men "of all parties and opinion the values of those primary forces that lie beneath all political action," but will also reveal "what wrong is intolerable, what wrong makes and breeds all this bad blood" (*J*, 15: 298, 299–300, 141, 202, 300–1). As he states in the letter to Cabot cited above, "gulf as it is, the war with its defeats and uncertainties is immensely better than what we lately called the integrity of the Republic, as amputation is better than cancer. . . . If the abundance of heaven only sends us a fair share of light and conscience, we shall redeem America for all its sinful years since the century began" (*L*, 5: 263).

For Emerson, America's unredeemed sin is the persistence of slavery in a nation that was to be founded on the virtues of freedom, liberty, and equality. The divine mission of America might support antislavery in the name of independence, but it could also require devotion to a Union that served to extend slavery. This inconsistency was central to the issues of a growing capitalist economy, social and sexual reform, westward expansion, and Manifest Destiny in nineteenth-century America. It not only produced, in the wording of Eric Sundquist, "a national ideology riddled with ambiguities and tension," but also "year by year distort[ed] the course of American democracy." [12] Whether thought in cultural, economic, or ideological terms, slavery presented an unavoidable ethical question that helped to precipitate the conflict that finally brought the force of American nationalism to its civil crisis. No other sectional factor had a greater effect in dividing the North from the South. As David Potter suggests, "the slavery issue gave a false clarity and simplicity to sectional diversities which were otherwise qualified and diffuse." [13] As Emerson would have it, "If the war goes on, it will be impossible to keep the combatants from the extreme ground on either side. In spite of themselves, one army will stand for slavery pure; & the other for freedom pure" (*J*, 15: 145). Although slavery worked to polarize the many points of conflict on which sectional interest diverged, the North continued to oscillate between a commitment to antislavery and the commitment to a Constitution that protected slavery, to a Union that manifested its complicity with slaveholders. This indecision was so deeply rooted in the rhetoric of the period that, on the eve of the Civil War, Abraham Lincoln could on the one hand claim that slavery was morally wrong and on the other pledge himself to enforce the fugitive-slave clause of the Constitution, promising to protect slavery in states that chose to retain it. [14] This ambiguity is already evident in his famous House Divided Speech of 1858. There, after speaking for the perpetuity of the Union, he goes on to describe a Union that, even in the North, is divided between free soil and proslavery interests, between abolitionists and Republicans who accuse the South of despotism and a legal machinery whose support of both the Nebraska Bill in 1854 and the recent Dred Scott decision works to extend slavery into the territories. [15] Responding to the Union's failure to rid itself of slavery, Emerson writes that "the late history shows how wide is the departure of the practice of government from the theory . . . what avails the correctness of the theory, when the practice is despotism" (*J*, 14: 421–22). For him, Lincoln's Union—as divided as Lincoln himself—no longer exists as a union, if it ever did.

Moreover, the North's ambivalence toward the issue of emancipation provoked a kind of political paralysis that prevented any real challenge to the widening sectional rift. Rather than being confronted head on, the choice between emancipation and slavery was displaced and diffused by legal questions concerning the relation of Congress and the states to territories, leaving slavery to be challenged where it did not yet exist rather than where it did.[16] The slave power and its injustices were effectively left untouched, even as the issue of slavery became, as Lincoln would have it, "*the* question, the absorbing topic of the day."[17] It is within this atmosphere of political indecision and confusion that the Confederacy opened fire on the American flag on the morning of April 12, 1861. Within three days Lincoln issued a proclamation to call forth "the militia of the several states of the Union" in order to suppress the rebels. At the same time, he made an appeal "to all loyal citizens to favor, facilitate and aid this effort to maintain the integrity, and the existence of our National Union."[18] The same day, the *New York Times* wrote that the North had responded to the attack on Fort Sumter with a "rapid condensation of public sentiment in the Free States," an "intense, inspiring sentiment of patriotism" that "fused all other passions in its fiery heat." The attack, it went on to say, had made the North "a unit."[19] Emerson himself later repeats this point by claiming that "at the darkest moment in the history of the republic, when it looked as if the nation would be dismembered, pulverized into its original elements, the attack on Fort Sumter crystallized the North into a unit, and the hope of mankind was saved."[20]

This recourse to the language of nature and climate—condensation, heat, crystallization—in order to figure not only the conflict between the North and the South but also the passion and power of public opinion was pervasive during the early stages of the war and became a primary means for evoking what for many was the war's turbulent necessity. The *Syracuse Daily Courier and Union* proclaimed that the outbreak of war had "startled the public like the burst of thunder in a still and cloudless night." The *Springfield Daily Republi-*

can praised the men now surrendering themselves "to the patriotic thrill that leaps from heart to heart like lightning along a chain." "To talk of peace now," the *Brooklyn Daily Eagle* reported, "would be to talk to the tempest and reason with the hurricane." [21] In the July issue of his review, Orestes Brownson called the conflict "the thunderstorm that purifies the moral and political atmosphere," and in *Drum Taps* Walt Whitman claimed to have "witnessed the true lightning" as "torrents of men" went to war in the name of a democracy that was now bursting forth in what Emerson would soon call "a whirlwind of patriotism." [22]

When news of the Fort Sumter attack reached Emerson on April 13, he was in the midst of a series of lectures in Boston on the relationship between "Life" and "Literature." Four days earlier, in the first of his lectures, he had spoken of "the downfall of our character-destroying civilization," and, a few days later, in his second lecture, he referred to "the facility with which a great political fabric can be broken." [23] He had planned to deliver the "Doctrine of Leasts" on April 23, but on hearing the news of Sumter he changed his topic to "Civilization at a Pinch." The outbreak of the war had relieved him of his apprehension that another compromise would be sought, that "the union would be patched up when no real union existed," [24] and his prose now seemed as impassioned as ever:

How does Heaven help us when civilization is at a hard pinch? Why, by a whirlwind of patriotism, not believed to exist, but now magnetizing all discordant masses under its terrific unity. It is an affair of instincts; we did not know we had them . . . now a sentiment mightier than logic, wide as light, strong as gravity, reaches into the college, the bank, the farm-house, and the church. It is the day of the populace. . . . I will never again speak lightly of a crowd. We are wafted into a revolution which, though at first sight a calamity of the human race, finds all men in good heart, in courage, in a generosity of mutual and patriotic support. We have been very homeless, some of us, for some years past,—say since 1850; but now we have a country again. Up to March 4, 1861, in the very place of law we found, instead of it, war. Now we have forced the conspiracy out-of-doors. Law is on this side and War on that. It was war then, and it is war now; but declared war is vastly safer than war undeclared. [25]

Emerson is most struck by the "spontaneity" of the public's reaction to the war—what he calls here, and in his earlier essay "Self-Reliance," "Instinct" (*W*, 2: 64). This force is neither strictly formal nor institutional: it coincides instead with a movement of gathering that redefines "patriotism." "Before the war," he states in a later journal entry, "our patriotism was a firework, a salute, a serenade, for holidays and summer evenings, but the reality was cotton thread and complaisance. Now the deaths of thousands and the determination of millions of men and women show it real" (*J*, 15: 454). In condemning patriotism prior to the war, Emerson's metaphors are those of performance or outer display—fireworks, salutes, and serenades. For him, the "reality" of patriotism is embodied in the materiality of cotton threads—that is, in the economic system that ties North and South together. Death makes patriotism real, at one level, because it is the truth behind the "holidays and summer evenings" of a false patriotism. As the *Buffalo Daily Courier* noted on April 22, 1861, in response to what it called "the portentous cloud" that had recently broken over the land, "Patriotism, all but an obsolete word before, has a meaning now. The national flag which hung, an idle piece of bunting, in the time of peace, has been reconsecrated in the breath of war, and is again a holy thing."[26] Despite the death that war inevitably brings, it works to open our eyes to what previously had prevented us from distinguishing the banners and decorations of a patriotism based on greed and oppression from a patriotism that responds to the exigencies of the moment according to a law of generosity. The spirit of the war—this "sentiment" that is "mightier than logic"—is a source of independence, virtue, and life. Beyond reason, this deep force, this fountain of action and thought, breaks into institutions that are either without vitality or already dead and calls forth living men who, like the forces of light and gravity, can then "repel the enemy as by Nature" (*J*, 15: 221). If "there is nothing real or useful that is not a seat of war" (*W*, 3: 100), it is because the war has a positive value as the avatar of an eternal principle that teaches the populace to win their physical and mental independence. As he suggests, even as early as his 1838 speech "War," delivered to the Boston Peace Society: "War educates the senses, calls into action the will . . . brings men into such swift and close collision in critical moments that man measures man" (*W*, 11: 152).[27] For Emerson, the outbreak of war, the first southern attack on the Union, transformed the North—even despite itself—into a "whirlwind of patriotism," a "spasm to throw off slavery" (*L*, 5: 322). As one newspaper reported, the impact of the assault on Fort Sumter was "carried on the wings of lightning to the most remote corners of the land," provoking "a revolution in public sentiment never before equalled." "Henceforth," it went on to say, "let no man doubt that the latent fires of patriotism burn as brightly as ever in American bosoms."[28]

The North retaliated against the South with a vigor and swiftness that inspired Emerson to announce the nation's return to itself. "We are coming," he writes in a journal passage of the same period, "thanks to the war, to a nationality" (*J*, 15: 326). The war effort gives integrity and honesty back to a country which, "say since 1850," had failed as a nation—and thereby deprived its inhabitants of a home—by establishing laws whose immorality enabled slavery to persist. For Emerson, only the abolition of slavery can insure peace and a real Union, only by guaranteeing the freedom of each of its citizens can America realize the aims of its founding. He makes the same points in his earlier essays and speeches against the 1850 Compromise—a compromise that reaffirmed even as it redefined the Fugitive Slave Law. In his address of May 3, 1851, in Concord, he says, "But one thing appears certain to me, that, as soon as the Constitution ordains an immoral law, it ordains disunion. The law is suicidal, and cannot be obeyed. The Union is at an end as soon as an immoral law is enacted" (*AS*, 67–68).

For Emerson and others, the law, rather than promise political freedom, betrays the founding principles of virtue and liberty which were to define the social revolution that gave America its significance. "We are losing," he writes in 1854, "for the sake of the Union, the good which the Union was adopted to guard" (*J*, 14: 419). In achieving national unity at the expense of the freedom of fugitive slaves, the Compromise suggests that the maintenance of the Union depends, in an essential and fundamental way, on the exploitation and exclusion of certain individuals living within its boundaries. For Emerson, the Compromise pushes America toward the blood bath of a fratricidal war as legal conflicts over states' rights, the rights of slaves, the constitutional basis of slavery, and efforts to nullify the Fugitive Slave Law clashed and, in so doing, defined the political and moral climate of the period.[29] In his 1856 speech on Sumner, anticipating Lincoln's words by two years, he describes the fearful conclusion to which such episodes were leading: "I do not see how a barbarous community and a civilized community can constitute one state. I think we must get rid of slavery, or we must get rid of freedom. Life has no parity of value in the free-state and in the slave-state" (*AS*, 107).[30]

However, the arbitrariness with which he seems to date America's homelessness—"say since 1850"—suggests that we might date it from another time. He may have in mind the 1793 Fugitive Slave Law that the 1850 law revised, but he certainly refers to the ambiguity already structured into a Constitution that establishes the conditions for both freedom and slavery.[31] The establishment of the Compromise, rather than effect a new sense of national unity, evokes a number of questions concerning the moral integrity of America's founding documents. In this respect, Emerson claims, "the crisis had the illuminating power of a sheet of lightning at midnight. It showed truth. It ended a good deal of nonsense we had been wont to hear and to repeat, on the 19th April, the 17th June, and the 4th July" (*AS*, 55). It suggests that perhaps more is amiss with America than a temporary discrepancy between what the country has stood for and present practices. Emerson's sensitivity to the constitutional questions involved in the issue of slavery led George Bancroft to proclaim, after Emerson's 1856 "Kansas Relief Meeting," that "Emerson as clearly as anyone, perhaps more clearly than anyone at the time, saw the enormous dangers that were gathering over the Constitution"(*W*, 11: 597n.). Phillips and even Lincoln were by this time interpreting the Constitution as a document that conspired with the cause of slavery even as it claimed to advocate freedom. As Robert Cover explains, "the judicial claims and successes of proslavery forces between 1840 and 1860—the gag-rule [itself initiated during the nullification crisis in South Carolina in the 1830s], the *Amistad* and the *Creole*, the Mexican War, the new Fugitive Act of 1850, *Kansas-Nebraska*, and finally *Dred Scott*—[gave] this vision . . . a degree of credibility. Taken one at a time, these developments need not be given the interpretation of a proslavery Constitution. But Phillips and the Garrisonians would not permit the events to be viewed seriatim."[32] Douglass points to the duplicity inscribed within American political discourse in his 1852 speech "The Meaning of July Fourth for the Negro." There, in one of the most remarkable and politically motivated weather passages of the period, he gives voice to the rage of the black man, whose body and life bear the consequences of the contradictions to which Emerson and others referred:

At a time like this, scorching irony, not convincing argument, is needed. O! had I the ability, and could I reach the nation's ear, I would, to-day, pour out a fiery stream of biting ridicule, blasting reproach, withering sarcasm, and stern rebuke. For it is not light that is needed, but fire; it is not the gentle shower, but thunder. We need the storm, the whirlwind, and the earthquake. The feeling of the nation must be quickened; the conscience of the nation must be roused; the propriety of the nation must be startled; the hypocrisy of the nation must be exposed; and its crimes against God and man must be proclaimed and denounced.

What, to the American slave, is your 4th of July? I answer: a day that reveals to him, more than all the other days in the year, the gross injustice and cruelty to which he is the constant victim. To him, your celebration is a sham; your boasted liberty, an unholy license; your national greatness, swelling vanity; your sounds of rejoicing are empty and heartless; your denunciation of tyrants, brass fronted impudence; your shouts of liberty and equality, hollow mockery; your prayers and hymns, your sermons and thanksgivings, with all your religious parade, and solemnity, are, to him, mere bombast, fraud, deception, impiety, and hypocrisy—a thin veil to cover up crimes which would disgrace a nation of savages. There is not a nation on the earth guilty of practices, more shocking and bloody, than are the people of the United States, at this very hour.[33]

As Emerson would put it, "America, the most prosperous country in the Universe, has the greatest calamity in the Universe, negro slavery" (*AS*, 57). Referring in a journal entry from the mid-1850s to the same duplicity and hypocrisy that Douglass does, he emphasizes the slave power's capacity to overcome resistance, especially when it comes from men who may claim to support an individual's right to freedom but whose actions betray their endorsement of the institution of slavery. "These men meant well," he writes, "but they allowed the Missouri Compromise; meant well, but allowed Texas; meant well, but allowed Mexican War; meant well, but allowed Fugitive Slave Law. They resisted Nebraska, but it is too late—Let them resist forever. They must now be convinced that we have no guards,—that there is no proposition—too audacious to be offered us by the Southerner" (*J*, 14: 380).[34] In response to this duplicity, Emerson turns much of his rhetorical energy during this period against the laws and political decisions that for him worked to maintain the institution of slavery. As he writes soon after the passing of the Fugitive Slave Law, "All I have, and all I can do shall be given &

done in opposition to the execution of the law" (*J*, 11: 343–44). This activism is legible throughout the 1850s in his two addresses on the Fugitive Slave Law, in his lectures against slavery in general, and in his responses to the passing of the Kansas-Nebraska Act, the assault on Charles Sumner, and the heroism of John Brown. As David Robinson has recently suggested in a remark that, directed toward the Fugitive Slave Law addresses, can be said of all of these texts, Emerson "found that he could turn his intellectual influence and rhetorical ability into stinging denunciations of the law. . . . These closely related addresses called up reserves of invective that many readers may not have known Emerson had, and despite their relative obscurity, they are among his most impressive rhetorical performances, crucial texts for charting the increasing grounding of his idealism in ethical and pragmatic action." [35]

Arguing against the proslavery bent of the Constitution, Emerson and others began to argue for disunion. [36] The Union is not an end, they claimed, but a means toward realizing the "original" goals of the founders: Liberty is to be privileged before the Union. Emerson repeatedly shows himself ready, if necessary, to sacrifice the Union for the abolition of slavery, and, as one of his biographers, Gay Wilson Allen, suggests, this explains why "he was slow to work up enthusiasm for Lincoln." [37] The election of 1860 posed a number of difficulties for Emerson and the abolitionist cause in general. Abolitionists were dissatisfied with Buchanan and confused by Lincoln. On the one hand, Buchanan had supported steps to assure the return of fugitive slaves and to protect slavery in the states where it already existed, and he had openly taken sides against the North's interference with states' rights in the South. [38] John P. Hale of New Hampshire exclaimed that Buchanan "has acted like the ostrich, which hides her head, and thereby thinks to escape danger." [39] Emerson himself writes that Buchanan was not a man of ideas (*J*, 14: 335) and that he really belonged to "the Southern party" (*J*, 15: 401). On the other hand, Lincoln claimed to be against slavery and its expansion but refused to approve immediate and total abolition. [40] Nevertheless, many became convinced—because of what Potter has called Lincoln's "frosty opposition" both to compromise and to slavery's expansion [41]—that a Republican triumph would indirectly be a victory for the abolitionist cause. Abolitionists began to proclaim the Republican party as "the embodiment of the Anti-Slavery sentiment of the country." Lincoln's inauguration on March 4, 1861, they believed, could inaugurate "the beginning of the end of slavery."[42] As Phillips declared the day after the election: "Not an Abolitionist, hardly an antislavery man, Mr. Lincoln consents to represent an antislavery idea. A pawn on the political chess board, his value is in his position."[43] According to Allen, Emerson, too, "by the eve of the election . . . had accepted the Republican ticket as the best means of attaining abolition."[44] A few days later he recorded in his journal that "the news of last Wednesday morning (7th) was sublime, the pronunciation of the masses of America against Slavery" (*J*, 14: 363).

The first southern attack on the Union only reinforced this sentiment. In his speech "The State of the Country," delivered in Boston in December 1863 and echoing Emerson's own rhetoric of crystallization, Phillips recalls the beginning of the war: "When the war broke out, the first blow the South aimed at the North, as if according to chemical law, crystallized that level of democracy into an antislavery mould."[45] When confronted by a choice between a potentially antislavery war and a proslavery peace, most abolitionists did not hesitate to choose war. Abolitionist rhetoric now served the Union. Prowar abolitionists further justified the war with arguments that "slavery itself was the worst form of war imaginable, and that a civil war, however terrible, was worth the cost if it held out a chance of abolishing slavery."[46] "The war existed," Emerson claims in his October 12, 1862, address "The President's Proclamation," "long before the cannonade of Sumter and could not be postponed. It might have begun otherwise or elsewhere, but war was in the minds and bones of the combatants, it was written on the iron leaf, and you might as easily dodge gravitation" (*AS*, 133). War existed as soon as "the rights of Man" were "recited," since "every one of them is a declaration of war," since "every principle is a war-note" (*J*, 15: 353). In characterizing the institution of slavery as a form of war—consisting only in part of the various legal conflicts already mentioned—Emerson appropriates and exploits the abolitionist rhetoric of Phillips, who in February 1861 declared that "Slavery is a form of perpetual war," as well as that of his friend Moncure Conway, a Virginia-born abolitionist who grew up on a slave plantation and who in 1862 announced that "Slavery is perpetual war. . . .

A single day of Slavery and its rule in this country witnessed more wrong, violence, corruption, more actual war, than all that civil war even could bring."[47] For Emerson and others, Lincoln's call for troops only brought into the open a condition of war that was already in existence. No longer hidden, its sinister effects might be addressed more directly. "It was war then and it is war now," he writes, "but declared war is vastly safer than war undeclared." Phillips, in his February 17 speech "Progress"—two months before Emerson's "Civilization at a Pinch"—had already argued that "with the slave, it is only war in disguise. Under that mask is hid a war keener in its pains, and deadlier in its effects, than any open fight. As the Latin adage runs,— *mars gravior sub pace latet*,—war bitterer for its disguise."[48]

By bringing together in urgent form the issues of civil liberties, republicanism, and slavery, the war—once declared—"forced" the conspiracy behind government policies that favored slavery's interests "out-of-doors" and, as Emerson claims the Fugitive Slave Law had done in 1850, "unglued the eyes of man" (*AS*, 89). Now, "read by the light of war fires by eyes in peril" (*J*, 15: 179–80), the institution of slavery aroused the moral and ethical energies of the people in the direction of its opposition. But, as William Goodell (a member of the Radical Abolitionist party, which included Douglass amongst its leaders) argued, the war had legal as well as moral sanction. According to Goodell, from the very moment that the seceding states seized federal property, the South declared war on the United States and was then answerable for her actions. The acts of the seceding states absolved the Republican Party of its promise not to interfere with slavery in the South. The war was now on the side of the North and responsibility for the war lay to the South. "Here are the threats of invasion," Emerson declares in his January 1861 lecture "Cause and Effect," "they are calls to duty. If a number of malcontents will disturb the government and union of the States, it may easily become the duty of every able and bodied citizen to go directly to the spot where the burglar breaks in. If that is our duty, war, violence can be no impediment. Run all the risks of war: it may become necessary to take life, or to lose life—that is neither here nor there."[49] After Lincoln's call for troops, Garrison himself proclaimed that "all my sympathies and wishes are with the government, because it is entirely in the right, and acting strictly in self-defense and for self-

preservation."⁵⁰ "The proof that war . . . is within the highest right,"
Emerson claims, that war "is a marked benefactor in the hands of the
Divine Providence, is its *morale*" (*J*, 15: 342). Sanctioned by human
legislation and motivated by spiritual laws, the war, which at first
seems "a calamity of the human race, finds all men in good heart, in
courage, in a generosity of mutual and patriotic support."

By June 1863, though, what had begun as a war of promise—a
war that promised to end slavery as well as to ground the nation in
the freedom of all its citizens—seemed for many to promise only
more suffering and confusion. The North was still recovering from
the defeats and losses of the previous year and still undergoing a period of economic distress. Moreover, since the summer of 1862 the
anti-emancipation "Copperhead" movement had been growing in
strength. Capitalizing on the North's growing weariness with the
war, the movement gained momentum in the spring of 1863 when, as
James McPherson notes, "the Army of the Potomac, decisively de-
feated at . . . Chancellorsville, seemed mired in the incompetency of
its generals."⁵¹ Nevertheless, despite his sensitivity to the country's
complaints "of the inefficiency of the army" and its leaders, the
motives behind the draft riots in New York, the various skirmishes
over Lincoln's Emancipation Proclamation, as well as many of the
other major factors contributing to the North's distress, Emerson
still maintains his conviction in the moral and ethical benefits that the
war brings with it. As he writes in a letter of June 17, 1863, to the
parents of a colonel who had been killed during the recent Union
attack on Port Hudson, Louisiana, "there are crises which demand
nations, as well as those which claim the sacrifice of single lives. Ours
perhaps is one and that one whole generation might well consent to
perish, if, by their fall, political liberty & clean & just life could be
made sure to the generations that follow" (*L*, 5: 332).⁵² The war is the
cruel but inevitable price of the nation's recovery of moral health. In
the face of personal and national fears—and in spite of his varying
estimate of America, which, as he says, "sometimes runs very low,
sometimes to ideal prophetic proportions" (*J*, 15: 166)—Emerson
encourages both himself and others to reaffirm the moral forces of
the North's early responses to the war. "There never was a nation
great," he writes in his journal, "except through trial" (*J*, 15: 298).
Though the war is still going badly for the North, he claims to detect

a renewed enthusiasm for liberty. He finds this enthusiasm in the raised hopes of the North and the weakening of the Copperhead movement that followed the Union's capture of Vicksburg and the victory at Gettysburg in July. Once the progress toward Liberty is in motion, he insists, nothing can interfere with it.

Weathering History

As Emerson explains in a brief but remarkable passage that both crystallizes and expands a number of his major themes concerning the meaning of the war to the nation, the war is "not an unmitigated evil; it is a potent alternative. . . . I see it come as a frosty October, which shall restore intellectual and moral power to these languid and dissipated populations" (J, 15: 379–80).[53] He offers in these few lines an intricate and powerful allegory of the war and its ambiguities. At a time when the war has reached another of its many crises, when the war's demands have weakened and scattered the North's energies, he figures the war as a powerful process of transformation that marshals the populace forward along a path of improvement, rekindling the light of moral and intellectual truth, and thereby summoning into existence a vital and energetic future. The progress of the war may bring death to many, but at the same time it enlivens people who have become spiritless, who are slow to respond to the war's imperatives because they can no longer sustain the vigorous patriotism and dedication the war requires. In the autumnal season of the war, when hopes seem to fall and wither along with the leaves of trees, the war comes according to an inexorable and compensatory law to turn the colors of weariness into those of hope and encouragement—and it does so in the name of nature. This conviction that the war comes with the force of nature to help restore the country to its founding principles was shared by many of Emerson's contemporaries and is given expression in numerous newspaper editorials aimed at characterizing what the April 29, 1861, *New York Herald* called "The Salutary Effects of the War":

All are disposed to recognise the disastrous effects of war, particularly of civil war, in those States which become the theatre of action. But the ultimate beneficial influences of war to society are for the most part overlooked in its present devastations and horrors. In the wise arrangements of Providence war seems to be a necessity—the result of a natural law for the preservation of society—just as much as storms and tempests, and whirlwinds and thunder, are the results of natural laws, and purify the atmosphere and render it salubrious to man and beast, while partially destructive to both. . . . Without war society would become stagnant and corrupt, just as would the air we breathe without the agitation of the winds.[54]

Like the frost, which is often figured as the breath of God, the war comes as a natural manifestation of spiritual and moral power, "a marked benefactor in the hands of divine Providence." Like the natural process of frost, the movement of the war works its effects according to local causes, transforms the objects or surfaces on which it acts, and brings death as well as life. For Emerson, "there is nothing lucky or capricious in these analogies" (*W*, 1: 27). They "pervade nature" and obey the laws of correspondence that govern the relationship between natural history and human history. As he claims in his November 4, 1833, lecture "The Uses of Natural History," "the laws of moral nature answer to those of matter as face to face in a glass."[55] "Such is the saturation of things with the moral law that you cannot escape it," he says elsewhere, "every change and every cause in nature is nothing but a disguised missionary," every natural process is "a version of a moral sentence," "every animal function from the sponge up to Hercules, shall hint or thunder to man the laws of right and wrong, and echo the Ten Commandments" (*J*, 15: 296; *W*, 1: 41, and 1: 40–41). Linking together the workings of nature—and in particular those of frost—with the movement of history, he suggests that the extraordinary nature of the war lies in its coincidence with the laws of nature's progress.[56] This coincidence is reinforced by numerous accounts and anecdotes that he gathered from his readings in horticulture, geology, chemistry, physics, literature, and political writing. Together they offer a basis for understanding more fully the strength and pertinence of his analogy.[57]

This pertinence is in part due to the link, in both proslavery and antislavery propaganda, between a rhetoric of morality and that of another intellectual tradition, which understood character and temperament to be dependent on environment. In particular, Emerson's figure draws on commonplace notions of the role and place of climate in determining not only moral and racial differences but also sectional differences. Like the analogy between politics and frost with which we began, this passage also exploits the political divisions between the so-called frostbelt and sunbelt states that had begun to be asserted as early as the revolution.[58] Within these debates over the differences between frosty climates and hot ones, "intellectual and moral power" was attributed stereotypically to the North, while the South was peopled by "languid and dissipated populations." What remains idiomatic in Emerson's use of these notions here is that he extends the epithet "languid and dissipated populations" to include not only southerners but also northerners who, he thought, were weakening in the face of the war's trials. In this way, he shifts the epithet from its more sectional and racist associations—it also was often used to describe the character of blacks and other ethnic minorities—in order to suggest a complicity between northern and southern interests in slavery, in order to suggest that the war requires a change of mind in both the North and the South.[59] What is at stake for Emerson in his analogy is the possibility of turning a language that has been used to reinforce slavery and discrimination against itself. This possibility can more often be read, as in this instance, in his practice of writing, in his staging and treatment of the language of slavery and war, than in any explicit and straightforward arguments.

This is why, if he deliberately chooses this analogy to name—even if only in broad outline—the historical and political meaning of the war for America, we may trace further the contours of this meaning by noting that the meteorological or atmospheric conditions most conducive to the formation of frost in the United States themselves allegorize the topographical elements of the civil conflict. The occurrence of frost is usually preceded by northerly winds accompanied by high barometric pressure, and especially by the coincidence of these conditions with the near approach, or passing, of a storm from the south or west. If Emerson figures the coming of the war as the coming of a "frosty October," he does so because the analogy helps him delineate a moment in American history when "the irresistible conflict" between the North and the South—primarily over the persistence of slavery in the Union and its expansion in the western territories—has provoked the political storm that now hovers over the country, casting its shadow over the populace. This allegory becomes less farfetched if we recall that the years between 1830 and 1871—the year that the United States Weather Bureau was established—witnessed unexampled activity in the study of storms, especially in relation to questions of navigation and agriculture. This activity led to an increased understanding of "the winds of the world"—what H. Hildebrandsson and L. Teisserene de Bort later called "dynamic meteorology"[60]—and to growing speculation about the relationship between storms and the variable, and sometimes violent, course of political history. One writer of an essay on "The Winds and the Weather" in the January 1858 issue of the *Atlantic Monthly* provides an example of such analogies when, at once emphasizing the "republican principles" that govern the power of the winds and the rain and the "lawlessness" and "incalculable fickleness" of the weather, he claims that "Man finds himself everywhere mirrored in nature."[61] Such speculation belongs to a long tradition of *reading* the weather in America.[62] Given the strength of this tradition, it took little imagination to link the country's political and social movements to the rhythms and crises of the weather. Not only were "military hopes" understood to "rise and fall with the rising and falling of the metal of the thermometer's tube," but "all military operations" were said to depend for their issue, to a greater or lesser extent, "upon the softening or the hardening of the earth, or upon the clearing or the clouding of the sky."[63]

One of the more prominent "weather prophets" of Emerson's day was James Pollard Espy. Publishing a controversial volume called *The Philosophy of Storms* in 1841, Espy became a regular lecturer on the popular lyceum circuit, where he was known as "The Storm King."[64] In a letter of January 14, 1843, to Lidian Emerson, Emerson describes having attended a lecture by Espy in Washington, D.C., and claims that the speaker amused him "with storms & inductive metaphysics" (*L*, 3: 123).[65] Espy's most notorious speculations concerned rainmaking. Observing that smoke rising above urban manufacturing areas often produced rain clouds, Espy believed that rain could be provoked artificially by fire. In order to relieve the current drought-like conditions in the mid-Atlantic States, he suggested that forest land be burned in order to precipitate rainfall. Although Congress did not approve his proposal, it is not without significance that the suggestion was made during a time of westward expansion. The weather was not only seen as an essential component in the progress of the growing nation, but this growth could also go so far as to "create" the weather.[66] Emerson's allegory of the nation's crisis seems almost

tame when compared to Espy's grandiose vision of the relation between the weather and America's unfolding history.

This link between the weather and politics had great circulation
in the journals, reviews, poetry, and even cartoons of the day, especially during moments of great civil crisis. In the May 1862 issue of
the *Atlantic Monthly*, for example, C. C. Hazewell wrote a historical
essay named "Weather in War," in which he discussed the role and
consequences of the weather in the operations of the war between
the Persians and the Greeks, the war between Spain and England, the
Napoleonic Wars, America's conflict with England, and the present
secessionist battle between the North and the South. This essay was
followed half a year later by an article in the January 1863 issue of the
New York Evening Post entitled "The Weather and the Army," which
argued for the importance of meteorology to the outcome of the war.
Whitman also devoted a section of *Specimen Days* to the question of
whether or not the weather "sympathizes" with the events of the war:

Whether the rains, the heat and cold, and what underlies them all, are affected with what affects man in masses, and follow his play of passionate
action, strain'd stronger than usual, and on a larger scale than usual—
whether this, or no, it is certain that there is now, and has been for twenty
months or more, on this American continent north, many a remarkable,
many an unprecedented expression of the subtle world of air above us and
around us. There, since this war, and the wide and deep national agitation,
strange analogies, different combinations, a different sunlight, or absence of
it; different products even out of the ground. After every great battle, a great
storm. Even civic events the same. On Saturday last, a forenoon like whirling
demons, dark, with slanting rain, full of rage; and then the afternoon, so
calm, so bathed, with flooding splendor from heaven's most excellent sun,
with atmosphere of sweetness; so clear, it show'd the stars, long, long before
they were due. As the President came out on the capitol portico, a curious
little white cloud, the only one in that part of the sky, appear'd like a hovering
bird right over him. Indeed, the heavens, the elements, all the meteorological
influences, have run riot for weeks past. It is a common remark that (as last
summer was different in its spells of intense heat from any preceding it), the
winter just completed has been without parallel. It has remained so down to
the hour I am writing.[67]

Emerson's own "strange analogies" between the weather and the
war may begin to be understood within the context of such medita-
tions. The parallels that he draws between the phenomenon of frost

and the war become especially striking when we recall that in New England an October frost is commonly referred to as a "killing frost," in order to suggest the immense and prodigious power of frost to damage and destroy crops, such as corn, vegetables, and fruits, as well as trees and other vegetation. This killing force is described in explicitly militaristic terms in various passages that Emerson might well have read in the set of encyclopedias that he owned, as well as in some of the horticultural journals to which he subscribed. In the entry "Frost" in the 1820 edition of the *Encyclopedia Americana*, for example—the edition that Emerson had in his library—the breaking up of ice on lakes is said to be accompanied by "a noise not less loud than if many guns were discharged together" and the cracking of ice-laden trees, the entry goes on to say, is "often attended with dreadful noises, like the explosion of fire arms."[68] These statements are corroborated by an article on frost in the August 1847 issue of *The Horticulturalist*, also in Emerson's library. There, the author claims that "severe cold has the effect occasionally of rending the entire trunks of large trees with a loud noise like the report of a cannon."[69] If these statements address the destructive character of frost, then Emerson's studies in geology and natural history—his readings in Georges Cuvier's *Discourse on the Revolutions of the Surface of the Globe*, John Playfair's *Illustrations of the Huttonian Theory of the Earth*, and Mrs. Sarah Lee's *Memoirs of Baron Cuvier* in the early 1830s, to name only a few—helped him to articulate the role that frost plays within the economy of nature. "The same process that destroys in different circumstances," he says, "is made to reproduce. And few phenomena in nature are more full of interest than the series of changes by which new strata are formed and consolidated and mineralized again to be decomposed" (*EL*, 1: 55).

The phenomenon of frost, Emerson knows, includes the processes of freezing as well as the effects of these processes. As he says of the law that demands that heat be released "whenever gases are converted into fluids or fluids into solids," frost, both destructive and beneficial, "is of the utmost importance in the economy of nature" (*EL*, 1: 59). It enters the crevices and minute cracks in rocks and rends them apart. Aiding and hastening their disintegration, it converts the rocks and solid materials of the earth into soil. Its capacity to loosen and pulverize the soil—by entering it and forcing the particles of compacted soil apart through its expansive action on the particles of moisture disseminated therein—was well known by Emerson's time and was considered to be of inestimable value to both agriculture and humanity.[70] As he remarks in his 1833 lecture "Water," the third of his four lectures "The Uses of Natural History":

Water everywhere "appears as the most active enemy of hard and solid bodies; and in every state, from transparent vapour to solid ice . . . it attacks whatever has emerged above the level of the sea, and labours incessantly to restore it to the deep." . . . The mechanical action of the waters reduces continually the immense mountain chains of granite and porphyry and forms from their ruins a habitable region, and fruitful fields. (*EL*, 1: 53–55)

In part citing Playfair's *Illustrations of the Huttonian Theory of the Earth*,[71] Emerson here provides a background against which we can continue to sharpen our understanding of his analogy between the war and frost. Like the frost that breaks up the hardened and solid elements of the earth and returns them "to the deep," the war, as he states in his 1865 speech at Harvard commemorating the Harvard sons who had survived the war, "passes the power of all chemical solvents, breaking up the old adhesions and allowing the atoms of society to take a new order" (*W*, 11: 341). The virtue of this new order is that it returns the country to the profundity of its founding principles, principles underlying the acts of transformation that, for Emerson, define the event of the American Revolution. The war loosens and disintegrates the hardened convictions that have led to the country's civil crisis. Like the frost that destroys in order to bring about a new state, the war is a force of crystallization that, even as it kills, consolidates and brings together the North's moral sentiment, directing it toward the abolition of slavery. Turning America from its destructive course toward its principled beginnings, the war rejuvenates the land, making it again habitable and fruitful. Like the frost that compensates for its ruinous effects, the "war heals a deeper wound than any it makes" (*J*, 15: 63).

Emerson's apparent desire to control the ambiguity and instability of war leads him to invoke, in the name of that control, the ambiguous figure of frost: the natural history of frost crystallizes the elemental questions of the war into the question of the relationship between life and death. In other words, the analogies that he draws between frost and the movements of war or politics suggest that for him the politics of war are founded on the natural coincidence of life and death. This coincidence constitutes the process of transformation that he terms "progress." If the war heals, it is because it brings "intellectual and moral power" to a weakened nation. Showing "the bankruptcy of all narrow views" and thereby undoing rigid beliefs, the war's expansive action helps men and women resist "the tendency to consolidation and rest" (*EL*, 2: 218) by provoking them into rethinking their relation to the war's questions. The war's own consolidating and crystallizing action is directed at transforming the way the populace thinks rather than reinforcing its present lack of vigor.[72]

As always, for Emerson, men are what they think. "It is a law which is found to hold in history," he states in his notebook "Liberty," "that it is not . . . their race, not their government, or their employment, which determines the destinies of men, but their credence. As is their way of thinking and belief, will their power and fortune be" (*J*, 14: 421). In suggesting a complicity between the genealogy of the war, between slavery as a social institution and the subtler forms of war and slavery at work in certain ways of thinking, Emerson here anticipates Phillips's claim, in his "State of the Country" address of 1863, that "we have not only an army to conquer . . . but we have a state of mind to annihilate."[73] For Emerson and Phillips the war can only bring victory and glory if it is conducted by men and women whose thinking is informed by ethical and moral sentiment. "Cannons think in this day of ours," Phillips proclaims in December 1861, "and it is only by putting thought behind arms that we render them worthy, in any degree, of the civilization of the nineteenth century."[74] "When the cannon is aimed by ideas," Emerson writes, this time echoing Phillips's rhetoric, "then gods join in the combat, then poets are born. . . . When men die for what they live for, and the mainspring that works daily urges them to hazard all, then the cannon articulates its explosions with the voice of a man . . . and the better code of laws at last records the victory" (*AS*, 142). "The whole battle," he claims elsewhere, "is fought in a few heads" (*W*, 12: 121). Thinking has the capacity to transform whatever it acts upon and, depending on its present state—of mind as well as of government—it can provoke either right or wrong. It can encourage either life or death. The demands of the war coincide with the aims of Emerson's rhetoric: each requires the transformative regeneration of a way of thinking that wants moral force, that is not yet organized around the ethical imperatives of nature. However much a natural necessity, the war will be transformative only insofar as it is at the same time a war of thought, a war that provokes thought, a war that can be rendered intellectually and morally significant. In more ways than one, the Civil War was, for Emerson, an ideological war.

Given the importance of the relationship between nature and thinking in Emerson, it is scarcely surprising that frost and the mind are figures for one another. As he claims in his first book in 1836: "Every appearance in nature corresponds to some state of mind . . . the whole of nature is a metaphor of the mind" (*W*, 1: 26, 32). Nature metaphorizes the processes of the mind at the same time that it is itself a figure produced by these processes. "The laws of [man's] mind," he explains, "the periods of his actions externized themselves into day and night, into the year and the seasons" (*W*, 1: 71). He brings together the action of frost and the processes of thinking in an early journal entry from January 1832. "There is a process in the mind," he writes, "very analogous to crystallization in the mineral kingdom" (*J*, 3: 316).[75] He repeats this point in a passage that links the process of crystallization to man himself: "Nature is the incarnation of a thought, and turns to a thought again, as ice becomes water and gas. The world is mind precipitated, and the volatile essence is forever escaping again into the state of free thought. Hence the virtue and pungency of the influence on the mind of natural objects, whether inorganic or organized. Man imprisoned, man crystallized, man vegetative, speaks to man impersonated" (*W*, 3: 196). This relay between thought and nature, between man and nature, follows the divine order of a nature that is what it is only to the extent that it already impersonates man. In other words, thought begins in a confusion of multiple associations that, upon reflection, organize themselves according to the force of nature's decree, the dictates of divine providence—what Emerson terms "God's architecture." Like the frost, which consolidates different elements into a force of dispersion, thinking works to crystallize the undefined or floating character of its own expansive movement. Linking together disparate elements, like nature, thought comes in the form of a metaphor. "A man conversing in earnest," Emerson says, "if he watch his intellectual processes, will find that always a material image, more or less luminous, arises in his mind, cotemporaneous with every thought, which furnishes the vestment of the thought. Hence, good writing and brilliant discourse are perpetual allegories" (*W*, 1: 31). Thought emerges with rhetoric. It is not only brought into existence along with rhetoric, but it also depends on rhetoric for its existence. Thinking cannot exist without the rhetoric that both reveals and conceals it. This fact is of great importance in Emerson's efforts to provoke the faint minds of the land back to life, for if he proclaims the coming of a war that will "restore intellectual and moral power" to the "languid and dissipated" minds of the populace, he at the same time suggests, through his own declaration, that the means of such restoration correspond to an act of rhetorical persuasion, an act that is governed by the inevitable advance of nature's ethical aims.[76]

This point is reinforced when we note that, in Emerson's formulation, the war itself appears rhetorically. His claim that he sees the war "come as a frosty October" does not say that the war *is* a frosty October. Neither does his statement suggest that the two terms of the simile are strictly analogous to one another. Although the war comes *as* a frosty October and therefore in its action and movement resembles those of this particular seasonal phenomenon, the same claim also suggests that the similarity between the terms lies in their manner of *coming*. The war comes as (in the same way as) a frosty October comes. Like the thought that measures its progress and outcome, the war comes in the form of a metaphor. The war comes with metaphor. Or, better yet: whether the war comes *as* a frosty October or whether it comes in the same way that "a frosty October" comes, it comes as a metaphor (comes). The rhetoric of war—the rhetoric that is war—corresponds to the force of its coming. There is no war without rhetoric. There are no campaigns without words. This does not mean that acts of war—the various acts of killing, suffering, and fighting, for example, that usually announce the fact of war—are only words, but rather that they have to come with words. They require the acts of persuasion, the arguments, the debates, the commands, and the legislation that are at once the force, provocation, and effects of the war. Rhetoric is never "to be distinguished from action," Emerson writes, "it is the electricity of action. It is action, as the general's word of command or chart of battle is action" (*W*, 8: 115). Calling attention to the war's rhetorical dimension—that is, to the war's capacity to declare, to institute, and to promise—Emerson emphasizes the essential tie he sees between language and politics and, in particular, the role that rhetoric has played within the history of American politics.

America's Logocracy

From the scriptural and covenantal community of the Puritans to the writing of a Constitution that enabled America to speak itself into being, and from this to the era between the Revolution and the Civil War that Edward G. Parker refers to as the "golden age of American oratory," America has been, as its first poet laureate, Washington Irving, notes, governed by words: "the simple truth of the matter is that their government is a pure, unadulterated *logocracy* or *government of words*. The whole nation does everything *viva voce*, or, by word of mouth, and in this manner is one of the most military nations in existence. . . . The country is intirely defended *vi et lingua*, that is to say, by *force of tongues*." "In a logocracy," Irving goes on to explain, "every offensive or defensive measure is enforced by wordy battle and paper war; he who has the longest tongue, or readiest quill, is sure to gain the victory."[77] The pervasiveness and place of political oratory, sermons, lyceum addresses, public dialogues, legal arguments, and commemorative orations within America's efforts to invent its cultural and national identity, and the respect given to such political orators as Patrick Henry, Edward Everett, William Ellery Channing, Daniel Webster, Frederick Douglass, Charles Sumner, and Wendell Phillips, to name only a few of the many who gained national literary reputations for their rhetorical abilities, seem to support Irving's claim. America has been a country of tongues and quills.[78] As Thomas Gustafson explains, "guided by the Word of God or by the words of the Declaration and the Constitution, Americans have conceived of themselves as the 'people of the Word,' and whether that word is understood as the Word of God or the words of the founding fathers, it has been their calling to rise up and live out the meaning of those words."[79]

In a republic that exists to define and maintain freedom, public expression and rhetoric are not only encouraged but indispensable. "By the eternal constitution of things," John Quincy Adams declared, in what was perhaps America's first formal treatise on rhetoric, "it was ordained, that liberty should be the parent of eloquence; that eloquence should be the last stay and support of liberty; that with her she is ever destined to live, to flourish, and to die."[80] Emerson himself writes that oratory "is eminently the art that only flourishes in free countries." "If there ever was a country where eloquence was a power," he adds, "it is the United States" (*W*, 8: 110, 132). Free men need to be persuaded rather than coerced. That this also lends, according to Daniel Walker Howe, "a particular importance to oratory as a means of social control" may account for Emerson's conviction that any analysis of political authority must at the same time address the rhetorical means whereby such authority is established. The same rhetoric that renders freedom possible may also restrict it.[81] We could even say that the history of the American experiment, from its beginnings on through the Civil War, can be read as the confirmation of this truth. The colonists shared with Locke and other Enlightenment writers an understanding of the ways in which the struggles for interests and power are conducted by linguistic means. In the *Federalist Papers*, for example, Alexander Hamilton notes that people can be governed as much by words as by force. "In the ancient republics," he writes, "when the whole body of the people assembled in person, a single orator, or an artful statesman, was generally seen to rule with as complete a sway as if a scepter had been placed in his hand."[82] As Emerson would have it, the orator may become "the organ of a multitude," "taking sovereign possession of it" with "that deceptiveness which poets have celebrated in the 'Pied Piper of Hamelin' " (*W*, 7: 66–67). This is why Emerson so often works to expose the counterfeit claims of America's republican rhetoric, a rhetoric most obviously revealed in the promise of its legal system to provide liberty and justice for all. As Emerson writes after the passing of the Fugitive Slave Act, "The popular assumption that all men loved freedom was found hollow American brag" (*AS*, 55).

If Emerson's claim that the war comes "as a frosty October" recalls the centrality of language within American politics, it does so not only to announce a contradiction in the meaning of America but also to locate this contradiction within language. For him, the power of language resides in its capacity to affect, if not to determine, the unstable but necessary course of historical and political events. In his two addresses on the subject, emphasizing the persuasive aspect of all rhetoric, he claims that "Eloquence" aims at altering, "in a pair of hours, perhaps in a half-hour's discourse, the convictions and habits of years" (*W*, 7: 64). This view, widely accepted in Emerson's day, reflects a not entirely groundless hope, or fear, that a single individual might be able to provoke major social change by sheer rhetorical force. The moral rectitude of such rhetoric depends on whether it directs the men and women whose convictions and habits it transforms toward greater freedom or greater enslavement. If the aims of an orator's eloquence correspond with those of nature, he might lead a people to discover the conditions of their liberty, but if his moral power falters, he can only jeopardize these same conditions. Emerson's appeal to the beneficent and transformative powers of the war arises from this context, responding as it does to the imperative that rhetoric be infused with ethical direction. If the nation is to be encouraged to favor liberty over slavery, its citizens must recall the moral nature of its revolutionary founding. His campaign to provoke the North into reconsidering its relation to the demands of nature's ethics is also an effort to alter the rhetoric of a North whose "national spirit" has become "drowsy, preoccupied with interest, deaf to principle" (*AS*, 86) and thereby forgetful of its moral beginnings. The restoration of "intellectual and moral power" to the "languid and dissipated" minds of this populace coincides with the coming of a powerful rhetoric whose moral force in turn corresponds to that of the war. This plea that rhetoric be reinvigorated by the moral spirit of the war is reinforced by Emerson's deliberate choice of the word "languid." If he chooses the word to name his sense of the North's spiritual weakness, he also wishes to emphasize the linguistic dimension of moral and intellectual power. Not only is a "languid" mind one which uses a language wanting in force or direction but, according to *The Oxford English Dictionary*, the word "languid," in its substantive form, is a corruption of *languet*, a diminutive form of French *langue*, which refers to the small talk of little tongues. Emerson had already established this link between the use of language and the measure of intellectual or mental power in an early journal entry from January 11, 1832. "The manner of using language," he writes, "is surely the most decisive test of intellectual power and he who has intellectual force of any kind will be sure to show it there" (*J*, 3: 319).

Men and women are not only what they think. They are also what they write and speak. Or, to be more precise, what they think is shaped by their language.

Emerson's recourse to a rhetoric grounded in nature and its laws allows him to make a powerful and complex appeal to the people of his country to rethink their relation to nature, politics, and language in terms of the prevailing issues of justice and injustice he wishes to address. Such a reflection, he claims, is requisite to any moral and ethical reform with regard to the issues of slavery and westward expansion that have led to the present national crisis. "All our political disasters," he tells us in another journal entry from the summer of 1863, "grow as logically out of our attempts in the past to do without justice, as thistles & nettles out of their seeds" (*J*, 15: 298). His persistent use of natural imagery is one and the same with his insistence that we measure our actions and thoughts according to the laws of nature. This persistence belongs to an entire rhetorical tradition that acknowledges the persuasive power of such imagery. "This immediate dependence of language upon nature," he notes, " . . . never loses its power to affect us" (*W*, 1: 29), because natural imagery gives way to the power of human activity, whether in poetry, oratory, or political controversy. As he writes in a journal entry from 1835, comparing the oratorical skills of Edmund Burke to those of Daniel Webster, "let a man make the woods and fields his books then at the hour of passion his thoughts will invest themselves spontaneously with natural imagery" (*J*, 5: 106).[83] If the greatest orators learn their skills in the fields and open air, the measure of their greatness lies in their being able to translate these skills into what he calls, at the end of his essay "Experience," "practical power" (*W*, 3: 86). As he explains in a famous passage from *Nature*, which brings together many of the issues pertinent to an understanding of the politicality of Emerson's rhetoric, both during the war and before:

The poet, the orator, bred in the woods, whose senses have been nourished by their fair and appeasing changes, year after year, without design and without heed,—shall not lose their lesson altogether, in the roar of cities or the broil of politics. Long hereafter, amidst agitation and terror in national councils,—in the hour of revolution,—these solemn images shall reappear in their morning lustre, as fit symbols and words of the thoughts which the

passing events shall awaken. . . . And with these forms, the spells of persuasion, the keys of power arc put into his hands. (*W*, 1: 31–32)[84]

In this passage from the mid-1830s, Emerson anticipates the approach to the question of the relationship between politics and representation that he will refine and develop throughout his career.
During moments of historical and political crisis, he suggests, the
poet or orator exhibits an almost incantational power, which calls
forth the images he once received from nature in order to figure the
thoughts and minds of others. He had already made this point in
"The Uses of Natural History." There, referring to the "power of
expression that belongs to external nature," to the "correspondence
of the outward world to the inward world of thought and emotions,"
and to the "secret sympathy which connects men to all the animals
and to all the inanimate beings around him," he suggests that the poet
draws his language from nature. "Nature is a language," he goes on
to say, "and every new fact one learns is a new word; but it is not a
language taken to pieces and dead in the dictionary, but the language
put together into a most significant and universal sense. I wish to
learn this language not that I may know a new grammar, but that I
may read the great book which is written in that tongue" (*EL*, 1: 39,
44, 46). As a child of nature, then, as a witness to nature's transformative and prodigal power, the poet gives way to the natural imagery
that, as a force of gathering and provocation, compels the minds of
the populace to awaken to the hour's passing events. The politicality
of Emerson's use of natural imagery coincides with its revolutionary
emergence and finds its forceful enactment in his efforts to address
the political and social issues of the day. Precisely this language of
nature is at the heart of the theories of rhetoric that prevailed in
America between the Revolution and the Civil War. As John Adams
notes in a diary entry from 1758, the orator, in order to "gain the Art
of moving the Passions, must attend to Nature, must observe the
Sounds in which all sorts of People, express the Passions and sentiments of their Hearts, and must learn to adapt his own Voice, to the
Passions he would move."[85]

In the broil of politics, Emerson the poet never speaks without
measuring what he says or what he refers to against the movement
and laws of nature. In the process, these natural metaphors take on

specific historical, political, theological, and literary connotations that, in the long run, will require us to return to the relationship between these domains and questions of language. Always in Emerson the suggestion that we align ourselves with the laws of nature corresponds to the necessity that we be attentive to the rhetorical dimension of our historical and political existence. Natural metaphors within his writings are not merely tropes but also principles of articulation among language, politics, and history. These principles account for both the force of tropes on whatever we might call the "reality" of history or politics and the essential figurality at work within the movement and constitution of either history or politics. This is why, he suggests, "the schools of poets and philosophers are not more intoxicated with their symbols than the populace with theirs. . . . The people fancy they hate poetry, and they are all poets and mystics." "We are symbols and inhabit symbols," he goes on to say, "workmen, work, and tools, words and things, birth and death, all are emblems" (*W*, 3: 16–17, 20).

The specular structure of frost, therefore, figures a more general structure that involves natural metaphors as historically and politically marked articulations of knowledge. Whatever nature may be within such articulations, it is inseparable from the political, historical, and rhetorical motivations that help determine what it is. Both the North and the South, for example, in associating the violence of the war with the volatile and sometimes violent storms of nature, attempt to naturalize the bloodshed resulting from the violent conflict in which they are engaged. Not only do nature and the weather help us explain events or crises that would otherwise appear traumatic in their contingency, but they are involved essentially in the provocation and enactment of these events or crises as figures. They are involved essentially in the historical acts of the production of meaning. Their links with knowledge give them their force and hence their consequence within the domains of history and politics. Emerson's obsession with the rhetoric of nature's laws is, therefore, less an attempt to reorient man's spiritual and moral life away from history toward higher, absolute principles—although it is this, too—and more an appeal for the necessity that we view the concept of nature as essentially historical. His "political" project does not merely articulate the ideal and immutable conditions of our existence as historical and political beings, it also traces a connection between transcendental idealism and empirical realism, between the aims of philosophy and the aims of history, and does so through a rigorous investigation of the nature of representation.

Nature's Ethics

If Emerson's invocation of the laws of nature corresponds to his wish to demonstrate the historical character of the notion of *nature*, it is because he wishes us to understand the rhetorical and political dimensions of any effort to define such a concept. His appeal to "natural law," especially in his writings of the 1850s and 1860s, not only links his texts with a historically marked tradition of late-eighteenth-century writing that used the natural law arguments of earlier figures such as Hugh Grotius, Samuel von Pufendorf, John Locke, Montesquieu, Lord Mansfield, and William Blackstone to argue against slavery but also recalls the revolutionary effort to found American politics in nature.[86] During the war, Emerson allies his so-called transcendentalist argument with historical debate concerning the relationship between natural and positive law in the wider discussion of slavery and antislavery that had transpired across the previous three-quarters of a century. He aligns himself with the abolitionists or legal theorists who argued that natural law makes any "positivist" or pragmatic legal decision essentially immoral if that decision goes against an individual's "natural right" to freedom. For Emerson and others, to speak of slavery as an institution opposed to natural law, even though the immediate legal consequences of such rhetoric might be limited, is to exhibit the moral defect of the legal system and so begin the important work that necessarily precedes any legal reform. As Phillips writes, "alas, the ostrich does not get rid of her enemy by hiding her head in the sand. Slavery is not abolished, although we have persuaded ourselves that it has no right to exist . . . . The Constitution will never be amended by persuading men that it does not need amendment. National evils are only cured by holding men's eyes open, and forcing them to gaze on the hideous reality."[87]

The persistent recourse to the virtues of natural law or natural right in order to convey the immorality of slavery suggests the strength of a common tradition and a set of meanings for the word "natural" that historically has associated moral force with the rhetoric of nature. For Emerson, the ambiguity and richness of the language of natural law is precisely what makes it so dangerously attractive as a means for expressing moral concern over slave law. In the 1780s, the language of natural law was both pervasive and overdetermined in discussions of slavery. Practically all of the literature written either to oppose or to support slavery was based on an interpretation of natural law. As Cover notes, "Both the rhetoric of the revolution and many basic sources for legal education raised natural law and natural rights questions about slavery."[88] During the period between the Revolution and the beginning of the Civil War, not only abolitionists and more moderate opponents of slavery but also judges chose the language of natural law to register their moral questions about slavery. As Emerson writes, the issue of slavery, especially upon the enactment of the Fugitive Slave Law, "made every citizen a student of natural law" (AS, 64). The specific instances may have addressed different circumstances, but almost all of the arguments were organized around the proposition that slavery is contrary to natural law. It rests on no other support than that of human legislation, and is such, Garrison proclaimed, that "the laws of nature and of spirit are violated, the moral government of the universe is rebelled against, and God is insulted and dethroned, by the usurpation of his power and authority."[89] Following Garrison, Gerrit Smith, in a letter of 1839 to Henry Clay, argued that "slavery is a war against nature" and a "devourer of the rights of nature"; Horace Mann, in his speech in the House of Representatives in 1848 on the necessity of excluding slavery from the territories, claimed that "the institution of slavery is against natural right"; and Sumner, in his 1852 speech against the Fugitive Slave Law, found slavery to be "repugnant to the Law of Nature and the inborn Rights of Man."[90] According to Emerson, what is needed is a universal effort to stop the slave traffic. In order to accomplish this, he suggests, "the nations should league themselves in indissoluble bonds, should link the thunderbolts of national power to demolish this debtor to all Justice human & divine" (J, 3: 10).

If slavery was morally wrong, however, positive law nevertheless sanctioned its existence. The rhetoric of natural law became, for Emerson, a powerful means of expressing the disparity between law and morality, and the failure of a revolution that had promised to realize natural rights. Rather than focus solely on the glory of the nation's early beginnings, he reminds us of the unfinished work of the revolution: the eradication of slavery. As Bernard Bailyn has demonstrated, attacks on slavery, joining the growing cry for freedom from the "slavery" of British rule, had by 1774 become "a commonplace in the pamphlet literature of the northern and middle colonies."[91] Colonial rhetoric repeatedly pointed to the inconsistency between slaveholding and the many revolutionary assertions of the natural right to liberty. Thomas Paine's first piece of public writing in America, the short essay "African Slavery in America," was a strong natural law attack on slavery. Written only a few weeks after he arrived in the country late in 1774 and authored in the name of "Justice and Humanity," the essay denounces what he calls the "monstrosity" of slavery, claiming that slavery is "contrary to the light of nature" and in violation of "a natural, perfect right" to freedom.[92] Emerson's own efforts to bring together the rhetoric of revolution and the varied tradition of natural law on slavery therefore has its source in an important strain of political writing that, like his own, had before it the revolutionary end of independence. As Donald Pease reminds us, the revolutionary fathers repeatedly declared liberty to be a self-evident truth, defining it as "a natural right protected by natural law." By natural law, he goes on to explain, they meant "a system of law binding on men by virtue of their nature, independent of any convention or positive law."[93] Nature's law required a correspondence between the rule of government and the workings of nature that would then define America's special character. "The United States of America," John Adams pronounced, "have exhibited, perhaps, the first example of government erected on the simple principles of nature."[94]

By Emerson's time, however, slaveholders and their supporters were invoking natural law in the name of slavery. By claiming the right to property guaranteed by natural law as the basis for their natural right to hold slaves, they justified what others considered an "unnatural" institution. The growing abolitionist movement in the 1830s, along with the spread of the cotton industry, the struggle for control of the territories, and the contest to continue southern power in the Senate, had pressured the leaders of southern thought, as Calhoun stated in 1838, "to look into the nature and character of this great institution, and to correct any false impressions that *even we* had entertained in relation to it."[95] As Benjamin Wright tells us, "Instead of lamenting and even apologizing for its existence as a necessary if unnatural evil, they came to proclaim it as a great good and as the most natural of institutions."[96] Citing the Bible, Aristotle, and many of the natural law theorists—Grotius, Pufendorf, Locke, and Blackstone, to name only a few—writers from Thomas R. Dew, whose 1833 *Review of the Debates in the Virginia Legislature* fueled the Southern defense of slavery, to George Fitzhugh, whose 1854 *Sociology for the South* and 1857 *Cannibals, All!* argued that slavery was "natural" to civilized society, found justification for the institution in the laws of nature and of God.[97] That natural law could be used to justify as well as to question an institution supported by positive law made it clear to Emerson that natural law could correspond with whatever institution one wanted to claim as natural. He registers this point as early as November 1822 when, in his journal, he states that what is needed is an analysis "of slavery as agreeable or contradictory to the analogies of nature" (*J*, 2: 44–45). The national debates over slavery, in which statesmen redefined liberty in terms of positive law and thereby made it subject to governmental legislation, reinforced this point for him. As Pease explains, "The Fugitive Slave Law distinguished the natural right of liberty from a state's right to self-rule. Liberty was toppled from the realm of nature, where it was protected by nature's law, into the realm of political expediency, where it could not be the principle for deciding the debates on slavery. Politicians distinguished liberty as a natural right from liberty as a political convention by turning liberty into an ideal principle, quite separable from the realm of legal practices. Once set apart from the practical realm, natural liberty could be honored while ignored in practice."[98] That Daniel Webster, for example, could express his conviction that all men should be free, while voting the Fugitive Slave Act into law, led Emerson to exclaim, in a journal entry from 1851: "Let Mr. Webster for decency's sake shut his lips once and forever on this word. The word *liberty* in the mouth of Mr. Webster sounds like the word *love* in the mouth of a courtezan" (*J*, 11: 346). "All the great cities," he adds in his second address on the Fugitive Slave Law, "all the refined circles, all the statesmen, Guizot, Palmerston, Webster, Calhoun, are sure to be found banded against liberty; they are all sure to be found befriending liberty with their words; and crushing it with their votes" (*AS*, 86).

Emerson's sensitivity to the rhetorical and political duplicity of words such as *nature* and *liberty*, to their persuasive capacity either to support or to question the social institution of slavery in terms of its correspondence to immutable features of human nature, ought to be seen as part of his broader concern with the relationship between issues of politics and questions of representation. What is essential for Emerson is never solely the "reality" of a particular historical or political situation. It is also necessary to consider the way in which that situation is represented to others. This is why, concerning the question of slavery, he tells us in his 1844 address on the emancipation of the British West Indies that the history of slavery can be read in the history of language. In other words, there can be no institution of slavery, for Emerson, without a concept of race, without an argument or articulation in language that justifies racial oppression. As he explains: "From the earliest time, the negro has been an article of luxury to the commercial nations. So has it been, down to the day that has just dawned on the world. Language must be raked, the secrets of slaughter-houses and infamous holes that cannot front the day, must be ransacked, to tell what negro-slavery has been" (*AS*, 9).[99] According to Emerson, neither slavery nor race can be natural categories. They are born instead when institutions and individuals, trusting the rhetoric of nature and liberty to dissimulate their political interests, work to persuade others that these interests are "natural." Arguing that slavery is a natural institution, for example, they justify not only conceptions of the black man's inferiority but also the necessity of maintaining the institution of slavery. This is why, Emerson declares one year later, "the objection of an inferiority of race" can be summarized in the word *niggers* (*AS*, 36). "What arguments," he explains, "what eloquence can avail against the power of that one word *niggers*? The man of the world annihilates the whole combined force of all the antislavery societies of the world by pronouncing it."[100] "They who say it and they who hear it, think it the voice of nature and fate pronouncing against the Abolitionist and the Philanthropist. . . . And what is the amount of this conclusion in which the men of New-England acquiesce? It is, that the Creator of the Negro has given him up to stand as a victim of a caricature of the white man beside him; to stoop under his pack, and to bleed under his whip. If that be the doctrine, then, I say, if He has given up his cause, He has also given up mine, who feel his wrong" (*AS*, 36). While Cornel West and others have argued that Emerson's earlier thoughts on race betray an ambivalence toward the black man's capacity for self-improvement, there can be little doubt that by the early 1840s he is not persuaded by arguments for racial determination.[101] In his 1844 address, for instance, he speaks for "the annihilation of the old indecent nonsense about the nature of the negro" and cites William Wilberforce's claim that, with the emancipation, "we have already gained one victory: we have obtained for these poor creatures the recognition of their human nature, which, for a time, was most shamefully denied them" (*AS*, 29).

This is not to say that there are not discursive elements in Emerson that lend themselves to racist reappropriations. West is right to discern in Emerson's language an association between Emerson and the racism of his time. This cannot be ignored. At the same time, however, many other elements of Emerson's thought, even sometimes the very same elements, cannot be reduced to the project of racism—that is, there are *other* possibilities in Emerson which cannot be said to be determined by the history of racism. Emerson's texts are open, multiple, and fragmented. Parts of these texts connect with racism, and parts resist racism, are stronger than racism. If he states in 1822 that "Nature has plainly assigned different degrees of intellect to different races, and the barriers are insurmountable" (*J*, 2: 44), he says in 1854 that races "must be used hypothetically or temporarily, as we do the Linnean classification, for convenience simply, and not as true and ultimate" (*J*, 13: 288). In 1836 he praises the heroism of a Columbus whose act of imperial expansion joins the beauty of the natural scene to the beauty of his deed: "When the bark of Columbus nears the shore of America;—before it, the beach lined with savages, fleeing out of all their huts of cane; the sea behind; and the purple mountains of the Indian Archipelago around, can we separate the man from the living picture? Does not the New World clothe his form with her palm-groves and savannahs as fit drapery? Ever does natural beauty steal in like air, and envelope great actions" (*W*, 1: 20–21). Yet in 1849 he claims that slavery begins in America with Columbus: "You know very well who introduced slavery into this country; Christopher Columbus,—the foremost man in the world of his time. After his discovery, he sent back three ships loaded with slaves to Ferdinand and Queen Isabella, to pay the expenses of the cargoes sent out. Soon after, Bartholomew Columbus, his brother, sent out other vessels loaded with slaves. This was in 1495" (*AS*, 48–49). In a journal entry from the late 1830s he writes: "It cannot be maintained by any candid person that the African race have ever occupied or do promise ever to occupy any very high place in the human family. Their present condition is the strongest proof that they cannot. The Irish cannot; the American Indian cannot; the Chinese cannot. Before the energy of the Caucasian race all the other races have quailed and done obeisance." Yet in the same passage he speaks of our duty "to assert" the slave's "right in all companies" (*J*, 12: 152). If we can read this passage as a symptom of Emerson's racism, we can also read it as a condemnation of white imperialism. Rather than giving a certain privilege to the Caucasian race, in other words, it can be said to condemn the Caucasian wish to subjugate other races to its rule. Emerson's ventriloquization here implies that the superiority of the Caucasian race lies only in its greater energy, in its greater capacity for violence and force, in its desire to have all the other races submit to it in fear. It is *because* of such racism—which has always informed the conditions under which, for example, the African race lives—that the African has never occupied nor promises to occupy a high place within the human family. This is why, he tells us elsewhere, "race in the Negro is of appalling importance" (*W*, 5: 48). It is also why he does not necessarily imply that the black man's inferiority will lead to his extinction when he writes in 1854: "The dark man, the black man declines. The black man is courageous, but the white men are the children of God, said Plato. It will happen, by and by, that the black man will only be destined for museums like the Dodo" (*J*, 13: 286). Rather, he suggests that racism belongs to the history of the West, to the history of Western thought, beginning at least from as far back as Plato. This racism accounts not only for the black man's decline but also for the threat to his existence in general.

If the complicities in these passages cannot be denied, it is because, for Emerson, no political discourse can escape this law of complicity. Just as "there is no conservative, no man who from the beginning to the end of his life maintains the defective institutions," so "there is no pure reformer" (*W*, 1: 314).[102] We can never entirely escape the "defective institutions" we wish to overcome, he suggests, because some measure of complicity is always inevitable, no matter what we might try to do. This is why responsibility cannot lie in our denial of this complicity, in our effort to claim that this or that line of thought or action is free from it. It must instead consist in acknowledging this complicity, in recognizing its necessity, in trying to measure, from *within*, the extent to which a particular discourse remains linked to what it works to question—and then in attempting to act accordingly. Responsibility can only begin, for example, when we recognize that the terrifying effects of racism are at work everywhere and try to confront this fact directly. Rather than avoiding racism by denying its complexity—by claiming that we know exactly what it is and where its borders are—we should approach it through an act of thinking that is also an act of politics. This means—and this is what I have tried to use Emerson to suggest—that our political gestures are inseparable from the thought and discourse without which they could never take place. As Emerson's writings so often remind us, this thinking and this discursivity take time. Not only does it take several sentences to begin to unravel implications and consequences—sometimes sentences that seem to contradict one another—but thought and discourse can never be confined to a single moment or point. "We must reconcile the contradictions as we can," Emerson explains in his essay "Nominalist and Realist":

but their discord and their concord introduce wild absurdities into our thinking and speech. No sentence will hold the whole truth, and the only way in which we can be just, is by giving ourselves the lie; Speech is better than silence; silence is better than speech;—and all things are in contact; every atom has a sphere of repulsion;—Things are, and are not, at the same time;—and the like. All the universe over, there is but one thing, this old Two-Face, creator-creature, mind-matter, right-wrong, of which any proposition may be affirmed and denied. (*W*, 3: 245)

It is because "all things are in contact," he suggests, that we must at every moment make complex gestures to signal that, despite this contact or complicity, we are acting in this particular way, because we believe that it is better to do this than that, that a particular decision is in this situation more likely than another one to accomplish what we want. These gestures should not be understood as pragmatic resolutions to given situations. They are strategic evaluations which attempt to respond to the formalization of the two-faced system we seek to unsettle at any given moment. That we always encounter a system composed of an entire network of propositions that, even within the system, can be neither simply affirmed nor denied suggests a protocol for reading that requires every statement to be read in relation to other ones—especially when they seem to contradict one another. This protocol names a task of thinking that begins in the belief that truth can never reside in a single statement. It presumes that there can be no evaluation or reading of a given statement without a passage through thought. If Emerson tells us time and time again that there is no distinction in his work between thought and action, it is because these acts of reading and evaluation are *actions of thought*. These acts of thinking are meant to prepare the way for a political decision and to do so within the parameters of an inevitable complicity. This is why, he states in his 1844 address on the emancipation of the British West Indies, "ideas only save races" (*AS*, 31).

For reasons that should now be clear, what Emerson says on this or that political issue—and, in particular, on the issue of race—will *always* run the risk of being understood unfavorably. His statements cannot fail to be read in relation to others that give his the lie, cannot fail to lead to misunderstandings, according to the law of contact or complicity (what Emerson elsewhere calls the law of compensation), which requires every statement to point to its contrary. There is no way out. "Every thought is a prison also," he explains, "I cannot see what you see, because I am caught up by a strong wind, and blown so far in one direction that I am out of the hoop of your horizon" (*W*, 2: 339). We can register the strength of his writing, then, the courage of his political engagements, in his willingness to assume the risk of being misunderstood, in his willingness to continue to think and confront the conditions of our most difficult responsibilities. Without risk, he suggests, there is nothing.[103] In regard to slavery and racism, he adds, this risk is to be measured in relation to the fact that the program of racism, and the biologism or naturalism that attends it, remain very strong—at times even within his own writing. We could even say, again according to the same law of complicity, that many of the features of this program belong to the majority of the discourses which, still today, claim to be opposed to racism. As Emerson would have it, even if all forms of complicity are incommensurable with one another, they remain irreducible. This means that our most urgent and serious responsibility is that of trying to evaluate which is the least dangerous of these forms of complicity—and to do so even as we know that this effort can never escape the danger we seek to overcome.[104]

This is why Emerson can suggest that, because Americans have been born into a language traversed by the rhetoric of nature that helped to found their republican system of government, they are more easily made subject to interests like those of slavery—which were defended explicitly by recourse to this same natural language. To the degree that all of Emerson's writings can be said to be directed toward a reading of the logic of this language, they are to be read as eminently political acts, even when they are articulated in linguistic or philosophical terms rather than in explicitly political ones. If his analysis of the place of nature within the arena of the historical or the political signals the strength of his social criticism, it also indicates his indebtedness to various eighteenth-century attacks on natural law, particularly that of David Hume. Hume's influence on Emerson is well known, but it usually has been considered only in terms of the skepticism that led Emerson to leave the ministry late in 1832. I want to suggest that what most attracted Emerson to "the Scotch Goliath" (L, 1: 138) was Hume's intense scrutiny of the meaning of nature. Throughout his life, from his early *Treatise of Human Nature* through his *Political Discourses* of the 1750s, Hume called into question the "naturalness" of nature, arguing that its laws were derived from human convention. Focusing on the ease with which the meaning of nature shifts according to whoever is referring to it, he points to its temporal and historical character. Although the principal aim of government, he suggests, is to force men to observe nature's laws, the laws themselves are "an effect of the institution of government." It is fruitless, he claims, to seek "in the laws of nature, a stronger foundation for our political duties than interest, and human conventions," since "these laws themselves are built on the very same foundation."[105] The laws of nature find their force in the rhetoric that helps convince the public of their inevitability. When nature is invoked to explain the bases for political obligation or the ethical standards by which law is measured, it exhibits its rhetorical character. As in Emerson, nature is a metaphor whose significance depends on the political or historical context in which it is used. The recourse to natural law, during Hume's day and on through to Emerson's, came to signal not an appeal to commonly accepted sources of principle but rather party affiliation.[106]

This is why the rhetoric of nature obliges us to rethink our relation to it: its ambiguity can be turned to both revolutionary and reactionary purposes. This is also why, for Emerson, the laws of nature require that we think the rhetoricity of natural law, and that we do so within the specific sociopolitical context in which such laws are evoked. This twofold requirement defines the ethics of nature. Emerson demonstrates this claim in the understanding of the Compromise of 1850 set forth in his two speeches on the Fugitive Slave Law. For him, the law goes against the principles on which America was to be founded. A law that kills law, he goes on to suggest, the Fugitive Slave Law is itself fugitive insofar as it runs away from justice. "What is the use of admirable law-forms and political forms," he writes, "if a hurricane of party feeling and a combination of monied interests can beat them to the ground. What is the use of courts, if judges only quote authorities, and no judge exerts original jurisdiction, or recurs to first principles? What is the use of a Federal Bench, if its opinions are the political breath of the hour?" (AS, 56).[107] Running away with sentiment in support of slavery, the law's very existence raises questions, for Emerson, concerning the moral integrity of America's founding documents. It makes America itself fugitive, exiling and banishing it from itself, from the promise it was founded to realize. "The law is suicidal," he writes, "and cannot be obeyed. The Union is at an end as soon as an immoral law is enacted. . . . Here was the question: Are you for man, and for the good of man; or are you for the hurt and harm of man? It was a question, whether man shall be treated as leather? Whether the negroes shall be, as the Indians were in Spanish America, a species of money? Whether this institution, which is a kind of mill or factory for converting men into monkeys, shall be upheld and enlarged? And Mr. Webster and the country went for quadruped law" (AS, 67–68, 79). This is why, he says elsewhere, we can say that "Webster truly represents the American people just as they are, with their vast material interests, materialized intellect, & low morals" (J, 11: 385). If this law is to be repealed, it must be transgressed, and this transgression, for Emerson, must involve an impassioned effort to think about what has led to the passing of the law. Coming with "the illuminating power of a sheet of lightning at midnight," the law reveals its truth, a truth that requires us to think the relation between rhetoric and politics. Emerson clarifies this obligation in his 1854 address on the Fugitive Slave Act. "There are always texts and thoughts and arguments," he writes:

but it is the genius and temper of the man which decides whether he will stand for Right or for Might.

Who doubts the power of any clever and fluent man to defend either of our parties, or any cause in our courts? There was the same law in England for Jeffreys and Talbot and Yorke to read slavery out of, and for Lord Mansfield to read freedom. And in this country one sees that there is always margin enough in the statute for a liberal judge to read one way, and a servile judge another. But the question which History will ask is broader.

In the final hour, when he was forced by the peremptory necessity of the closing armies to take a side, did he take the side of great principles, the side of humanity and justice, or the side of abuse and oppression and chaos? (*AS*, 78)

Emerson offers in this passage a profound reflection on the ethical dimension of our historical and political existence. What is at issue, he says, speaking of Webster's "unexpected" decision to throw "his whole weight on the side of Slavery," is "not a question of ingenuity, not a question of syllogisms, but of sides." "Nobody doubts that Daniel Webster could make a good speech," he writes, but the question is how he came to take sides with slavery (*AS*, 78). The question is how "at last, at a fatal hour . . . on the 7th March, 1850, in opposition to his education, association, and to all his own most explicit language for thirty years, he crossed the line, and became the head of the slavery party in this country" (*AS*, 66). In order to begin to answer this question, Emerson states that, although our existence is inseparable from the texts, thoughts, and arguments that define it, it is ultimately not rhetoric but a man's "genius and temper" that "decides whether he will stand for Right or for Might." This beginning, however, only complicates matters since, as he explains elsewhere, "genius and temper" are the names of what is at once peculiar to this man and "the voice of the Soul that made all men, uttered through a particular man" (*EL*, 3: 70). Together they simultaneously affirm and call into doubt his or anyone else's individual authority over his rhetoric or his history. This is why, he notes, "there is less intention in history than we ascribe to it" (*W*, 2: 134). What is at stake, it would seem, is the very nature of a decision. What can a decision be if the activity that gives birth to it both belongs and does not belong to the individual who makes it?

As Emerson explains in "Considerations by the Way," "so much fate, so much irresistible dictation from temperament and unknown inspiration enters into it, that we doubt we can say anything out of our own experience whereby to help each other" (*W*, 6: 245). Insofar as man is subject to both rhetoric and history—his own, as well as that of others—his "genius and temper" are always unpredictable. Forfeiting control over himself at the same time as he forfeits the ability to assert himself as the origin of history, he is unable to provide a basis for evaluating the rightness or wrongness of his actions or thoughts through rhetoric alone. Its capacity to define what is "right" according to the interests and needs that motivate all definition makes any claim based on moral categories untenable. This is not to say that Emerson's writings contest or destroy the value of truth. Rather, this value is resituated within a more powerful, more stratified context, but a context which cannot be saturated. "The philosophy of six thousand years," Emerson tells us:

> has not searched the chambers of the soul. In its experiments there has always remained, in the last analysis, a residuum it could not resolve. Man is a stream whose source is hidden. Our being is descending into us from we know not whence. The most exact calculator has no prescience that somewhat incalculable may not balk the very next moment. I am constrained every moment to acknowledge a higher origin for events than the will I call mine. (*W*, 2: 159)

If the conditions for our decisions are broader than our own will, Emerson suggests that this context is nevertheless interpretive by citing the debates over the decisions that led to the emancipation of the British West Indies. Relying on research done for his 1844 address on the matter, he focuses on the rhetorical dimension of the political and legal conflicts among Jeffreys, Talbot, and Yorke, who had argued that the continuance of slavery was perfectly in keeping with the English Constitution, and Lord Mansfield, whose decision to the contrary—based on his belief that "the claim of slavery never can be supported" by "tracing the subject to natural principles"—"established the principle that the 'air of England is too pure for any slave to breathe'" (*AS*, 11). If Mansfield's decision had no direct impact in the Indies—"the wrongs in the islands were not thereby touched" (*AS*, 11), Emerson says—it nevertheless drew public attention in that direction. Still, for Emerson, that the same law could be used to support either slavery or freedom shows that laws cannot by themselves be of any use. "I fear there is no reliance to be had on any kind or form of covenant," he tells us, in a passage that also suggests the ways in which religion is used to justify slavery, "no, not on sacred forms, none on churches, none on bibles. For one would have said that a Christian would not keep slaves, but the Christians keep slaves. Of course they will not dare read the bible. Won't they? They quote the bible and Christ and Paul to maintain slavery. . . . These things show that no forms, neither Constitutions nor laws nor covenants nor churches nor bibles, are of any use in themselves; the devil nestles comfortably into them all." "There is no help," he adds, "but in the head and heart and hamstrings of a man. Covenants are of no use without honest men to keep them. Laws are of no use, but with loyal citizens to obey them" (*AS*, 83). Before any juridical, political, or religious discourse, before the letters of any positive law, the laws of Emerson's nature speak within the voice of conscience. This voice speaks in us, but before us, because it is written within the depths of the heart. It corresponds to the immediate and unfailing sentiment of justice that, maintaining our balance and enabling us to move forward, defines the moral fiber of our character. But this justice is not the justice offered to us by the legislators of the Fugitive Slave Act. The "head and heart and hamstrings of a man" are rather the place of a categorical imperative, of a morality and justice incommensurate with the strategies of self-interest at work within this or that civil law.

Still, we should not be inattentive to the rhetorical dimension of this place. Emerson's claim that our only hope is in "the head and heart and hamstrings of a man" evokes a complicated rhetorical and historical matrix that he has already noted in *Nature*. "We say the *heart* to express emotion," he explains, "the *head* to denote thought; and *thought* and *emotion* are words borrowed from sensible things, and now appropriated to spiritual nature." "Most of the process by which this transformation is made," he goes on to say, "is hidden from us in the remote time when language was framed" (*W*, 1: 25–26). Emerson's appeal to the "head and heart and hamstrings of a man" is an appeal to rhetoric, to a rhetoric that historically has been associated with the issues of conscience and passion.[108] With this appeal, he hopes to draw us to our hidden resources—here figured as "the hamstrings" of our being (suggesting physical force, these hamstrings imply the active political stance to which Emerson wishes to direct his audience)—in order to involve us in an impassioned struggle against slavery, in the name of conscience. There is no help, he seems to suggest, but in this appeal, in a rhetoric informed by the laws of conscience rather than the laws of the nation. Moreover, the necessity of this rhetoric, within the specific ethico-political urgency of addressing the issue of slavery, is itself sanctioned, as it were, by the turmoil of the moment. As he suggests, again in *Nature*, "the moment our discourse . . . is inflamed by passion and exalted with thought, it clothes itself in images. . . . The imagery is spontaneous. It is the blending of experience with the present action of the mind. It is proper creation" (*W*, 1: 30–31). Emerson's appeal, like all "proper creation," appeals to a rhetoric with a history, to a rhetoric that draws its resources from historical experience. Though this history risks evoking the same values of "conscience" and "passion" on which others rely in their arguments for slavery, he nonetheless commits himself to his conscience and his passion.

For Emerson, institutional forms and laws declare the will of the moment in which they were born and in which they exist (*AS*, 56). The "law of Nature and rectitude"—the law of Emerson's conscience—requires us to ask about all institutional laws or virtues that claim more time for themselves. There are no fixtures in nature. Every institution "looks permanent until its secret is known," until we "see that it is founded on a thought which we have" (*W*, 2: 303, 161). Every institution seems immutable and permanent until we recognize that it is the result of human thought and labor. As Emerson tells us in his essay "Politics": "In dealing with the State we ought to remember that its institutions are not aboriginal, although they existed before we were born . . . every one of them was once the act of a single man; every law and usage was a man's expedient to meet a particular case . . . they are all imitable, all alterable; we may make as good, we may make better" (*W*, 3: 199). To say that laws are always conditioned by the historical presuppositions and interests of those who legislate and interpret them is to question their being based on a set of eternal and rational principles.[109] Emerson consistently feels obliged to recall us to this question, because our capacity to use these same presuppositions and interests to argue for the inevitability of interpreting the law in one way rather than another is, for him, one of the primary means of reducing our independence. The laws of Emerson's nature urge us to rethink our relation to time and history. It is because we are subject to history, it is because we are subject to languages that cannot overcome this history, that "we ought to remember" that there is nothing final in nature. This act of memory defines our ability to resist the imposing force of institutions, as they, and the individuals of which they consist, try to represent their values as permanent. Only through such remembrance can we distinguish between respect for the laws of nature and submission to positive law. Nature's ethics requires an act of memory that is also a promise. This promise is the promise of a nation whose very being would consist in this memory. It is nothing less than the promise of liberty and independence. In order for this promise to be promised, nature's ethics demands that we think the questions of history, nature, and representation together.

Emerson continues to engage his own responsibility to this demand by addressing the current legal and moral controversies over the Fugitive Slave Act. The virtue of liberty, he suggests, subject as it is to interpretation, may mean "freedom" to one and "slavery" to another, depending on his or her "genius and temper." But this does not free us from the necessity of evaluating these interpretations. We must take a stand for or against them, even though we know that, when we do, we too will be subject to evaluation. "In the final hour," we are obliged to take on the responsibility of deciding. As he notes in his essay "Power," "in our flowing affairs a decision must be made,—the best, if you can; but any is better than none" (*W*, 6: 76). In the name of "humanity and justice," then, Emerson decides against Webster's decision to support the Fugitive Slave Act. If he reminds us that the meaning we attribute to the virtues of "humanity and justice" is the result of human labor and not the manifestation of an absolute law that remains unaltered through history, he does so to provoke us into the courage to measure what this labor has created. He pronounces the necessity for ethical decision in the name of "humanity and justice" at the very moment he suggests that such words shift their historical and rhetorical significance according to

the needs of the people or institutions that use them. His own recourse to "humanity and justice" is therefore unable to justify itself
by reference to fixed principles. As he tells us in his essay "Circles,"
"there is no virtue which is final" (W, 2: 316). His appeal to the necessity that we confront and decide on the central issues of the day
defines an obligation that he cannot legitimize within the domain of
his "own" rhetoric, an obligation whose authorization is perfectly
undecidable. To decide within the context of such undecidability is
not merely to experience the tension between two decisions—for
example, that between what might support slavery and what might
go against it. It is also to experience that which, exceeding what we
could calculate in advance, must still give way to this impossible decision. A decision that does not undergo this trial would not be a free
decision—it could only be the effect of a determined program.

This is why, for Emerson, the ethical moment emerges only in
the absence of fixed criteria or principles. Only within this situation
of undecidability—the only situation in which a decision yet remains
to be made—can an individual both decide and be answerable for his
or her decision.[110] In his essay "War," speaking on the issue of "individual action in difficult and extreme cases," he proclaims, "A wise
man will never impawn his future being and action, and decide be-
forehand what he shall do in a given extreme event. Nature . . . will
instruct him in that hour" (W, 11: 169). He refers again to the help
that we can expect from nature in our struggle against slavery in his
1855 "Lecture on Slavery." He writes: "by every new creation to
those shameful statutes which blacken the code of this country, the
opposition will never end, never relax, whilst the statutes exist. As
long as the grass grows, as long as there is Summer or Winter, as long
as there are men, so long will the sentiments condemn them" (AS,
174). In a situation whose outcome has already been decided, the
freedom of decision is not possible: there is no room for either the
risk of decision or responsibility. If the decision to take a particular
side or stance is ultimately unjustifiable, however, it is nevertheless
unavoidable. As David Robinson has noted, "this affirmation of the
ethical imperative to act, even within the framework of a less than
absolute surety, is a fundamental premise of his later thought."[111] I
would only suggest that this affirmation is fundamental to all of
Emerson's writings. His appeal to the ethics of nature announces an

ethics, but one that is neither an ethics in the sense of a set of moral principles or values that might in advance determine one's thoughts or actions in any given situation, nor a practice that might be the realization or application of a given theory. Instead, nature's ethics corresponds to a thinking of the ethicality of ethics. Like the virtues of liberty and justice that it is supposed to encourage and support, ethics is itself subject to the demands of history, is itself the effect of human institutions and legislation, is itself defined by men in time. The ethics of nature, in its requirement that we think the relationship among history, nature, and politics, that is, that we think the question of representation, requires another way of thinking than that which would lead to an ethics, to a final moment of knowing. "There is no end in nature," Emerson writes, again in his essay "Circles" (*W*, 2: 301). He responds to this law, here and now, by phrasing his appeal to "humanity and justice" in the form of a question rather than in the form of an answer. That he ends with the question of an obligation and of a freedom recalls to us the necessity that we guard the issues of obligation and liberty as questions. We must remain sensitive to the ways in which the rhetoric of obligation and liberty forms a powerful means of furthering "abuse and oppression and chaos." Nevertheless, in order to take the risk of deciding, he suggests that we must also act and think according to the singular and equivocal nature of what we believe in. In this passage, Emerson demonstrates the correspondence between nature's ethical demand and a thinking that concerns itself with the relationship between questions of representation and politics. He also urges us to abandon ourselves to this demand, to think our being in time by asking about the ethics of representation.

The Frost of Slavery

The passionate urgency that Emerson attaches to this question clearly coincides with the volatility and momentousness of the issues of slavery and war that so preoccupied him during the 1850s and 1860s. But throughout his life he was concerned with the different ways in which the relationship between questions of political history and issues of representation manifested itself, not only in "the broil of politics," as his first book suggests, but also in the various theological, philosophical, and literary debates of the eighteenth and nineteenth century in America. Emerson's writings provide a strong genealogical analysis of the way in which these debates, influenced as they were by continental Romanticism, are transformed into statements with profound implications for epistemology, theology, and politics. These statements are inseparable from a thinking of the nature of representation. Indeed, the various debates in eighteenth- and nineteenth-century England and America over the meaning and concept of representation themselves joined the political, philosophical, and literary connotations of the term. Emerson makes this point in an entry from his 1835 journals, written approximately one year before the publication of *Nature*. "It is remarkable," he notes,

> that all poets, orators, and philosophers, have been those who could most sharply see and most happily present emblems, parables, figures. Good writing and brilliant conversation are perpetual allegories. . . . Webster is such a poet in every speech. "You cannot keep out of politics more than you can keep out of frost," he said to Clifford. All the memorable words of the world are these figurative expressions. Light and heat wave passed into all speech for knowledge and love. The river is nothing but as it typifies the flux of time. Many of these signs seem very arbitrary and historical. (*J*, 5: 63–64)

Citing Webster in this discussion of the metaphorical and allegorical dimension of concepts, Emerson again emphasizes the essential link that, for him, exists between politics and issues of representation. The force of political language, he suggests, depends on "figurative expressions." A good figure, he says elsewhere, "is a missionary to persuade thousands" (*W*, 8: 13). These expressions or analogies may "seem very arbitrary," but they are scarcely "capricious." They "must follow fate" (*W*, 8: 20). Their being arbitrary does not imply that the associations they claim are left entirely to the person who invokes them. Instead, Emerson suggests that the two terms of the analogy have no natural attachment. That this attachment is not "natural" works to question the idea of naturalness rather than that of attachment. In other words, while the associations between light and knowledge, heat and love, rivers and time, and even politics and frost exist, they do not refer to a "nature" that is strictly separate from human history. They are no more natural than cultural. They are no more physical than psychic. "Nature is itself a vast trope" (*W*, 8: 15), Emerson tells us in his late essay "Poetry and

Imagination." From the moment that there is meaning, there are "emblems, parables, figures," and allegories. The strength of this claim lies in its recognition that these "figurative expressions" are essentially historical. They gain their strength and currency in history as they are "remembered and repeated" (*W*, 8: 12). For Emerson, a thinking of representation can no more break with history or politics than be reduced to either one of them. These associations are natural only insofar as they are necessary, only insofar as Necessity operates within both language and history, according to ways and powers that belong to what he terms "nature." That we have seen this Necessity at work in his writings on slavery and war may help us begin to understand the relationship between his writings of the 1850s and 1860s and those of the 1830s and 1840s. For the very themes that have been taken as evidence of the difference between Emerson's early and late writings—the themes of history, society, race, slavery, politics, and so forth—if they are thought in terms of the necessity to think the question of representation, appear as consistent with his perspectives of the 1830s. To say this, however, is not to say that Emerson's treatment of these themes is exactly the same from one instance to another. It is not. Instead, it is a question of our being able to see how Emerson thinks the relationship of these themes to the issue of representation at different times and in different places.

We are obliged to think this question by his citation of Webster. Pointing to Webster as the source for the 1863 journal entry with which I began, this earlier passage reminds us that, in reading Emerson, we ought also to look for the sources of his writings in places that are neither strictly literary nor strictly philosophical. The significance of Emerson's use of the line in 1863, however, is not exactly the same as his use of it in 1835. Although in each case Emerson emphasizes the link between politics and language, we should not forget that by 1863 Emerson had denounced Webster publicly for having supported the Fugitive Slave Law. The Webster that he cites in 1835 is not the same Webster that he echoes in 1863. If he cites Webster's line in his war journals among a series of passages that mobilize the tropes of politics and frost within an antislavery argument, he does so in order to turn Webster against himself. He resituates Webster's line within an argument that aims at realigning the force of Webster's rhetoric, as well as that of others, with the moral and ethical forces of nature. He already had noted the way in which the moral forces of nature—and, in particular, of frost—were against slavery in his 1849 antislavery address at Worcester. Referring to the 1846 Wilmot Proviso—which sought to exclude slavery from any of the territories acquired as a result of the Mexican War—he writes, "Mr. Wilmot! It would take millions of . . . men to make the 36th degree of latitude the line of slavery. It is in the ordinance of the universe. Wherever a cooler climate, wherever frost—which is good alike for apples and for men—comes in, slavery cannot subsist" (*AS*, 49). That Emerson turns Webster's own natural metaphor against him suggests that what often has been understood as Emerson's characteristic method of composition—the recirculation of phrases, sentences, and passages from one place to another—here corresponds to a movement of transformation that defines the nature and politics of Emerson's efforts. I will return to this later, but for the moment I want to suggest that his concern over the relationship between the institution of slavery and the rhetoric that sustains it already is evoked by the Romantic context within which he cites Webster in 1835.

For if Emerson invokes Webster's statement within a romantic discussion of allegory and representation in order to reinforce the relationship he sees between politics and language, he does so not only because Webster is both a politician and a poet, not only because Webster draws an analogy between politics and the figure of frost, but also because, by 1835, "frost" is already a romantic trope for both figurative language and slavery.[112] In Coleridge's "Frost at Midnight" and "The Rime of the Ancient Mariner," for example, the enactment of frost's "secret ministry" coincides with the movement of figuration.[113] The "rime" of the latter poem's title itself refers to both rhyme and hoarfrost. It is no accident that, when Life-in-Death—"she / who thicks Man's blood with cold"—freezes the Ancient Mariner, he is from then on destined to rhyme the story of his own riming. Not only is the rhymer of Coleridge's poem a piece of frost, but, as Arden Reed has suggested, the "rime itself (in the strict sense of hoarfrost and independent of the pun) is *already* a name for language," as it gives voice to the polar ice. "The plot of the poem," Reed goes on to say, "alludes to this linguistic meaning of rime because the moment Life-in-Death freezes the Ancient Mariner is likewise the moment she condemns him to wander the earth and tell his tale. She freezes or rimes him precisely so that he can go on rhyming indefinitely." [114] Damned to an endless, mechanical repetition of his tale, the Mariner is imprisoned by his own rime, by his own frozen language. The figure of frost is a figure for language, as well as a figure for the freezing, enslaving capacities of an imagination and language that have, like the Mariner, transgressed the laws of nature. As Emerson explains in "The Poet," "the quality of the imagination is to flow, and not to freeze. . . . For all symbols are fluxional; all language is vehicular and transitive" (*W*, 3: 34). For both Coleridge and Emerson, rhetoric that does not obey nature's laws—that is, rhetoric that does not remain loyal to the laws of transition and metamorphosis, to the laws of writing in general—may only condemn us to slavery.

This association between frost and slavery was widespread among the romantics. From Coleridge's "Rime" to Wordsworth's "Immortality Ode" to Shelley's "Mont Blanc" and "Hellas," the figure of frost represents the various forms or processes that work to freeze us under their authority—whether rhetorical, mental, historical, or social. [115] Perhaps the most striking and powerful instance of this association is offered in "Hellas," a poem that is throughout concerned with the issues of slavery and war. The pertinence of the poem to this discussion of Emerson becomes clearer when we recall that in it Shelley associates the Greek struggle for independence in 1821 with a conception of America that organizes the issues of freedom and slavery specifically around the question of representation. Emerson's own interest in the Greek revolution can be seen in numerous journal passages from 1822 to 1826, and reappears in his war journals of the 1860s. [116] His early interest coincided with a kind of Greek fever, which spread across the United States, especially after the Messenian Senate of Calamata appealed to the United States for support and recognition on May 25, 1821. "Having formed the resolution to live or die for freedom," it wrote, addressing its appeal "to the citizens of the United States," "we are drawn toward you by a just sympathy; since it is in your land that Liberty has fixed her abode, and by you that she is prized as by our fathers. Hence in invoking her name, we invoke yours at the same time, trusting that in imitating you, we shall imitate our ancestors, and be thought worthy of them if we succeed in resembling you." [117] Responding to this appeal, public gatherings, sermons, publications, and fundraisings brought widespread sympathy for the Greek cause. Edward Everett, for example, looked into the background and progress of the Greek revolution, addressed the topic in some of his public lectures in Boston, and published a long article on the subject in the October 1823 issue of the *North American Review*. In the article—a review of a recent edition of Aristotle's *Ethics*, dedicated to "the newly constituted government of all the Greeks"—Everett claimed that the Greeks had caught "the contagion of liberty" from America and, because of this, their appeal "must bring home to the mind of the least reflecting American, the great and glorious part, which this country is to act, in the political regeneration of the world." "There is that in the cause of the Greeks," he added, "which ought to speak in the heart of every free man."[118]

Nevertheless, despite the justice of the Greek cause and its appeal to America's revolutionary past, the Monroe administration promised no official assistance because of America's long-standing policy of nonintervention in Europe. Inspired by Everett's essay and encouraged by Clay, Webster decided to attempt to persuade Congress to commit itself on behalf of the Greeks. He delivered his speech to the House of Representatives on January 19, 1824. Moved by the widespread enthusiasm for the Greek revolt, he implored his listeners to "take occasion of the struggle of an interesting and gallant people, in the cause of liberty." Reminding America of "her duty towards those great principles which have hitherto maintained the relative independence of nations, and which have, more especially, made her what she is," he called upon her as "the leading republic of the world" to lend official sanction to the Greek cause. He called upon her authority as a free country to voice the "prevailing spirit of the age" against oppression. "The great question is a question of principle," he claimed, "Greece is only the signal instance of the application of that principle."[119] Although some members of the House supported Webster's argument, he was finally unable to carry his resolution. Emerson himself refers to this failure in a journal entry from 1862. The passage, written only a few days before an early version of the 1863 passage with which I began this chapter, is closely connected to many of the issues I have been discussing. Referring to America's tendency to forget the virtue of Liberty that "made her what she is" in favor of her own commercial and selfish interests, he writes:

Governments are mercantile, interested, & not heroic. Governments of nations of shopkeepers must keep shop also. There is very little in our history that rises above commonplace. In the Greek revolution, Clay and Webster persuaded Congress into some qualified declaration of sympathy. . . . These were spasmodic demonstrations. They were ridiculed as sentimentalism. They were sentimentalism, for it was not our national attitude. We were not habitually & at home philanthropists. No, but timorous sharp shop-men, and each excuses himself if he talks politics, for leaving his proper province, & we really care for our shop & family, & not for Hungary & Greece, except as an opera, private theatricals or public theatricals. And so of slavery. (*J*, 15: 175–76)

Linking America's unwillingness to declare its full support for Greece with its unwillingness unequivocally to rid itself of slavery, Emerson indicts an America that has cared more for its commercial interests than for the human right to freedom. While America has represented itself as a country grounded in the virtues of freedom and independence, it has, in reality, supported institutions and interests that promote slavery. For Emerson, aside from a few "spasmodic demonstrations"—of which the Civil War, itself "a spasm to throw off slavery," is of course one of the most important examples—there is very little in American history that is truly American. That is to say, there is very little in America that is true to the democratic spirit it was founded to realize. As he writes in a journal entry from September 1836 (the month of *Nature*'s publication), "when I . . . speak of the democratic element I do not mean that ill thing vain & loud which writes lying newspapers, spouts at caucuses, & sells its lies for gold, but that spirit of love for the General good whose name this assumes. There is nothing of the true democratic element in what is called Democracy; it must fall, being wholly commercial" (*J*, 5: 203). The cries for Liberty that punctuate the American scene—whether for Hungary, for Greece, or for America itself—are, for Emerson, more often than not mere "theatrical" flights of rhetoric aimed at disguising the selfishness that characterizes American history. This selfishness has prevented both the country and the individuals that comprise it from overcoming slavery. For Emerson, we can free our-selves only by caring for the freedom of others. He makes this claim in a passage that associates the Greek struggle for independence with the issue of slavery, which brought America to its present civil crisis, not only indicating his interest in the Greek revolution but also reinforcing the thematic and rhetorical links that he sees between this revolution and the Civil War: each has something to do with the meaning of America. For Emerson, both the Greek revolution and the Civil War are figures for the revolution that was to give America its significance. That he makes this association by introducing the issue of representation returns us to Shelley's "Hellas," a poem whose themes and metaphors anticipate much of his own thinking during the war. In particular, Shelley, too, mobilizes the figure of frost to think the relationship between freedom and slavery. Shelley, too, sees a contradiction in the meaning of America.

In his Preface to "Hellas," Shelley writes, while referring to the outbreak of the Greek struggle for independence, that the poem was "written at the suggestion of the events of the moment."[120] Nevertheless, the poem throughout weaves together the drama of the war for Greek independence with the revival of ancient Greek freedom and the future reenactment of this revolutionary event in another place, namely, America. This helps to explain why Shelley entitles his drama "Hellas," the spirit of freedom, rather than "Greece." "Greece is but one local habitation of the eternal Hellenic spirit," Earl Wasserman notes, "not the country to which it is limited." Greece is "wherever Freedom is."[121] Still, if Shelley chooses to name his poem "Hellas," it is also because the struggle between Greece and the Ottoman Turks is not yet resolved. The poem dramatizes this ongoing conflict by having the action of the drama depict the present battles of the war, and the choruses give voice to the language and vision of universal prophecy. The specific historical events of the struggle are no more important than their relation to the spirit of history in general. This entanglement between contemporary history and universal history prevents a final resolution in the present and instead looks to the promise of freedom's victory in a new and "brighter Hellas" (l. 1066). Despite his inability to foresee the war's outcome, Shelley announces that even "If Greece must be / A wreck, yet shall its fragments reassemble / And build themselves again . . . / In a diviner clime" (ll. 1002–5). Since for Shelley so much of Europe, even England, aggressively or tacitly supports Ottoman oppression, "Freedom and Peace" shall "flee far / To a sunnier strand," following Hesperus westward "To the Evening-Land" of America (ll. 1027–30).

That Shelley prophesies the more glorious renewal of Hellas in America reveals his hope in an America whose revolution and republican government have inspired Europe's own stirrings for liberty, in particular those of Greece. "Kingless" and "sinless as Eden," America emerges as a figure for a process of continual self-renewal, announcing the coming of "another Athens," which will inaugurate a new beginning for the world and "bequeath . . . the splendor of its prime" to "remoter ages" (ll. 1084–87). Evoking and exploiting the myth of America as the "new Eden," Shelley suggests that America will be the birthplace of a perfect equality among men. His America corresponds to an experiment in the capacities of man. With its primeval forests, vast plains, and unscaled mountains, it evokes the image of a pristine and long-forgotten nature. From Locke's pronouncement that "in the beginning all the world was America" to Paine's belief that America has it in her power "to begin the world all over again," to Whitman's claim that America is "a world primal again," America is understood as the promise of possibility.[122] America is to be, in Anne Norton's words, "what all the world once was, and what all men might be."[123]

For Shelley, however, what the world once was and what men might become are as engaged with the possibility of slavery as they are with that of freedom. He indicates this inconsistency in an extraordinary way when he has his chorus address slavery directly, in terms that bring together the figure of frost and the institution of slavery. "O Slavery!," the chorus cries, "thou frost of the world's prime, / Killing its flowers and leaving its thorns bare! / Thy touch has stamped these limbs with crime" (ll. 676–78). The power of the analogy that Shelley draws between frost and slavery lies in its suggestion that neither the Greece that was the "world's prime," nor the Greece of 1821, nor the America that will begin the world anew are yet free of slavery. In each case, the glory of Greece and the glory that America might become are born alongside slavery (ll. 682–87). The America that inaugurates the beginning of a new world is from the very beginning beset with slavery—and not least because America is Greek. To say that America is Greek is, of course, not to say that America is only Greek, but rather that any understanding of America must include an understanding of the example of Greece. For "we are all Greeks," Shelley tells us in his Preface to "Hellas," "our laws, our literature, our religion, our arts have their roots in Greece."[124] "What we are and hope to be," he says elsewhere, "is derived, as it were, from the influence and inspiration" that Greece—as the "world's prime"—has bequeathed to "remoter ages."[125] Webster and Everett add to this claim by suggesting that America also owes its representative form of government to Greece. It owes its ideals of the popular assembly, the practice of free debates and public discussions, and its forms of political oratory to the Greek example.[126] For Shelley, though, as these few lines suggest, America is also Greek because, like the Athens it is supposed to recall and renew, it has not yet overcome the institution of slavery.

That slavery existed in the ancient world had long been a problem for humanists and orthodox Biblicists. Its existence posed serious challenges to abolitionist arguments in the 1830s concerning the corruption that slavery was said inevitably to bring along with it.[127] As I have already noted, proponents of slavery found justification for the institution in the writings of Aristotle, Plutarch, Livy, and Pliny, each of whom claimed that slavery was necessary for the achievements of freedom and civilization. For these writers, slavery provided slaveholders with the leisure necessary for politics, philosophy, and the arts.[128] As the early-nineteenth-century Göttingen philosopher and historian Arnold Heeren notes, "without the instrument of slavery, the culture of the ruling class in Greece could in no way have become what it did."[129] For Shelley, however, that slavery existed in Greece and exists in America means that Greece and America, as places where the ideals of freedom were to have been realized, either have never existed or do not yet exist. Again, it is no accident that he chooses to name his poem "Hellas" rather than "Greece," and that he refers to America only as "another Athens," a "young Atlantis," the "Evening-Land," rather than by name. As he explains in his *Philosophical View of Reform*, while "the system of government in the United States of America" was to be "the first practical illustration" of a government organized around the principle that "liberty and equality" are the "forms according to which the concerns of human life ought to be administered," it is at the present moment still "sufficiently remote . . . from the accuracy of ideal excellence" that its representative character was formed to fulfill.[130] If America is to fulfill its destiny, if it is truly to be *another* Athens, it must overcome the

"institutions and opinions, which in ancient Greece were obstacles to
the improvement of the human race."[131] It must not be too Greek: it
must instead eradicate slavery. For just as "personal slavery, and the
inferiority of women, recognized by law and opinion" in Athens reduced "the delicacy, the strength, the comprehensiveness, and the accuracy of their perceptions in moral, political, and metaphysical science, and perhaps in every other art and science,"[132] so too has
slavery prevented America from realizing the dream of its founding.
America must redeclare its independence, from Greece as well as
from itself. It must repeat its founding statements, but this time with
the greatest of all sincerities. This time, "America" must address
and include all of its inhabitants—the slave, the Native American,
women, ethnic minorities, immigrants, the poor—for such was its
founding promise. Or as Emerson has it in his journals, addressing in
particular the conditions for overcoming slavery: "This time no compromises, no concealments, no crimes that cannot be called by name
shall be tucked in under another name, like 'persons held to labor,'
meaning persons stolen, & 'held,' meaning held by hand-cuffs, when
they are not under whips" (*J*, 15: 302). This time, he suggests, our
language must prevent us from fixing the meaning of the words *liberty*, *democracy*, *representation*, *community*, *people*, *nation*, or *humanity* in
a way that could lead to the subjugation of others.

The features of this obligation are illuminated in "Hellas" in a
remarkable way—immediately after the chorus has identified the
frost that is slavery with the beginning of the world—by Liberty's
own declaration of freedom:

> O Slavery! thou frost of the world's prime,
> . . .
> These brows thy branding garland bear,
> But the free heart, the impassive soul
> Scorn thy controul!
> Let there be light! said Liberty,
> And like sunrise from the sea,
> Athens arose!
>
> (ll. 676, 679–85)

At stake in this declaration is the existence of Athens herself. In a
repetition of the original creative fiat, Liberty proclaims the light that
will give birth to Athens. Athens is founded in an act of language that

wishes to accomplish the realization of its declaration. That is to say, Athens does not exist before this declaration, which is declared by Liberty. Liberty authorizes the declaration of independence, even though she does not exist before the "Let there be light!" of her own declaration. Liberty repeats America's own declaration of independence outside the bonds of slavery and in so doing hopes to bring both herself and Athens to the light of day.[133] Unfortunately, however, Liberty's declaration takes place in a poem whose entire action occurs at sunset. There is no sun in Greece to melt away the frost of slavery. "Darkness has dawned in the East" (l. 1023), Shelley writes, and we must turn westward to America if we are to find the "lamp of the free" (l. 1041). If Athens is without the light that will guarantee its birth and if America is still to be sought, neither Athens nor America yet exists. That Liberty nonetheless proclaims the rise of Athens and that the poem continues to project the realization of a "brighter Hellas" in America reveals a profound act of faith. Hellas is this act of faith. It is Liberty's declaration of independence. Neither Greece nor America, it is the spirit of freedom in each. This spirit corresponds to an activity of continual self-renewal that, within the context of Shelley's poem, is the process whereby a nation comes to declare itself into existence. Shelley's "Hellas" is a powerful allegory of a nation's invention of itself. This invention corresponds to the various acts that declare the promise of a nation to come. These acts are acts of language, acts that institute a nation's history. Since there are many such acts, there are many versions of this history. We may never know, Shelley writes, "the Greeks precisely as they were."[134] Or rather, the Greeks we may know will be the Greeks of our own invention.

That "Hellas" dramatizes a nation's coming into existence by means of its war against slavery recalls Emerson's own allegory of the Civil War as the means whereby America may finally fulfill its own promise of freedom. What Shelley calls "Hellas," Emerson calls "America." For both writers, "Hellas" and "America" are figures for the process of self-renewal announced by the forces of the American Revolution. For Shelley, these forces may correspond to Greek and American declarations of independence, but they are linked, more particularly, to the American Constitution itself. The virtue of America is that Hellas, as the progress of the spirit of freedom, is written into its Constitution. This is made clear in Shelley's *Philosophical View of Reform*, where, following Paine, he claims that what makes America different "from all other governments which ever existed" is its Constitution. America, he goes on to say, "constitutionally acknowledges the progress of human improvement, and is framed under the limitations of the probability of more simple views of political science being rendered applicable to human life." "There is a law" in America, he writes, "by which the constitution is reserved for revision every ten years."[135] That the American Constitution can be revised through direct acts of writing enables it to be continually renewed across time.[136] Able to benefit from experience, to prevent the accumulation of errors, and to help the government meet the always-changing circumstances of its people, this Constitution articulates itself in relation to the future possibilities of the nation it calls into being. As Paine notes, "Here we see a regular process—a government issuing out of a constitution, formed by the people in their original character; and that constitution serving, not only as an authority, but as a law of control to the government."[137] The realization of an America that would be true to its founding requires that Hellas, as an activity of continual redefinition, be actualized as America. Shelley's "Hellas" declares what Emerson's America is. That it also conceives America in terms of the relation between politics and issues of representation returns us to Emerson. If the promise of America lies in its capacity to revise its Constitution, then Shelley's hope for this capacity suggests his sensitivity to the ways in which language can become a means of furthering class distinction and slavery. America conceives itself in terms of the possibility that language may be revised and thereby reveals its commitment to the possibility of continual moral and political reform.[138] In a truly free government, no political or civil regulation should be perpetual, for people have no right to make laws for those not yet in existence. "I find it to be a mischievous notion of our times," Emerson remarked, "that men think . . . the world is of a constitution unalterable, and see not that in the hands of genius old things are passed away and all things become new" (*J*, 5: 349). As Noah Webster claims, speaking of the consequences of this "mischievous notion," "the very attempt to make perpetual constitutions, is the assumption of a right to control the opinions of future generations."[139] For both Emerson and Webster,

America can be vigilant against the "ever-watchful spirit of avarice and tyranny"[140] only as long as it remains faithful to a thinking of representation, to a thinking of man's relation to time. The idea of America coincides with this obligation, with this fidelity; it corresponds to what I have earlier called "nature's ethics."

The Representation of America

Following the "logic" of this ethics, both Shelley and Emerson suggest that governments, as well as the people who comprise them, are obliged to think their relation to language and history. The virtue of America lies in its recognition that language is an essential element in the constitution of a political and cultural unity among its citizens. The American Revolution gathered its momentum through a deluge of pamphlet literature that emphasized the strong association between the written word and political activity. "A vocal minority of colonists," Gustafson tells us, "turned to sermons, speeches, and pamphlets primed with the language of evangelical religion and republican ideology to protest against (and later free themselves from) what they viewed as a long train of artifices and prevarications perpetrated by King George III and the British government to defend indefensible acts of tyranny and make them pay obeisance (and taxes) to a representative institution that did not represent them."[141] In addition, within this literature, the arguments took on a distinctly linguistic cast, as they were often concerned with defining such words as *constitution*, *liberty*, and *representation*.[142] As John Adams writes, in a letter of September 5, 1780, to the president of Congress, just as forms of government have an influence on language, so "language in its turn influences not only the form of government, but the temper, the sentiments, and manners of the people."[143] Madison repeats this point when he suggests that "if the meaning of [the Constitution] be sought in the changeable meaning of the words composing it, it is evident that the shapes and attributes of the government must partake of the changes to which the words and phrases of all living languages are constantly subject."[144] The point is made again just three years before the publication of *Nature*, in an article from the *North American Review* entitled "The Union and the State."[145] There, the author writes that "questions involving the meaning of political words lie at the very foundation of political society, and accordingly as they are settled in one way or another, the whole fabric must assume a different shape and character." Emerson's insistence on the necessity that we think the relation between politics and language therefore belongs to a tradition of thought that throughout has concerned itself with the place of language within our political and historical existence.[146] Such thought, he suggests, recalls us to the meaning of America's founding. For him, it is precisely because America was conceived in terms of a thinking of the nature and concept of representation that representation can explain the uniqueness of American politics.

The question of representation was central to the controversy between England and America, and its answer continued to be sought among Americans, even in the years following independence. Ideas about representation were linked to different conceptions about the form of the government and the nature of the political process. As Gordon S. Wood notes, "Behind every differing statement concerning the right of taxation, the force of law, or the sovereignty of the legislative authority lay a varying idea of representation."[147] Representation defined men's ideas about their relation to the government. "The principle on which all the American governments are founded," wrote Samuel Williams of Vermont, "is *representation*."[148] Only the American scheme, wrote Paine, was based "wholly on the system of representation."[149] In the wording of Wood, "nearly all of the great debates of the period, beginning with the imperial controversy in the 1760s and ending with the clash over the new Federal Constitution in the 1780s, were ultimately grounded in the problem of representation. Indeed, if representation is defined as the means by which the people participate in government, fulfillment of a proper representation became the goal and measure of the Revolution itself, 'the whole subject of the present controversy,' as Thomas Jefferson put it in 1775."[150] For Alexander Hamilton, John Jay, and particularly James Madison in the *Federalist Papers*, representation was "the pivot" on which the whole system moved.[151] According to these authors of the *Federalist Papers*, the question of political representation necessarily arose out of the impossibility of assembling large numbers of people in a single place and out of the right of every individual to representation. The issue was to reconcile the paradox of representative legislature. On the one hand, the representative body is composed of persons who are supposed to govern the nation and pursue the national interest, and, on the other hand, this same body is supposed to respect and represent the various constituencies and individuals that have themselves legislated its existence. The debates oscillated between a concept of virtual representation that assumed a people whose heritage of liberty and independence implied a single, transcendent concern, and a concept of actual representation that assumed a relationship between constituents and representatives that preserved the "spirit of *locality*" evident in elections in small districts or towns.[152]

Rather than destroy the liberty that is essential to the existence of any faction or give "to every citizen the same opinions, the same passions, and the same interests," Madison argues that faction is an inevitable, if not natural, result of a representative government. As he explains, "as long as the reason of man continues fallible, and he is at liberty to exercise it, different opinions will be found." What is at stake is not so much the prevention of factions that might try to impose their own interests upon others—factions, Madison tells us, are a natural result of liberty—but rather how to control them. For Madison this can only be done through a kind of representation that gives power to property owners. "The diversity in the faculties of men, from which the rights of property originate," he suggests, "is not less an insuperable obstacle to a uniformity of interests. The protection of these faculties is the first object of government. From the protection of different and unequal faculties of acquiring property, the possession of different degrees and kinds of property results; and from the influence of these on the sentiments and views of the respective proprietors ensues a division of the society into different interests and parties. The latent causes of faction are thus sown in the nature of man."[153] Emerson makes a similar argument when he claims in his essay "Politics" that "the same benign necessity and the same practical abuse appear in the parties, into which each State divides itself." "Parties are . . . founded on instincts," he adds,

and have better guides to their own . . . aims than the sagacity of their leaders. They have nothing perverse in their origin, but rudely mark some real and lasting relation. We might as wisely reprove the east wind or the frost, as a political party, whose members, for the most part, could give no account of their position, but stand for the defence of those interests in which they find themselves. Our quarrel with them begins when they quit this deep natural ground at the bidding of some leader, and obeying personal considerations, throw themselves into the maintenance and defence of points nowise belonging to their system. (*W*, 3: 208)

For both Emerson and Madison, parties themselves are not really the issue. The difficulty arises when parties betray the liberty that provided for their existence in the first place, when their leaders "reap the rewards of the docility and zeal of the masses which they direct" (*W*, 3: 209). Echoing Madison's definition of a faction, Emerson explains that the corruption of parties occurs when they fail to "plant themselves on the deep and necessary grounds to which they are respectively entitled," and instead "lash themselves to fury in the carrying of some local and momentary measure, nowise useful to the commonwealth" (*W*, 3: 209).[154] That parties are as inevitable as the natural laws that give us frost, that they reveal, even if only in a rude way, a "real and lasting relation," recalls to Emerson that representation in America can never be virtual or inclusive. Always subject to the corruption of personal interest, representation may only be *actual*, that is to say, provisional and partial. There can be no representation that is not subject to this partiality, because there is no representation that is not subject to time. As Emerson explains, "A mob cannot be a permanency; everybody's interest requires that it should not exist" (*W*, 3: 212). When political parties attempt to represent a "local and momentary measure" to the people as permanent, they forget America's fundamental truth: its Constitution proclaims that there can be nothing final in America. America must continually "make and mend its law" (*W*, 3: 213). "The old statesman knows that society is fluid," he writes. "The law is only a memorandum. . . . The statute stands there to say, Yesterday we agreed so and so, but how feel ye this article today? Our statute is a currency which we stamp with our own portrait: it soon becomes unrecognizable; in process of time it will return to the mint" (*W*, 3: 199–200). When parties use the freedom bequeathed to them by the founding documents of the republic to restrict the liberty of others, they forget the spirit of self-renewal that gives America its meaning. This point is made more generally in Rousseau's *Social Contract*. Claiming that the moment "a people allows itself to be represented it is no longer free: it no longer exists," he suggests that there can be no representation in which a people does not lose its autonomy and self-reliance, in which it does not become subject to a representative that does not represent it.[155]

Nevertheless, even though Emerson admits that parties exist and that they are "perpetually corrupted by personality" (*W*, 3: 212), by the desire to make their interests the interests of others, he still maintains his hope in the promise of a representative republic. Although much since the revolution "has been blind and discreditable," he explains, "the nature of the revolution is not affected by the vices of the revolters; for this is a purely moral force" (*W*, 3: 219). Parties that abuse their liberty make our return to the republic's founding ethical and moral principles all the more urgent and necessary. At issue is not the restriction of parties or the liberty that brings them into existence, but rather the evaluation of what happens in the name of liberty. As I have already suggested in relation to Emerson's response to the Fugitive Slave Law, "texts, thoughts, and arguments" can never serve to guarantee liberty. The same constitution may be read by one party to support freedom and by another to support slavery. "Written constitutions and bills of rights could never be effective guarantees of freedom," Noah Webster writes in his 1788 essay "Government," "Liberty is never served by such paper declarations; nor lost for want of them."[156] In Hamilton's words, "The sacred rights of mankind are not to be rummaged for among old parchments or writing records. They are written, as with a sunbeam, in the whole *volume* of human nature, by the hand of Divinity itself, and can never be erased or obscured by mortal power."[157] Emerson notes the often "flippant mistaking for freedom of some paper preamble like a 'Declaration of Independence,' or the statute right to vote, by those who have never dared to think or to act" (*W*, 6: 23). We have here an ethical question: to what end are these "texts, thoughts, and arguments" used? For Emerson, the inevitable entanglement between questions of political and moral liberty and questions of representation obliges us to develop a conscience. The possibility of Liberty obliges us consistently to evaluate and measure the representations of persons, parties, and institutions in terms of whether they are meant to free or enslave others. This is what Emerson does when, writing of the forms of representation that have helped to instantiate the system of slavery, he states:

The fathers, in July 1787, consented to adopt population as the basis of representation, and to count only three-fifths of the slaves, and to concede the reclamation of fugitive slaves;—for the consideration, that there would be no slavery in the Northwest Territory. They agreed to this false basis of representation and to this criminal complicity of restoring fugitives: and the splendor of the bribe, namely, the magnificent prosperity of America from 1787, is their excuse for the crime. It was a fatal blunder. They should have refused it at the risk of making no Union. . . . The bribe, if they foresaw the prosperity we have seen, was one to dazzle common men, and I do not wonder that common men excuse and applaud it. But always so much crime brings so much ruin. A little crime, a minor penalty; a great crime, a great disaster. (*AS*, 99–100)

For Emerson, there can be no slavery without the system of representation that would justify and sustain it. The power of his analysis of the question of representation in America lies in its suggestion that to speak of a governmental body or system as "representative" is to say something broader and more general about the way in which this body or system operates as an institutionalized arrangement, about its consequences for the lives of its constituents. For him, any analysis of the notion of representation that necessarily belongs to a representative government must consider the inevitable relationship that exists between a philosophical or rhetorical notion of representation and the more usual concrete, practical, and historical understandings of political representation. This is why, he tells us, "the poet is representative" (*W*, 3: 5). As Gustafson explains, political representatives "stand in relation to their constituents as language does to the world. The classical ideal is mimesis: The 'representative assembly,' John Adams asserts, 'should be an exact portrait of the people at large.' The reality of representation, however, is not the sameness of an echo but the difference of a new voice. Political representatives can no more be equated with their constituents than a word can be equated with the thing it stands for. Just as a word replaces the presence of a thing, so too do political representatives replace the presence of the people."[158] This relationship between linguistic and political representation is already written into the American Constitution. It implies that the concept of representation is related not only to the realms of agency and political activity involved in the historical development of institutions but also to the thought and writing without which these institutions would never have been installed. Emerson's appeal that America return to its founding in the laws of nature coincides with an appeal that it return to the ethical obligation to think the nature and meaning of the concept of representation that defines the promise of America. America promises that representation will happen. Emerson's entire career needs to be read in terms of this promise, for it is there that he addresses the major political and social issues of his time. What generally has been read as Emerson's "retreat" from the arena of the political is instead an effort on his part to rethink or re-treat the nature of the political in terms of questions of representation. "Nothing remains," he says, "but to begin at the beginning to call every man in America to counsel, Representatives do not represent, we must take new order & see how to make representatives represent us" (J, 14: 423). This effort is particularly pertinent at a time when the major issues of the day—slavery, war, women's rights, the extermination of the native population, westward expansion, rapid urbanization and industrialization, the emergence of various secondary institutions (including schools, asylums, factories, and plantations), and the growing inequality in the distribution of wealth—are all centrally concerned with issues of the right to representation. Emerson's insistence that we think the question of politics in terms of representation corresponds to his wish that we rigorously take into account what, for him, is the essential tie between politics and representation. For Emerson, this tie is neither accidental nor simply historical. His retreat from a notion of politics whose domain is regarded as either isolated from philosophy or subordinated to an empirical realm in no way excludes wholly determined political intentions on his part, in no way suspends reference—to history, to the world, to reality. Instead, he clarifies the relationship between politics and representation in order to deny an unsound basis of power to those persons, parties, or institutions that would dissimulate the representational dimension of their interests. Emerson's engagement with the political is something other than a commitment to one or another politics. There is no single form of political engagement in Emerson.

For him, our passion for questioning the limits of both representation and politics is the condition of our salvation. It is the condition of our being "American." That this passion traverses even his earliest writings can be seen in a journal entry from September 1836, the very month of his first publication, *Nature*. There, Emerson's writing once again shows itself to be traversed by the major political and social questions of his day. There, his reflection upon these questions suggests that the climates of political history are inseparable from the words without which neither politics nor history nor America could ever exist:

Shall I write on the tendency of modern mind to lop off all superfluity & tradition & fall back on the Nature of things? . . . What is good that is said or written now lies nearer to men's business & bosoms than of old. What is good goes now to all. . . . Tamerlane and the Buccaneers vanish before Texas, Oregon territory, the Reform Bill, the abolition of Slavery and Capital Punishment, questions of Education & the Reading of Reviews; & in these all men take part. The human race have got possession, and it is all questions that pertain to their interest outward or inward, that are now discussed. And many words leap out alive from barrooms, Lyceums, Committee Rooms, that escape out of doors & fill the world with their thunder. (*J*, 5: 203)

Chapter Two

✺ Nature's Archives

> No man can quite emancipate himself from his age and coun-
> try, or produce a model in which the education, the religion,
> the politics, usages, and arts, of his times shall have no share.
> Though he were never so original, never so wilful and fantas-
> tic, he cannot wipe out of his work every trace of the
> thoughts amidst which it grew. The very avoidance betrays
> the usage he avoids. Above his will, and out of his sight, he is
> necessitated, by the air he breathes, and the idea on which he
> and his contemporaries live and toil, to share the manner of
> his times, without knowing what that manner is.
>
> —Emerson, "Art"

> A man is a bundle of relations, a knot of roots, whose flower
> and fruitage is the world. All his faculties refer to natures out
> of him. All his faculties predict the world he is to inhabit. . . .
> Insulate a man and you annihilate him. He cannot unfold—he
> cannot live without a world.
>
> —Emerson, *Journals*

In tracing the shifting relation between nature and history in
Emerson's writings, I have wished to suggest the ways in which his
words or sentences not only open onto the history sealed within them
but also, by this opening, work to engage already-changing historical
and political relations, what he elsewhere calls the "fugitive clouds of
circumstance" (*J*, 7: 532). In so doing, I have tried to elaborate on
what Emerson might mean when he writes in "The Poet" that "language is the archives of history" (*W*, 3: 21). Among other things, he
suggests that we can only give an account of history, of what makes
history history, by considering the ways in which it is preserved and
enacted within language. He also suggests there can be no historical
description, interpretation, or analysis of history that is not touched,
and therefore altered, by the movement and difficulties of the language it seeks to study. We could say, more broadly, that he proposes

a textual model of history. In other words, for him, a thought of history must begin with the presupposition that "all experience has become mere language" (*J*, 11: 374). Rather than understand history uncritically in terms of a concept of immediate experience or a representation that looks only toward the past, Emerson begins his thinking of history with what for him is the moment of linguistic inscription and figuration that grounds the capacity of every event to inaugurate history. That there can be no language that does not refer to history and no history that does not refer to language means that the task of reading historically involves tracing not only the manner in which a text shares its language with other language (how it is situated within a particular or general historical context, how it is inscribed in a chain of works) but also what remains idiomatic in the text (how it confirms this context even as it betrays it, even betrays it in order to respect it).

In my first chapter, I have tried to read Emerson's analogy between frost and politics in a way that remains faithful to his sense of how the activities of reading and writing are themselves historical events. I have followed the analogy as it appears in different contexts and forms in order to suggest the ways in which history and politics leave their traces in his language, the ways in which Emerson works to appropriate these traces and mobilize them in another direction. Such a reading involves, for Emerson, a transformation of "the point of view from which history is commonly read." The reader is now expected to transfer the view of history:

from Rome and Athens and London to himself . . . he must attain and maintain that lofty sight where facts yield their secret sense, and poetry and annals are alike. The instinct of the mind, the purpose of nature betrays itself in the use we make of the signal narrations of history. Time dissipates to shining ether the solid angularity of facts. No anchor, no cable, no fences avail to keep a fact a fact. Babylon, Troy, Tyre, Palestine, and even early Rome, have passed or are passing to fiction. The Garden of Eden, the Sun standing still in Gibeon, is poetry thenceforward to all nations. Who cares what the fact was, when we have made a constellation of it to hang in heaven an immortal sign? "What is history," said Napoleon, "but a fable agreed upon?" (*W*, 2: 8–9).

If history must be thought in relation to language, it is not surprising that Emerson's theory of history is at the same time a theory of reading and writing. If he focuses on what has been overlooked or hidden within history, on the transitoriness of events or historical facts, it is because he wishes to delineate the contours of a history whose chance depends on overcoming the idea of history as the mere reproduction of the past. It is because, for him, the past is never simply the past. History names the transit among the past, present, and future that happens whenever history is read and written "actively and not passively" (*W*, 2: 8). To say that there can be no history that is not also a history of poetry, narration, fiction, and fable is not to say that we are cut off from history but rather that we now have the chance to encounter a sense of historicity. Indeed, for Emerson, it is precisely the historicity or temporality inscribed within every fact that underlies the inability of historical truth to coincide with itself, that reveals history to be nothing more than "a vanishing allegory" (*J*, 11: 435).

Emerson suggests that a certain tradition of reading has worked against the instability of the history of facts—even if, he says, "no anchor, no cable, no fences avail to keep a fact a fact"—by converting these fables and tropes into "immortal signs," into signs no longer affected by their poetic origin. They try to forget that, like the deadest word that the etymologist can encounter, the fact was once, not a fact, but a "brilliant picture." "Language is fossil poetry," he explains in "The Poet." "As the limestone of the continent consists of infinite masses of the shells of animalcules, so language is made up of images, or tropes, which now, in their secondary use, have long ceased to remind us of their poetic origin" (*W*, 3: 22). Nietzsche later translates this passage in his discussion of the genealogy of truths or facts. In "On Truth and Lie in an Extra-Moral Sense," suggesting that philosophical and historical truth begins in poetic language, he writes:

What then is truth? A moveable host of metaphors, metonymies, and anthropomorphisms: in short, a sum of human relations which have been poetically and rhetorically intensified, transformed, and embellished, and which, after long usage, seem to a nation to be fixed, canonical, and binding; truths are illusions of which one has forgotten that they *are* illusions; worn out metaphors which have become powerless to affect the senses, coins which have their image *effaced* and now are no longer of account as coins but merely as metal.[1]

Pointing to the work of metaphor within discourse in general and history in particular, Nietzsche and Emerson suggest that a genealogy of historical truth would reveal its origins not only in metaphor but in the progressive erosion of metaphor. In their terms, a history founded on facts would correspond to the process whereby, in the face of the metaphorical sedimentation of historical concepts and truths, a fact is asserted nevertheless through the erasure of the metaphor in which it was born. History would here be a name for this obliteration of figures or tropes. The gesture of history erases "what the fact was"—a fable or trope—and thereby attempts to legitimize its artifice by ascribing it to a natural scheme, in this particular passage from "History," an astronomical one. For these two writers, however, the historian is a gatherer of fables and not of facts. Emerson here registers a genealogical anxiety within history which it is the purpose of nature to repress. However, nature (always in Emerson only another name for reading and writing) is unable to efface the traces of this anxiety and so betrays the artifice of any attempt to write its own genealogy, of its use of the narrations of history as signs of a genetic or natural order. The purpose of nature exposes not only the ruse of a rhetoric of nature but also a history whose temporality is caught between two moments, between those facts which have already been read as fiction and those facts which are in the process of becoming fiction. This is why, Emerson says, history is nothing but "an endless flight of winged facts or events" (*W*, 2: 32).

Like writing itself, history is therefore a palimpsest of several shifting figures. What does history become, though, when its facts and figures are transformed, displaced, and decomposed by conditions that no longer obey these facts and figures? Emerson's *Nature* is a text that attaches an unusually great weight to this question—unusual, at least, if measured in relation to the powerful tradition whereby *Nature* is read as a text that knows very little about itself as a historical phenomenon, about history as a whole. We might say, however, that the event of *Nature* belongs to the activities of reading and writing. We could even say that the questions of Emerson's first book are how reading and writing happen and why they make such a difference in and to history.

These questions emerge the moment we recognize that, in Emerson, writing forms an essential part of the motion that names nature and that nature names. In his essay "Goethe; or, the Writer," he suggests that the laws of nature are in fact laws of writing:

Nature will be reported. All things are engaged in writing their history. The planet, the pebble, goes attended by its shadow. The rolling rock leaves its scratches on the mountain; the river, its channel in the soil; the animal, its bones in the stratum; the fern and leaf, their modest epitaph in the coal. The falling drop makes its sculpture in the sand or the stone. Not a foot steps into the snow, or along the ground, but prints, in character more or less lasting, a map of its march. Every act of the man inscribes itself in the memories of his fellows, and in his own manners and face. The air is full of sounds; the sky, of tokens; the ground is all memoranda and signatures; and every object covered over with hints, which speak to the intelligent.

In nature, this self-registration is incessant, and the narrative is the print of the seal. It neither exceeds nor comes short of the fact. But nature strives upward; and, in man, the report is something more than print of the seal. It is a new and finer form of the original. The record is alive, as that which it recorded is alive. In man, the memory is a kind of looking-glass, which, having received the images of surrounding objects, is touched with life, and disposes them in a new order. (*W*, 4: 261–62)

Nothing exists in nature for Emerson that is not linked essentially to writing and the processes of inscription. Everything is a form of writing and therefore in need of being read. As he tells us in *Nature*, "by degrees we come to know the primitive sense of the permanent objects of nature, so that the world shall be to us an open book, and every form significant of its hidden life and final cause" (*W*, 1: 35). In order to read the history inscribed within nature, however, we need to read the language of nature, the means whereby nature registers whatever happens. In other words, that history leaves its traces in the writing that nature is—and here we can make the transit from nature to *Nature*—means that we can read *Nature*'s relation to history only by staying as closely as we can to the movement of its language. "We infer the spirit of the nation," Emerson explains in "Nominalist and Realist":

in great measure from the language, which is a sort of monument to which each forcible individual in a course of many hundred years has contributed a stone. And, universally, a good example of this social force is the veracity of language, which cannot be debauched. In any controversy concerning morals, an appeal may be made with safety to the sentiments which the language of the people expresses. Proverbs, words and grammar-inflections convey the public sense with more purity and precision than the wisest individual. (*W*, 3: 230–31)

This history of America can be read best in the ways in which it has become inscribed within the language that has also determined its course and, in particular, within the language of nature. This is why any reading that wishes to address Emerson's historical and political engagement must confront *Nature*, not simply because he there reveals the force of this commitment but also because readings of this text have been most responsible for perpetuating his reputation as an idealist who, wishing to retreat from society, revolts against tradition by cutting the threads that link him to history. Read as the primary source of both New England Transcendentalism and American modernism, *Nature* is a veritable encyclopedia of all the themes around which an American literary tradition has been defined.[2] The text has a particularly important relation to the institution of American letters, perhaps all the more so, I would argue, because it raises the question of its own relation to history. Nevertheless, if *Nature* has both a history and a politics, it is a history and politics that readers of the essay conspicuously refuse to take seriously.

Having set up a context for beginning to read the relationship between history and nature in Emerson, I will now turn to a discussion of *Nature*'s politics. Rather than read the entire text, however, to sharpen my focus I will restrict myself to considering primarily the opening of the essay, without pretending to exhaustiveness even in this circumscribed domain. Nonetheless, I would suggest, no reading of *Nature* can neglect the historical and political questions, the challenge to think the nature of history and politics, opened up within the essay's first few sentences. It would be no exaggeration to say that everything that follows in Emerson begins with these sentences, even if, within certain contexts and certain exigencies, his writings would seem to depart from their implications. Moreover, Emerson himself suggests that no matter how restricted our inquiry might seem to be, it can in principle open onto a world. As he writes in "The American Scholar," "One must be an inventor to read well. . . . There is then creative reading as well as creative writing. When the mind is braced by labor and invention, the page of whatever book we read becomes luminous with manifold allusion. Every sentence is doubly significant, and the sense of our author is as broad as the world . . . there is a portion of reading quite indispensable to a wise man. History . . . he must learn by laborious reading" (*W*, 1: 92–3). In what follows, I want to offer a reading of *Nature* as a text about the possibility of making a passage from writing to history. In reading some of the political, religious, and literary backgrounds to *Nature*, I focus on Emerson's relation to such figures as Thomas Paine and Daniel Webster as well as to certain theological and economic issues of the period. Again emphasizing the relationship among history, politics, and language, I suggest that the essay *Nature*—which generally has been read as Emerson's plea to the American writer to shed the burden of history in order to begin to write a literature that would be peculiarly "American"—inaugurates Emerson's revolutionary politics.

Nature's Jeremiad

In a letter of March 14, 1847, Theodore Parker wrote to Emerson of his conviction that the present political climate in America required a journal which would engage the real events of the time. In April, Parker and Emerson met with Sumner, Eliot Cabot, Channing, and Thoreau to discuss the possibility of starting this journal. The quarterly review was to address, more directly than the *North American Review* had ever done, the major political, theological, philosophical, and literary questions of the day. Parker wished it to be "the *Dial* with a beard" (*W*, 11: 622n.). Declining to assume the responsibilities of principal editor, Emerson nevertheless agreed to write an address to the public for the initial number. Written shortly after the annexation of Texas and during the progress of the Mexican War, Emerson's address was published in the first issue of the *Massachussetts Quarterly Review* in December 1847. In the address, he defines the aim of the journal as provoking the men and women of America into rethinking their relation to the questions of their age. Encouraging them to align themselves with the principles and virtues of nature rather than with the "delirium" and "maniacal activity" that, for him, characterize the growing expansionism of the day, the journal will recall them to the nation's beginnings in nature. At a time when the moral and intellectual powers of the country are not "on the same scale with the country's trade and production," the measure of the journal's courage and power will be the extent to which it can return the populace to the "true direction" of the nation's "first steps" (*W*, 11: 385, 388). Speaking in the name of the individuals responsible for the journal's existence, and of an America that would remain faithful to the aims of its founding, Emerson writes, "We are more solicitous than others to make our politics clear and healthful, as we believe politics to be nowise accidental or exceptional, but subject to the same laws with trees, earths and acids" (*W*, 11: 388). This correspondence between politics and nature in fact names the promise of America, a country governed by the ideas of a declaration and Constitution that claim to be grounded in the laws of nature—that is, in the laws of reading and writing.

For Emerson, nature's politics coincides with the politics of an America which remains true to its founding principle of natural liberty. Three years later, in his 1850 review of Emerson's writings, published in the March issue of the *Massachussetts Quarterly Review*, Parker suggests a similar understanding of the politics of these writings. "Mr. Emerson," he writes, "is the most American of our writers. The idea of America, which lies at the bottom of our original institutions, appears in him with great prominence. We mean the idea of personal freedom, of the dignity and value of human nature, the superiority of a man to the accidents of a man." He goes on to suggest that Emerson's writings are the "highest exponent in literature of the idea of human freedom and the value of man" and that, finally, "Emerson is more American than America herself."[3] For Parker, writing his review in the same month that Webster spoke out in favor of the Fugitive Slave Act, Emerson is "truer" to the revolutionary principles on which America was to be founded than Webster's America, than the America of the Compromise of 1850: the America that has sanctioned the Fugitive Slave Act has betrayed the laws of its founding. If Emerson criticizes America often, it is because he wishes to recall her to the glory of this founding. Keeping this wish in mind, we may begin to understand Margaret Fuller's seemingly paradoxical declaration, in a letter dated December 7, 1844, that "history will inscribe Emerson's name as a father of the country, for he is one who pleads her case against herself."[4] If Emerson indicts America in the name of America, it is because he believes, among other things, that the original relation among words, nature, and spirit has been betrayed by the founding fathers in the construction of a Constitution that sanctions slavery.

This is why Parker and Fuller suggest that Emerson's writings announce an ambiguity in his use of the word *American*—and by implication his use of the word *tradition*—that exceeds and thereby questions the possibility of either an "America" or an American tradition. If Emerson's writings work to establish a truly American tradition—be it in terms of politics, religion, economics, or literature—they at the same time suggest that such a tradition would reject the idea of any tradition or succession that might work to reduce either man or nature. For Emerson, Americans have always ordered their understanding of themselves in terms of this seeming contradiction—a contradiction that signals an immanent conflict in the meaning of America. His entire career might be understood as an effort to delineate the various ways in which this contradiction manifests itself in the major political, historical, religious, literary, and philosophical issues of his day. This effort is evident throughout all of his writings, but perhaps no more forcefully than in his first book, *Nature*. There, in the essay's famous opening lines, he writes:

Our age is retrospective. It builds the sepulchres of the fathers. It writes biographies, histories, and criticism. The foregoing generations beheld God and nature face to face; we, through their eyes. Why should not we also enjoy an original relation to the universe? Why should not we have a poetry and philosophy of insight and not of tradition, and a religion by revelation to us, and not the history of theirs? Embosomed for a season in nature, whose floods of life stream around and through us, and invite us by the powers they supply, to action proportioned to nature, why should we grope among the dry bones of the past, or put the living generation into masquerade out of its faded wardrobe? The sun shines to-day also. There is more wool and flax in the fields. There are new lands, new men, new thoughts. Let us demand our own works and laws and worship. (*W*, 1: 3)

The extraordinary strength of this passage no doubt coincides with its effort to inspire intellectual independence. The passage strikes the opening note of a revolutionary "hymn to power."[5] It attempts to provoke us into rethinking our relation to the past. Its revolutionary appeal encourages us to overcome the authority of the past by asking us to rethink the nature of our debt to previous forms and meanings. Attentive to the ways that the past can limit our independence, Emerson understands his age to be burdened by the memory of its past. No longer moved by the founding powers of nature, he suggests, America finds itself under the sway of its revolutionary fathers. As Donald Pease has explained, Emerson "thought the age excessively retrospective, too enthralled with the lives of its founders to accomplish anything on its own."[6] It has forgotten the promise of these founders—a promise that implicitly included freedom from their own authority: no one, not even the country's founding fathers, ought to presume to govern the thoughts and actions of future generations. *Nature* will be a reminder of this truth. Rather than reinforce the authority of the fathers, Emerson writes *Nature* in order to restore the power of nature to the American people. By recalling us to the revolutionary promise of independence, the essay comes to us as a work of reform that will help us recover the "poetry and philosophy of insight" that gives America its special meaning. It tells us that looking to the past is not simply a mistake but a means of ruin and death. "A new day," Emerson tells us in a journal passage that returns to the rhetoric of *Nature*'s opening, "a new harvest, new duties, new men, new fields of thought, new powers call you, and an eye fastened on the past unsuns nature, bereaves [us] of hope, and ruins [us] with a squalid indigence which nothing but death can adequately symbolize" (*J*, 8: 329).

Emerson's invocation of new lands, new men, and new thoughts corresponds to the "politics" of a nature whose end is the founding of America as a process of sheer possibility. In other words, nature's politics coincides with the politics of an America that remains faithful to the principle of Liberty. That this plea for independence gains its strength through its fidelity to earlier declarations of independence raises an issue that haunts all of Emerson's writings. As Pease suggests, even "in the apparently revolutionary question 'Why should not we also enjoy an original relation with the universe?' the 'also' implies a repetition if not an imitation at work in the very wish for independence, as if 'our' wish were first the fathers. . . . Consequently, when the tone of the paragraph finally eventuates in a command, it turns out to be one that demands that we do precisely what we feel compelled not to do, repeat the desires and actions of the fathers."[7] Emerson's revolutionary call for the end of histories and traditions that are not truly American emerges from a rhetoric and series of concepts that belong to the past, to an entire complex of historically marked traditions—be they political, theological, philosophical, or literary. That the possibility of revolution is here cast in the borrowed language of the past recalls Marx's famous metaphor in the opening of *The Eighteenth Brumaire*. "Men make their own history," he writes:

but they do not make it just as they please; they do not make it under circumstances chosen by themselves, but under circumstances directly encountered, given and transmitted from the past. The tradition of all the dead generations weighs like a nightmare on the brain of the living. And just when they seem engaged in revolutionizing themselves and things, in creating something that has never yet existed, precisely in such periods of revolutionary crisis they anxiously conjure up the spirits of the past to their service and borrow from them names, battle-cries and costumes in order to present the new scene of world history in this time-honored disguise and this borrowed language. Thus Luther donned the mask of the Apostle Paul, the revolution of 1789 to 1814 draped itself alternately as the Roman Republic and the Roman Empire, and the revolution of 1848 knew nothing better to do than to parody, now 1789, now the revolutionary tradition of 1793 to 1795. In like manner a beginner who has learnt a new language always translates it back into his mother tongue, but he has assimilated the spirit of the new language and can freely express himself in it only when he finds his way in it without recalling the old and forgets his native tongue in the use of the new.[8]

As Marx notes here, the conjuration of the past names an anxiety at the very moment it calls on this past to invent what "has never yet existed." Suggesting that this anxiety belongs to the possibility of revolution, he claims that it refers to the difficulty we experience in trying to overcome inherited representations, the uncertainty within which we must struggle with the past in order to give the future a chance. This dilemma is one that Emerson encounters throughout his career, as he suggests that any discourse must either conduct itself in an old language or reveal the new as a translation of the old.[9] As he writes in his late essay "Quotation and Originality":

Our debt to tradition through reading and conversation is so massive, our protest or private addition to tradition so rare and insignificant,—and this commonly on the ground of other reading and hearing,—that, in a large sense, one would say there is no pure originality. All minds quote. Old and new make the warp and woof of every moment. There is no thread that is not a twist of these two strands. By necessity, by proclivity and delight, we all quote. We quote not only books and proverbs, but arts, sciences, religions, customs and laws; nay, we quote temples and houses, tables and chairs by imitation. . . . The originals are not original. There is imitation, model and suggestion, to the very archangels, if we knew their history. (*W*, 8: 178–80)

If, on the one hand, the suggestion that there can be no revolution that does not belong to the structure of repetition drives Emerson to ask why we should "grope among the dry bones of the past, or put the living generation into masquerade out of its faded wardrobe," on the other hand, his sense that such repetition is indispensable, even inevitable, compels him to note that we must always pass through our inheritance in order to appropriate the life of a new language or enact a revolution. It is no accident that, like Emerson, Marx understands this doubled process in relation to the learning of a new language. For both thinkers, there can be no revolution that does not revolutionize language, that is not an appropriation and displacement of another language—that is, of other language. What gets evoked in their texts is the necessary risk involved in borrowing the language of what we wish to overcome—the risk of having our critical stance toward any particular form of cultural authority be neutralized by the dominant culture we set out to question. If this risk cannot be avoided, however, it is because it belongs to the possibility of reform. As Emerson puts it in his essay "The Conservative":

so deep is the foundation of the existing social system, that it leaves no one out of it. . . . All men have their root in it. You who quarrel with the arrangements of society, and are willing to embroil all, and risk the indisputable good that exists, for the chance of better, live, move, and have your being in this, and your deeds contradict your words every day. For as you cannot jump from the ground without using the resistance of the ground, nor put out the boat to sea, without shoving from the shore, nor attain liberty without rejecting obligation, so you are under the necessity of using the Actual order of things, in order to disuse it; to live by it, whilst you wish to take away its life. (*W*, 1: 304–5)

The desire for revolution destines us to this risk insofar as we are inscribed within history. For both Marx and Emerson, not to take this risk is to take others. Without taking into account the extent to which our actions and thoughts are caught within this history, within the history of reform, for example, we take the greater risk of being taken from behind—by history. In other words, in order to remain vigilant toward the possibility that our actions or thoughts may only confirm or consolidate what we wish to transform, we should neither declare our capacity to effect change before thinking our relation to the terms we are using nor imagine that we can think this relation without taking into consideration the relays that exist between anything "new" and everything "old." Emerson's response to this obligation can be read throughout his writings: in his persistent warnings about both the danger and inevitability of imitation; in his reluctance to join formally any of the growing number of reform movements in mid-nineteenth-century America, which, for him, often merely repeat the social ills they purport to address; and in his obsessive questioning of the entanglement between questions of slavery and those of freedom, between dependence and self-reliance, quotation and originality, and tradition and revolution. Whatever we might call Emerson's politics should take this response into account, should respect this commitment to respond to the obligation that history places on us all to think the risk of history. To refer to this commitment is to recognize, however, that Emerson's politics are not wholly of his time. This does not mean that his writings do not address the contemporary socio-political issues of his day—we have already begun to measure the extent to which his writings do little else—but rather that, for him, to address the "existing social system" requires an effort to understand the history of this system. We may never address our own time, in other words, without also thinking through the long and complicated histories that have contributed to what we call our current historical and political situation. "Man is explicable by nothing less than all his history," Emerson explains in his essay "History." "There is a relation between the hours of our life and the centuries of our time . . . the hours should be instructed by the ages, and the ages explained by the hours" (*W*, 2: 3–4).

What is at stake in reading Emerson's writings is therefore the possibility of reading the relation between the Orphic poet at the end of *Nature* who urges his listeners to "build their own world" and the Emerson who notes in a journal entry from January 10, 1832, that "the difficulty is that we do not make a world of our own but fall into institutions already made and have to accommodate ourselves to them to be useful at all," who tells us that "this accommodation is . . . a loss of so much integrity and of course of so much power" (*J*, 3: 318–19). Rather than denounce what in one sense or another has usually been understood as an incoherence in his language or a contradiction in his system, in what follows I want to suggest the meaning of an Emersonian necessity. As he would have it, whatever hope there may be for us to build our own world depends on our being able to renegotiate our relation to the historical and institutional circumstances within which we are always inscribed. This is to say again that we can only read Emerson if we learn how to read his language in relation to other language.

This is precisely what Emerson tells us in April 1835, approximately one and a half years before the publication of *Nature*. "Every man is a wonder," he writes, "until you learn his studies, his associates, his early acts and the floating opinions of his time" (*J*, 5: 30). He makes his point more precise, focusing on the question of how a writer should be read, when he later claims in "Quotation and Originality" that "we are as much informed of a writer's genius by what he selects" to quote "as by what he originates. We read the quotation with his eyes, and find a new and fervent sense" (*W*, 8: 194). Taken together, these two statements can provide us with directives for beginning to read at least some of Emerson's more paradoxical claims. They imply that we cannot begin to read his language until its intelligibility is shaken and we follow not merely what he seems to be saying, but its very movement as it refers elsewhere. As we have seen, the possibility that the meaning of any of Emerson's statements may lie in its relation to other statements, to other contexts beyond or before the text in which the statement is pronounced, opens his texts to questions of history. We can measure the justice of such directives in relation to the degree to which they bring forth the necessity of rereading these texts, the degree to which they oblige us to be responsible to these questions of history.

With *Nature*, we can begin to take on this responsibility by noting that the essay's opening paragraph takes the specific form of a New England jeremiad, a sermon form that by Emerson's day had become not only an important mode of political discourse but also a means of social integration. In the second quarter of the nineteenth century, Anne Norton explains, "the resurgence of evangelical Protestantism, the decline of anti-authoritarianism, and Whig efforts at universalizing New England's sectional culture, made it a more frequently employed rhetorical form." [10] As the name suggests, the jeremiad was derived from a prophetic model: by revealing present sin and future glory to an erring people, the prophet encouraged their reformation. Viewing themselves as actors in the penultimate scene of sacred history, the Puritans had used the jeremiad to define themselves in terms of the special mission they claimed had been assigned to them by God. They possessed a strong sense of their place within this sacred history, and so continually looked to the past for prophetic prefigurations of the present and intimations of the future. Historians such as Robert Middlekauf, Sacvan Bercovitch, and Perry Miller have documented the Puritan identification of colonial history and biblical prophecy and have suggested that it enforces an identity at once transitional and representative, since the community figures its migration from Europe to America in terms of the Hebrew redemption from slavery, the exodus from Egypt to the promised land.[11]

Although the actual form of the jeremiad alters slightly according to the historical circumstances it addresses, it usually begins, as Bercovitch has noted, with a scriptural precedent that defines communal norms. *Nature*'s opening sentences allude to chapter 11 of Luke and chapter 13 of Corinthians. This allusion to the scriptures is then followed by a series of condemnations and laments that describe the present state of the community and recall the covenantal promises that will lead to renewal. The sermon ends with a prophetic vision that unveils a promise and announces an errand of recovery. Bringing together secular and sacred history, "social criticism and spiritual renewal," the jeremiad works on a politico-theological level "to direct an imperiled people of God toward the fulfillment of their destiny."[12] Nevertheless, as Emerson well knows, the jeremiad had been resurrected by younger New England ministers in the late seventeenth century who were increasingly convinced—because of a crisis of confidence that arose over contradictions in the Puritan errand—that New England had failed its world-historical mission.[13] For these ministers, New England's fall separated the past from the present, leading them to feel estranged from the sources of religious authority that had given their lives meaning. Associating this authority with the past, with their dead parents, they increasingly idealized the founders of New England. This idealization of the fathers encouraged a sense of inadequacy among the sons, transforming their vision of history as well as their role in it. As David Scobey notes, "the Puritan intellectuals continued to identify themselves as latecomers on the stage of sacred history, but now they seemed less the harbingers of a new age than the afterthoughts of an old one."[14] We can perhaps begin to see that Emerson's revolutionary call for independence seems all the more pertinent at a time when Americans were being encouraged to revere the past, to imagine themselves unable to meet the same challenges their forefathers had met.

In choosing to frame his opening paragraph as a jeremiad, Emerson has already begun to announce all the issues with which his essay will be concerned. By invoking the myth of America in terms of this particular sermon form—the political sermon, as the New England Puritans sometimes called it, in order to suggest what they saw as both the practical and the spiritual dimension of their calling—he suggests that politics, theology, and rhetoric are inseparable in their relation to questions of nationalism. The paragraph exploits the possibilities and contradictions inherent in the traditional themes and features of the jeremiad in order to evoke the major themes and questions of his own essay—the relationship between secular and sacred history, national and universal history, mediation and revelation, as well as the nature of politics, literature, theology, and history and their relation to questions of language, to name only a few of the more persistent. The form reinforces his wish to recall America to its destiny as nature's nation. It gives him license to indicate existing elements or tendencies in contemporary America that, for him, betray its founding principles. It permits him to demand that these elements and tendencies realign themselves with the laws of nature. At the same time, his sentences invoke values that clarify, refine, and eventually question the jeremiad itself. Rather than furthering the jeremiad's tendency to promote the idealization of the past over the rights of the living, his "sermon" works to provoke each individual into rethinking his or her relation to this past. His jeremiad can be read as a sermon *against* the jeremiad. In order to understand the specific nature of Emerson's own revolution within the jeremiad form, however, we must consider not only the specific statements that comprise it but also their transformation.

The Sepulchres of History

The politics of Emerson's language becomes more legible when we recognize that several passages in *Nature* are drawn from earlier journal entries in which he analyzes Daniel Webster's political discourse.[15] Not only does *Nature* begin by evoking the natural rights of liberty and independence, but the essay's first two sentences return us to the scene of America's struggle for independence by alluding to Webster's 1825 speech at the groundbreaking ceremonies for the Bunker Hill Monument. These sentences read as a powerful response to Webster, whom Emerson once referred to as "Nature's own child" (*J*, 5: 33). As I will try to suggest, they also indicate that Emerson's admiration for Webster was not as unqualified in the 1830s as we have been taught to believe. Even if Emerson evokes Webster's speech in order to identify his essay with the powers that Webster claims for himself when he speaks—those of the American Revolution—he does so to different effect. Webster appeals to the revolutionary rhetoric of America's beginning in order to encourage his audience to defer to the authority of their forefathers, whereas Emerson appeals to this rhetoric in order to persuade his listeners that they too may effect similar if not more spectacular revolutions. For Emerson, in arguing for obedience and duty, Webster misunderstands and betrays the virtue of independence the revolution sought to guarantee. In order to measure the difference between these two appeals more exactly, we will need to situate them within the specific contexts in which they appear.

Fifty years had passed since the famous battle on the Charlestown peninsula. On June 17 nearly twenty thousand people gathered to witness the laying of the monument's cornerstone. Webster, the president of the monument association, was to be the principal speaker. "We are among the sepulchres of our fathers," he proclaimed. Saluting the surviving veterans of the Bunker Hill battle who were before him and then turning to his contemporaries, he continued:

We are on ground, distinguished by their valor, their constancy, and the shedding of their blood . . . it is natural, therefore, that we should be moved by the contemplation of occurrences which have guided our destiny before many of us were born, and settled the condition in which we should pass that portion of our existence which God allows to men on earth . . . the great event in the history of the continent, which we are not met here to commemorate, that prodigy of modern times, at once the wonder and the blessing of the world, is the American Revolution. . . . The society whose organ I am was formed for the purpose of rearing some honorable and durable monument to the memory of the early friends of American Independence. . . . We trust it will be prosecuted and that, springing from a broad foundation, rising high in massive solidity and unadorned grandeur, it may remain as long as Heaven permits the works of man to last, a fit emblem, both of the events in memory of which it is raised, and of the gratitude of those who have reared it . . . our object is, by this edifice, to show our own deep sense of the value and importance of the achievements of our ancestors . . . and to foster a constant regard for the principles of the Revolution. . . . We consecrate our work to the spirit of national independence. . . . We rear a memorial of our conviction of that unmeasured benefit which has been conferred on our land, and of the happy influences which have been produced, by the same events, on the general interests of mankind. . . . We wish that this column, rising towards heaven among the pointed spires of so many temples dedicated to God, may contribute also to produce, in all minds, a pious feeling of dependence and gratitude. . . . The leading reflection to which this occasion seems to invite us, respects the great changes which have happened in the fifty years since the battle of Bunker Hill was fought. . . . Any adequate survey, however, of the progress made during the last half-century in the polite and mechanic arts, in machinery and manufactures, in commerce and agriculture, in letters and in science, would require volumes. I must abstain from these subjects, and turn for a moment to the contemplation of what has been done on the great question of politics and government. . . . The *principle* of free governments adheres to the American soil. It is bedded in it, immovable as its mountains. . . . Let the sacred obligations which have devolved on this generation, and on us, sink deep into our hearts. . . . We can win no laurels in a war for independence. Earlier and worthier hands have gathered them all. Nor are there places for us by the side of Solon, and Alfred, and other founders of states. Our fathers have filled them. But there remains to us a great duty of defence and preservation; and there is opened to us, also, a noble pursuit, to which the spirit of the times strongly invites us. Our proper business is improvement. Let our age be the age of improvement. . . . Let us develop the resources of our land, call forth its powers, build up its institutions, promote all its great interests. . . . Let us extend our ideas over the whole of the vast field in which we are called to act. Let our object be, OUR COUNTRY, OUR WHOLE COUNTRY, AND NOTHING BUT OUR COUNTRY. And, by the blessing of God, may that country itself become a vast and splendid monument, not of oppression and terror, but of Wisdom, of Peace, and of Liberty.[16]

Webster's address works to create a sense of national identity by providing its audience with a series of images within which they can view themselves. An important narrative of national remembrance, the address is filled with references to blood and origins, to the past

and the present that is indebted to it. Although it evokes images of
the dead and memories of the survivors—in order to generate an affect which then can be mobilized politically—the history it presents
is less that of the veterans of Bunker Hill than of the audience which
has come to commemorate them. Taking its point of departure from
the memories of revolution, Webster's entire speech organizes itself
around what for him are the interrelated ideas of national memory
and progress. It derives its authority from the scene of the nation's
founding that serves as its frame. In evoking this scene, it suggests
that it springs from the same founding principles. Webster takes his
cue from the patriotic occasion and rehearses the special triumphs of
our political independence—all of which, he suggests, are perhaps
most visible within the realms of industry and manufacturing. If industrialization in America is different from industrialization elsewhere, it is because it has developed within the context of political
freedom. Webster's association between America's economic abundance and its republican form of government is essential to his attempt to account for the country's rapid commercial growth in terms
of existing socioeconomic conditions. He evokes the authority of the
revolution in order to sanctify and support emerging institutions in
the 1820s.

The revolutionary heritage provides him with a powerful trope of
independence. If he considers the revolution to be the primary source
of America's rapid economic advance, he does so to mobilize the
revolutionary values of independence and freedom in justification
of a set of values corresponding to the commercialism of his day.[17]
Economic and commercial growth, he suggests, is a consequence of
the work of the revolution. Aiming to restore the authority of the
revolutionary fathers, Webster tries to heal the divisions in American
life that, for Emerson and others, are the result of rapid urbanization, industrialization, and a growing inequality in the distribution
of wealth. He praises capitalist expansion and works to neutralize the
force of any opposition emerging from the growing numbers of men
and women whose lives—because of the declining social and economic status of laborers—are diminished by such expansion. Webster's speech in fact functions precisely by displacing materiality, by
abstracting the bodies that lost their life during the war and the la-
boring bodies that are now subject to the interests of capital. Webster

inscribes his audience into a series of images of the nation's dead founders and soldiers. These images gain their force through the absence of the actual bodies which are here evoked and redefined, which might refer to more violent and destructive histories than the one Webster wishes to present. This work also abstracts the bodies of Webster's audience, which, having been asked to see itself within these other images, is somehow removed from its own corporeality, placed within Webster's creation of the nation's political body, and asked to think of its nation as a site of commemoration and remembrance.[18] To suggest that the nation is a monument means that every present of the nation becomes traversed and even possessed by the past. Webster's speech in fact defines a moment in national history that is dominated and displaced by memory.

As Michael Rogin has suggested, Webster's speech is "a plea for the power of tradition in America" which attempts to shift authority "from living patriot heroes to their tombs."[19] Webster had already anticipated this argument in his 1820 speech "The First Settlement of New England." There, celebrating the landing of the Pilgrims at Plymouth, he claims that one of the first acts the Pilgrims performed after having arrived was the erecting of "sepulchres for the dead" on ground that thereafter became sacred.[20] In both speeches, Webster uses the memorials and monuments to which he refers in order to remind us of achievements that we cannot repeat. He asks us to submit to the value or authority accorded to these memorials. They not only perpetuate the authority of the revolutionary fathers over their descendents but also encourage a process of emulation that is at the same time a form of restraint. Emerson will make this point again twenty-one years later in his 1851 address on the Fugitive Slave Law. There, referring to Webster's obsession with the past, he writes:

Mr. Webster is a man who lives by his memory, a man of the past, not a man of faith or of hope. . . . He believes, in so many words, that government exists for the protection of property. . . . Happily, he was born late,—after the independence had been declared, the Union agreed to, and the Constitution settled. What he finds already written, he will defend. Lucky that so much had got well written when he came. For he has no faith in the power of self-government; none whatever in extemporising a government. Not the smallest municipal provision, if it were new, would receive his sanction. In Massachusetts, in 1776, he would, beyond all question, have been a refugee.

He praises Adams and Jefferson; but it is a past Adams and Jefferson that his mind can entertain. A present Adams and Jefferson he would denounce. (*AS*, 66–67).

For Webster, the Bunker Hill Monument will serve to establish a genealogical continuity between "fathers" and "sons." It will also remind the sons of their duties to the fathers. He emphasizes this continuity and duty by characterizing the Union as a hierarchical system based on deference and love. He attempts to reinforce these hierarchies by drawing an analogy between the father who watches over his children and the secondary institutions he wishes to support. Like other social reformers in the Age of Jackson, Webster justifies emerging institutions by claiming that the relation of order and protection that exists among factories, asylums, schools, plantations, political parties, and the people whose lives they affect corresponds to the natural relations of the family, if it does not improve them.[21] He reinforces this effort by appropriating the rhetoric of an American political religion for nineteenth-century industry and economics. Combining respect for the fathers, institutional conservatism, and capitalist progress, he joins the question of economic improvement to the move from a concern with liberty to a desire for prosperity. As Rogin suggests, he proposes "an organic, hierarchic image of authority reaching backward in time to the heroes of the founding, outward to new institutions, and forward to a prosperous future."[22] Investing the revolution and the landscape of nature with the virtues of liberty and independence, Webster assimilates the glory of the past into a vision of America's rapid and successful expansion. He further justifies the rapid economic and social changes taking place in nineteenth-century America by understanding this change in terms of an idea of natural progress.

As Carolyn Porter has noted, however, despite the powerful and patriotic rhetoric of Webster and others, "protests about the ill effects of the factory system, the declining status and waning autonomy of farmers and mechanics, the wage earner's impotence to halt the growing disparity between wages and prices—all effects of an expanding market economy which served the interests of the rising men of the period—persisted."[23] The development of the American manufacturing system from 1815 to the years just after the publication of *Nature* in 1836 was marked by an increased dependence of workers on owners. By the end of the 1830s, factory workers were protesting their decreasing wages, their loss of autonomy and self-respect, and the lack of education for their children. Like Webster, they, too, appropriated the revolutionary rhetoric of their forefathers, but to a different end. Declaring their independence from the oppression of manufacturing powers they believed had been imported from England, they spoke out against the threats to their humanity resulting from growing specialization and fragmentation within the manufacturing process. Rather than complementing the revolution, the factory system, they argued, betrayed its promises of liberty and independence.

If Emerson's *Nature* also invokes and appropriates a rhetoric of revolution, progress, economy, authority, family, and institutions, it is because he aligns himself with the cause of the laborer. Unlike Webster, he works to question the stability and ethics of such rhetoric. Although Emerson praises progress, for example, he sees the rise of commerce as a reduction of man and nature. As he writes in a journal entry from 1839, "this invasion of Nature by Trade with its Money, its Credit, its Steam, its Railroad, threatens to upset the balance of man and establish a new Universal Monarchy more tyrannical than Babylon and Rome" (*J*, 7: 268). The issue at stake in *Nature* is not only the explicit question of the meaning of nature, but also the implicit question of the aesthetic, intellectual, moral, religious, economic, and political uses to which it can be put—both as a resource and as a metaphor—in order to dissimulate the alienation that occurs when these uses have as their end the imposition of certain values on a people. Emerson's interest in nature, then, should be read in relation to his sense that natural language can be used to manipulate and control a populace as much as to liberate it.

This points to an important difference between Emerson's and Webster's conception of the ethics of nature's laws. When Webster speaks at the Bunker Hill Monument in 1825, he reminds his audience of their debt to their revolutionary fathers and proclaims that, as "a race of children," it is "natural" for them to defend and preserve what their fathers created. What Emerson finds most powerful in this speech—Webster's invocation of the power of the revolutionary moment—he also finds most dangerous.[24] Webster's identification of this power with the past as well as with himself works to seduce his audience into obedience. Emerson, by contrast, identifies this power with nature and suggests that it is available to the "race of children" in the same way that it was available to their fathers. The adherence to revolutionary principles, for him, should promote the virtue of self-reliance rather than the weakness of dependence. Webster's misuse of language here—his recourse to a language of nature, for example, that tends toward subjugation—betrays his corruption. As Emerson explains later in his essay, "the corruption of man is followed by the corruption of language. When simplicity of character and the sovereignty of ideas is broken up by the prevalence of secondary desires,—the desire of riches, of pleasure, of power, and of praise,—and duplicity and falsehood take the place of simplicity and truth, the power over nature as an interpreter of the will is in a degree lost; new imagery ceases to be created, and old words are perverted to stand for things which are not; a paper currency is employed, when there is no bullion in the vaults. In due time the fraud is manifest, and words lose all power to stimulate the understanding or the affections" (*W*, 1: 29–30). That Emerson has Webster in mind here can be seen from a journal passage that uses the same economic metaphor to associate corrupted language with paper currency, and does so within the context of the relation between quotation and originality: "Webster's speeches seem to be the utmost that the unpoetic West has accomplished or can. We all lean on England[;] scarce a word, a page, a newspaper but is writ in imitation of English forms, our very manners and conversation are traditional, and sometimes the life seems dying out of all literature & this enormous paper currency of words is corrupted instead" (*J*, 4: 297). It will be a matter, in these early sentences of *Nature*, of rejuvenating and mobilizing the language of Webster's speech—a language that, for Emerson, is directed toward death and corruption—toward the meaning of a revolution based on the principles of nature, but a nature that is devoted to radical transformation rather than to preservation.

Nature's opening remarks, then, should be read as a transformation of Webster's major themes: in them, Emerson tries simultaneously to question Webster's synthesis of the possibility of progress with monuments to the fathers and to indict Webster's plea for the authority of an American tradition.[25] We can read this transformation in his appropriation of Webster's rhetoric. By substituting his "Our age is retrospective. It builds the sepulchres of the fathers" for Webster's "We are among the sepulchres of our fathers," for example, he both acknowledges and revises his debt to Webster. More particularly, his substitution of the phrase "the fathers" for Webster's "our fathers" works to indict Webster's cultural provincialism as well as any strictly patriarchal form of authority. For Emerson, both provincialism and patriarchy are supported by a rhetoric aimed at enforcing particular and fixed structures of authority. (As he will remind us later in *Nature*, "man in all ages and countries" embodies notions of authority "in his language as the FATHER" [*W*, 1: 33].) Whereas a provincialist rhetoric attempts to produce the political power of a national identity at the expense of the genealogical heterogeneity that runs through the history of any people,[26] a patriarchal form of government, as he explains in his 1844 essay "The Young American," "readily becomes despotic, as each person may see in his own family. Fathers wish to be fathers of the minds of their children" (*W*, 1: 375). *Nature* suggests that Webster's evocation of the power of the revolutionary fathers forgets the force with which they themselves fought against patriarchy, not only in the name of America but also in the name of humanity as a whole. As he explains elsewhere, "the scraps of morality to be gleaned from [Webster's] speeches are reflections of the minds of others. He says what he hears said, but often makes signal blunders in their use" (*AS*, 67).

Emerson gives his argument a special twist at this point, since his first sentence also alludes to Paine's *Rights of Man*. Arguing for the rights of men over the rights of institutions and government, he recalls Paine's claims for the sacred rights of the individual. Like Emerson, Paine's "motive and subject"—as he describes it in a letter of 1806 to John Inskeep, the mayor of Philadelphia—had always been "to rescue man from tyranny and false systems and false principles of government, and enable him to be free."[27] Emerson evokes Paine at this moment in order to set the representative revolutionary father against a Webster who argues for the necessity that we obey the precedents established by these fathers—without thinking the principles of these precedents.[28] In the *Rights of Man*, the particular passage to which Emerson refers occurs in the context of a discussion of the different constitutions of men—in the context, that is, of a characteristically Emersonian pun. Paine writes that "since the Revolution of

America, and more so since that of France," the "preaching of the doctrine of precedents, drawn from times and circumstances antecedent to those events, has been the studied practice of the English government." He goes on to say:

by associating those precedents with a superstitious reverence for ancient things, as monks show relics and call them holy, the generality of mankind are deceived into the design. Governments now act as if they were afraid to awaken a single reflection in man. They are softly leading him to the sepulchre of precedents, to deaden his faculties and call his attention from the scene of revolutions.[29]

Although Webster evokes the glory of the revolution, his insistence that we become dependent on the authority of that revolution works to call us away "from the scene of Revolutions" toward the English Constitution against which the revolution was fought—toward the sepulchre that, for Paine, is that constitution.[30] For both Paine and Emerson, freedom is destroyed by dependence. Recalling that Paine's text is an indictment of Burke's pleas for the authority of tradition and hierarchy, we might even say that Webster is Emerson's Burke. Emerson's use of Paine against Webster is particularly pertinent at a time when Paine was enjoying a kind of revival, especially among labor groups, who were appropriating Paine's republican language in their arguments against the oppression of the factory and manufacturing systems. By the 1830s, Paine birthday dinners were being held in cities such as Boston, Philadelphia, Cincinnati, and Albany. As Eric Foner notes, "The dinners were closely associated with the emergence of the first class-conscious labor movement in American history. The ideology of the labor spokesman echoed the premises of Paineite republicanism—a belief in natural rights and human perfectability and a conviction that, in the absence of artificial privilege, republican government would ensure an economic abundance in which all classes would share." "Combined with these beliefs," he adds, "was an early version of the labor theory of value, coupled with an assertion of the right of the worker to the 'whole product of his labor.'"[31] Paine's rhetoric of radical egalitarianism encouraged urban workers to defend their right to enjoy the revolutionary promise of independence. In appealing to Paine, Emerson appeals to the cultural frame of reference of his audience. He attacks Webster in the same republican language that American working-class radicals were using to legitimize their demands for political and social reform. *Nature*'s first sentence begins to articulate the conditions for his own revolutionary call for independence—a call that is once again a memory as well as a promise. In suggesting that Webster has forgotten the lessons of the fathers, Emerson's evocation of Paine seems appropriate for another reason as well. Although Paine's language had pervaded American culture since he wrote *Common Sense* in 1776, no other revolutionary father had been more willingly forgotten until the 1830s revival. Republican and Democratic ideas could be obtained from Jefferson, many argued, without the added burden of Paine's aggressive anticlericalism. As I will suggest in a moment, however, the force of Paine's antiecclesiastical position may have played an important role in Emerson's attraction to him.[32]

Emerson's return to the language of the revolution reminds us of the necessity to remain vigilant toward any form of authority that threatens to tyrannize us and reduce all of our actions to empty repetitions—especially when that authority may gain its power over us by recourse to the rhetoric of freedom. For him, there can be no revolution that does not aim to protect an individual's self-reliance. "There is a time in every man's education," he writes in his essay "Self-Reliance," "when he arrives at the conviction that envy is ignorance; that imitation is suicide" (*W*, 2: 46). As Porter suggests, we should not be surprised that he shows "little patience with the 'Universal Whiggery' of New England."[33] Its constant invocation of the authority of the founding fathers leads him to denounce what he calls its "cant." As he writes, in a journal entry from October 14, 1841, that has some bearing on Webster's appeal to the founding fathers:

Is it a man that speaks, or the mimic of a man? Universal Whiggery is tame and weak. . . . Instead of having its own aims passionately in view, it cants about the policy of a Washington and a Jefferson. . . . What business have Washington or Jefferson in this age? You must be a very dull or a very false man if you have not a better and more advanced policy to offer than they had. They lived in the greenness and timidity of the political experiment. The kitten's eyes were not yet opened. They shocked their contemporaries with their daring wisdom: have you not something which would have shocked them. If not, be silent, for others have. (*J*, 8: 58)

If Emerson questions the authority of "European" traditions over "American" ones, he also questions that of any "American" tradition that might wish to govern the destiny of its "own" people, that might wish to subject them to the imperatives of the fathers. He reinforces this point by substituting an "age" which "builds the sepulchres of the fathers" for Webster's "we" who "are among the sepulchres of our fathers." He suggests that any authority we might attribute to the tombs of the revolutionary fathers can only be the belated result of an interpretive act. The meaning of this authority can only be imposed and established by rhetorical and institutional means. At the same time, he questions the possibility of a "national" identity by inscribing it within a historical moment which it shares with all other nations and over which it has no privileged authority. Whatever we might build, write, or speak, he suggests, can never belong to "us." Or rather, it belongs to us because it belongs to everyone. Linking America's national identity to the cause of humanity, he suggests that America's cosmopolitanism defines its national character.

This argument is complicated further in Emerson's next few sentences, in terms that reinforce and expand my discussion of his reading of Webster's speech. *Nature*'s fourth sentence—"The foregoing generations beheld God and nature face to face; we through their eyes"—alludes to I Corinthians 13: 9–13: "When I was a child, I spake as a child, I understood as a child, I thought as a child; but when I became a man, I put away childish things. For now we see through a glass, darkly: but then face to face." Both Emerson's sentence and the biblical passage to which it refers would seem to point to a temporal order between past and present that is characterized in terms of a shift from an earlier moment of revelation to a present condition of mediation. In I Corinthians, however, the face-to-face encounter with the divine is projected into the future at the end of history rather than into the past at history's beginning. In reworking the passage, Emerson reverses the priority of its temporal order so that he can once again emphasize the retrospective character of his age. By defining ourselves in terms of a past that we imagine as having had "an original relation" to the truths of revelation, we overlook the present divinity of nature's laws. We forget, Emerson suggests, the divinity of our own present creative potential. The belief that revelation occurred only in the past keeps us from exercising our power to experience it now. He explicitly repudiates the biblical lament, "now we see through a glass, darkly," in his essay "Illusions," claiming instead that "we see God face to face every hour" (*W*, 6: 324). This is why, he tells us in "The American Scholar," the notion "that we are come late into nature, that the world was finished a long time ago" is a "mischievous" one (*W*, 1: 105). He makes a similar point in a journal entry from August 1837. "Man is fallen Man is banished," he writes, "an exile; he is in earth whilst there is a heaven. What do these apologues mean? These seem to him traditions of memory. . . . We say Paradise was; Adam fell; the Golden Age; & the like. We mean man is not as he ought to be; but our way of painting this is on Time, and we say *Was*" (*J*, 5: 371). "The ruin or the blank, that we see when we look at nature, is in our own eye," he tells us toward the end of *Nature*. "The axis of vision is not coincident with the axis of things, and so they appear not transparent but opake" (*W*, 1: 73).

Emerson's indictment of the notion of the Fall recalls his concern over the implications of the jeremiad form, as well as those of Webster's Bunker Hill speech. For him, the danger arises whenever the rhetorical, political, and religious uses to which the concept of the Fall may be put invest the past with an authority that then determines the quality of our lives, now and in the future. This worry over the ethicality of the notion of the Fall, this insistence on the present realization of our creative powers, works to subvert, as Joel Porte has suggested, "the traditional Christian claim that full spiritual maturity and the direct apprehension of the divine, will be attained only at the end of time, when the veil is finally removed."[34]

The possibility of distinguishing between these moments—between a past, a present, and a future, between a moment of revelation and one of mediation—is further problematized by the opening syntactical constructions of Emerson's next two sentences. Instead of continuing to articulate the order of a before and an after, he presents a negative grammatical and rhetorical structure that entangles these two moments: "Why should not we also enjoy an original relation to the universe? Why should not we have a poetry and philosophy of insight and not of tradition, and a religion by revelation to us, and not the history of theirs?" Emerson's "Why should not we . . ." is a rhetorical form of inversion which ironizes the representation of a single, identifiable meaning—here, that of the possibility of an immediate vision or revelation—and thereby joins the past, the present, and the future. In this, the sentence requires us to rethink the nature of revelation. There can be no revelation that is not at the same time caught within history. If we are to enjoy an original relation to the universe, this relation must account for its relationship to history.

The necessity of this rhetorical strategy becomes clearer when we recognize that, in emphasizing the question of the possibility of revelation, Emerson echoes the vocabulary and arguments of the eighteenth- and nineteenth-century theological and epistemological debates among German biblical scholars such as Johann Gottfried Herder, Johann Gottfried Eichhorn, and Friedrich Schleiermacher and between orthodox Christianity and deism.[35] He would have been aware of the German debates first through the writings of Andrews Norton, George Bancroft, Theodore Parker, and Edward Everett, each of whom studied the Germans with great care, even if not always with great sympathy,[36] and second, through his brother William, who had traveled to Göttingen in 1823 to study theology. More particularly, though—in terms of his rhetorical aims as well as our reading of his reading of Webster—Emerson here echoes the vocabulary and arguments of such "founding fathers" as Paine, Franklin, and Jefferson, whose so-called "religious" writings comprised some of the most influential articulations of the deist tradition in America.[37]

In fact, Paine's *The Age of Reason*, first published in 1794, had such a wide and rapid circulation that Paine quickly became the greatest spokesman of popular deism. In the mid-1790s alone, Paine's text went through seventeen editions in America and sold tens of thousands of copies. As a result, deism, which had been confined primarily to the educated classes, became available and attractive to the populace.[38] Borrowing the critical vocabulary and rhetoric of such Enlightenment figures as Newton, Locke, and Spinoza, Paine's famous theological treatise attempts to bring together a political and religious radicalism in order to democratize deism. For him, the introduction and acceptance of deism in America is essential to the constitution of the new state. As he claims in his introduction to *The Age of Reason*: "Soon after I had published the pamphlet 'Common Sense,' in America, I saw the exceeding probability that a revolution in the system of government would be followed by a revolution in the system of religion" (*AR*, 51). Identifying political liberty with religious and moral liberty, Paine and other revolutionaries repeatedly identified freedom from the tyranny of George III with freedom from the tyranny of sin. His argument for the principles of deism must be read as one and the same with his denouncement of "despotic governments" (*AR*, 186). He reminds us of this correspondence in his *Letter to Mr Erskine*. "Of all the tyrannies that effect mankind," he writes, "tyranny in religion is the worst; every other species of tyranny is limited to the world we live in; but this attempts to stride beyond the grave, and seeks to pursue us into eternity." [39]

Encouraged by the downfall of both church and state in France, radicals in the 1790s wrote pamphlets disseminating the debates that had emerged from the earlier deist controversies. Paine himself began the *Age of Reason* in the fall of 1793 in St. Denis, during the rise of the Convention's efforts to dechristianize France. These efforts moved him to seek a mass audience for his religious views. [40] His deism appropriates and condenses earlier forms of deism, but also follows the deist attempt to understand religion in terms of a secular world view rather than a theological one and to replace a transcendent divinity with the self as the agent of personal order. [41] As a rationalization and demystification of religion, this shift from revealed religion to natural religion should be read in relation to the antiecclesiastical element in late forms of Puritanism. Both reject organized Christianity's emphasis on the values of revelation, tradition, and ecclesiastical authority, arguing instead in terms of the values of reason and social function. Paine's arguments against the conservatism of the clergy, against their defense of aristocratic and hereditary privilege, need to be read in this context. Throughout the *Age of Reason*, he tries to expose the false character of religious institutions—which, for him, are nothing more or less than "human inventions, set up to terrify and enslave mankind, and monopolize power and profit" (*AR*, 50)—by indicting the source of their authority: scriptural revelation.

For Paine, every religious institution establishes itself "by pretending some special mission of God," which has been "communicated" to certain of its members (*AR*, 51). The repetition and institutionalization of the meaning or truth which is attached to this

communication marks the "beginning" of religious traditions. Moreover, he suggests, even if it were true that:

something has been revealed to a certain person, and not revealed to any
other person, it is revelation to that person only. When he tells it to a second
person, a second to a third, a third to a fourth, and so on, it ceases to be a
revelation to all these persons. It is revelation to the first person only, and
hearsay to every other, and consequently they are not obliged to believe it. It
is a contradiction in terms and ideas, to call anything a revelation that comes
to us at second-hand, either verbally or in writing. Revelation is necessarily
limited to the first communication. (*AR*, 52)

By claiming the incompatibility between revelation and the telling
of that revelation in speech or writing, Paine argues against the
possibility of establishing a "genuinely" religious succession or tradition on the "hearsay" of revelation. He also emphasizes the necessarily rhetorical dimension of all religious institutions. He reinforces
this last point by discussing specific instances of the instability of
scriptural meaning: the exegetical difficulties that arise whenever one
tries to establish the authorship of the scriptures, the place and time
of their composition, the data included in them, or whenever one
tries to account for the various additions or deletions required to prepare these texts for inclusion within the biblical canon. The nature of
this rhetorical and fictional foundation precludes the transmission of
a univocal religious meaning by producing the instability and unreli
ability of the revealed truths on which churches of any kind are
founded. "The idea or belief of a Word of God existing in print, or
in writing, or in speech," Paine says, "is inconsistent in itself," due to
"the want of a universal: the mutability of language; the errors to
which translations are subject; the possibility of totally suppressing
such a word" (*AR*, 97–98).

If "the Word of God cannot exist in any written or human language," Paine recommends that we no longer search for revelation in
"the book called the Scripture, which any human hand might make,"
but rather in "the Scripture called the creation" (*AR*, 63 and 70). Here
he follows the deist replacement of the book of scripture by the book
of nature.[42] In the universal living gospel, which must neither be in-
terpreted nor preached nor translated into the languages of men, "we
cannot be deceived." The creation of nature is "an ever-existing

original" in which every man can read God's beneficence (*AR*, 69). As Paine proclaims, "the creation is the Bible of the Deist." This redefinition of divine authority corresponds to a redefinition of political authority. As an "ever-existing original," Creation questions the establishment of any tradition or institution which might support "the imposition of one man upon another" (*AR*, 185).[43] Paine here touches on the force of Emerson's own thinking of the nature of creation. Emerson more than once admitted his indebtedness to Paine. "Each man . . . is a tyrant in tendency, because he would impose his idea on others," he notes in his essay "Nominalist and Realist." "But Tom Paine," he goes on to say, "helps humanity by resisting this exuberance of power" (*W*, 3: 239).

Paine's persistent questioning of the authority of scriptural revelation, his emphasis on the belatedness of all writing or speaking, and on the necessity of believing in a "religion" of nature and creation, clearly anticipate Emerson's own meditation in *Nature* on the possibility of revelation, on mediation, and the nature of the act of creation. But if *Nature*'s opening remarks invoke the rhetoric of deism in general and the deist rhetoric of "revolutionary fathers" such as Paine in particular, it is not simply to echo the themes with which he is concerned—although this is certainly an important aspect of what he is doing. Emerson also wishes to use the rhetoric of the founding fathers against that of Webster. If Webster argues in his Bunker Hill speech for the power and modernity of an "American" tradition—characterized by a correspondence between the expansion of democracy and that of capitalism—by relying on the authority of *his* founding fathers, then Emerson reminds us that these same "fathers" argued against the establishment of any form of tradition or authority that wishes to impose itself on the destiny of a people, especially when that tradition or authority is patriarchal.[44] Benjamin Franklin makes this point when he suggests that any attempt to institute "Traditions of the Fathers" is in fact a forgetting rather than a remembrance of the "genius" of "the Fathers." Webster's "forgetting" of the "truth" of this genius makes him, in Franklin's words, one of the "multitudes among us, who are *zealous for the Traditions of the Fathers*, but yet are in a great measure ignorant of those Principles upon which our Ancestors settled in this Wilderness."[45] By exploiting the antiecclesiastical dilemma at the heart of American Puritanism, Franklin argues against the subjugation of an individual to an external authority that we have already seen Paine call the "imposition of one man upon another." "Every age and generation must be free to act for itself, *in all cases*, as the ages and generations which preceded it," he writes in his *Rights of Man*. "The vanity and presumption of governing beyond the grave, is the most ridiculous and insolent of all tyrannies. Man has no property in man; neither has any generation a property in the generations which are to follow. . . . It is the living and not the dead, that are to be accommodated. . . . I am contending for the rights of the *living*, and against their being willed away by the manuscript assumed authority of the dead."[46] As Emerson explains, reinforcing Paine's point, "The destiny of this country is great and liberal, and is to be greatly administered. It is to be administered according to what is, and is to be, and not according to what is dead and gone" (*W*, 11: 205). In 1836, Emerson appropriates Paine's republican rhetoric to further his attack not only on the common materialism of the day but also on the obsession with the past that he sees prevailing in antebellum America—a materialism and obsession he sees represented in Webster's Bunker Hill address.[47]

The Echolalia of Revealed Politics

Emerson evokes the rhetoric of the revolutionary fathers Franklin and Paine in order to appropriate, resituate, and then release its critical potential vis-à-vis Webster. That other texts become *events* inside his texts emphasizes the relationship that he envisions between the past and the present, between an event and its representation. This relationship corresponds to what Emerson terms "history" and accounts for Emerson's refusal to stay in any single context as well as for his insistent desire to seek new significances in different places. This refusal and desire should be read in relation to his belief in transformation in general and, in particular, in relation to his conviction of the transitory and fugitive character of nature. "What we call nature," he tells us in "The Poet," is a certain "motion or change" (*W*, 3: 22). Or, as he puts it in a journal entry from 1827, "The ground on which we stand is passing away under our feet. Decay, decay is written on every leaf of the forest, on every mountain, on every monument of art. Every wind that passes is loaded with the solemn sound. All things perish, all are the partakers of this general doom but man is . . . the prominent mark at which all arrows are aimed. In the lines of his countenance it is written 'that he is dying,' in a language that we can all understand" (*J*, 3: 73). This transitoriness has its analogue within Emerson's own language. What characterizes this language is the way in which its figures are always dissolving into one another, questioning their structure before any one of them has a chance to assert itself. They are evoked only to be transformed by different figures or mobilized into different contexts. We could even say that the shifting movement that we understand as the signature of Emerson's language is his way of remaining faithful to something that is always about to vanish or perish. In other words, like the nature whose decay is inscribed within every one of its phenomena, Emerson's language appears only in order to disappear. It becomes not only an archive of history but a sepulchre for both history and language. Such a sepulchre, though—no matter how much it is supposed to maintain history, to preserve it beyond its death—at best contains history's decomposing corpse. If all language is past, decayed, and disintegrated (as Emerson explains elsewhere, "Words cannot cover the dimensions of what is in truth. They break, chop, and impoverish it" [*W*, 1: 28]), this sepulchre can no longer even be said to be built out of something called language. Since this movement of decay belongs to history, if its linguistic sepulchre names the remains of everything that has passed away, then it is no simple metaphor. It is perhaps the first metaphor of language or history. There can be no language or history, in other words, that does not begin in the sepulchre. This is why history can only "be" history as long as it is the withdrawing trace of its own transience. Only when it is no longer history—that is to say, no longer an empirical, historical fact among others—can it survive as history. The sepulchre of history can be said to give birth to the possibility of history. Emerson makes this point in a journal entry from December 29, 1830, which identifies language with the figure of the sepulchre, cites Sir Thomas Browne's identification of America itself with this sepulchre, and evokes again the fugacity of all things. Discussing Browne's *Hydrotaphia: Urne-Buriall*, he writes:

Hydrotaphia of Sir Thos Browne smells in every word of the sepulchre. "That great antiquity America lay buried for thousands of years; and a large part of the earth is still in the urn unto us." . . . "There is no antidote against

the opium of time." . . . Every science is the record or account of the dissolution of the objects it considers. All history is an epitaph. All life a progress
toward death. The [sun] world but a large Urn. The sun in his bright path
thro' Ecliptic but a funereal triumph . . . for it lights men & animals & plants
to their graves. (*J*, 3: 219–20).

According to Emerson, the world of *Hydrotaphia* is one in which
everything passes away, in which all life progresses toward death. It
tells us that there can be no history that is not a history of death—
that is not a history of its own death. To be more precise, the true
history of the past is the one that is always in a state of passing away.
This is why "all history is an epitaph." This is also why we can say
that, like Browne's *Hydrotaphia*, Emerson's *Nature* comes in the form
of a sepulchre. An anthology of American figures and history, it is a
sepulchre of sepulchres—a history of the surviving language of the
past, in particular, of the linguistic phantoms of a nation's past. We
therefore should not be surprised to hear yet another echo in *Nature*'s first few lines. For Emerson's opening two sentences—"Our
age is retrospective. It builds the sepulchres of the fathers"—allude
not only to Webster's "We are among the sepulchres of our fathers,"
but also, as Porte reminds us, to Christ's angry words to the lawyers
in Luke II: 47–48: "Woe unto you! For ye build the sepulchres of the
prophets, and your fathers killed them. Truly ye bear witness that ye
allow the deeds of your fathers: for they indeed killed them, and ye
build their sepulchres." [48] The echolalia of *Nature*'s opening sentences
here becomes extraordinarily complicated, as each of the three passages works to contextualize and "read" the other two. When Emerson then invokes the revolutionary fathers, exchanges, recognitions,
and reverberations occur whose possibility is, as I will suggest, already
inscribed within Luke—a gospel to which Emerson again refers at
the end of *Nature*. Christ's speech to the lawyers is no doubt invoked
at this point as part of Emerson's opening meditation on the nature
of tradition, institutions, revelation, interpretation, and the language
of creation—since these are also the central concerns in Luke. But,
as we might now have come to expect, the text is also appropriated
as an aid in Emerson's indictment of such enlightened legislators as
Webster.

Christ's accusation of the lawyers is one of three woes that he
directs to these interpreters of the Mosaic law. Each of these woes

is concerned explicitly with the relations among law, prophecy, and wisdom. Together they repeat and echo the three woes which he has just directed to the Pharisees. He accuses both the Pharisees and the lawyers for their minute and legalistic interpretations of the Mosaic law as well as for their purported respect for the traditions of the elders. He claims that these interpretations create a mass of regulations and restrictions which then become burdens on the people. Moreover, such legalistic interpretation serves as a theological means to justify the policies and institutional practices of these so-called spiritual leaders. It leads to a complacency among such leaders which enables them to rationalize their subjugation of a people. Neither the Pharisees nor the lawyers realize that they are not what they seem to be. Christ metaphorizes this deception by comparing them to unmarked graves with bones of the dead within them—for although these graven leaders seem holy, they deceive others, burying them under the weight of their laws. Rather than hearing and honoring the words of the prophets, the lawyers work to memorialize themselves as well as their interpretations of the law.

Christ's rhetorical entombment of the Pharisees and the lawyers here anticipates his second charge against the lawyers: "Woe unto you! For ye build the sepulchres of the prophets, and your fathers killed them." The words of the lawyers and the Pharisees replace those of the prophets. They entomb the voices and wisdom of the true prophets. The building of monumental tombs for the honor and memory of the prophets—nothing less than the recording of the words of the prophets in the scriptures themselves—marks the lawyers' complicity in the crimes of their fathers. "The forms, the books, which are called religious," Emerson explains in an early lecture from the mid-1830s, "are nothing but the monuments and landmarks men have erected to commemorate these moments, and to fix, if it were possible, their too volatile Spirit" (*EL*, 2: 345–46). In honoring only dead prophets, the lawyers betray their approval of what their fathers have done to these mouthpieces of God. Christ reinforces this link between the lawyers' efforts to memorialize their interpretation of prophecy and the killing of the prophets in his next sentence: "Truly ye bear witness that ye allow the deeds of your fathers: for they indeed killed them and ye build their sepulchres." By indicating the lawyers' collaboration in the killing of the prophets, Christ not only announces the violence of all legalistic and scriptural interpretation, but he also allegorizes his own situation. As the latest of the prophets, he prophesies the Pharisees' and the lawyers' refusal either to listen to him or to acknowledge him. Christ's indictment works to provoke his listeners into transforming their relation to the past. He encourages them to begin to question the institutionalization of any interpretive tradition. For, separated as they are from the Word of God (the word "Pharisee" literally means "separated"), unless such a transformation occurs, they can neither enjoy an original relation to the law that commands—God himself—nor the justice or wisdom which this law communicates to those who listen well.

Although we can perhaps recognize many of the thematic and rhetorical elements in these passages from Luke, their relationship to those in the passages by Webster, Paine, and Emerson that I have already discussed is difficult to ascertain. The various appropriations and misappropriations which Emerson sets in motion by placing all of these texts in conjunction with each other enables each text constantly to reflect and defer each of the other ones. Still, within the constraints and limitations of this reading, I want to suggest some of the more important connections among them, even if only briefly. To begin with, the entanglement that Emerson produces amongst these texts demands that at some level we read Christ's indictment of the Pharisees and the lawyers as an allegory of Emerson's own indictment of Webster. We can begin to read this allegory by noting that the opening sentences of *Nature* replace Christ's attack on the lawyers for building "the sepulchres of the prophets" with an indictment of an age which "builds the sepulchres of the fathers." Porte is right to suggest that this substitution of "fathers" for "prophets" is an indication of Emerson's sense that, in building monuments to honor and remember the fathers, his age has neglected the prophets, "those with direct knowledge of God." Nevertheless, this suggestion cannot fully and precisely account for what Emerson might mean by either "prophecy" or "a direct knowledge of God." For while Porte goes on to claim that Emerson seeks an unmediated moment of "perfect sight,"[49] Emerson's insistence that "we do not see directly; but mediately" (*W*, 3: 75) is, as I have argued, less a plea for the transparency of vision and more a reminder of our irremediable belatedness. If Emerson's *Nature*—his own "Book of Revelation"[50]—reveals anything, it is perhaps the vision of the end of vision, the revelation that everything begins in a moment of mediation. What is at stake for Emerson is the possibility of seeing the world as mediated, for the law of nature's politics requires that we recognize the world as the result of man's own labor within time. That Emerson begins by substituting "fathers" for "prophets," and hence by deferring the question of prophecy, suggests that his age suppresses those "prophets" who see and write of the end of vision. But he also wishes to remind us that, in their most prophetic moments, Webster's "revolutionary fathers" speak out against the possibility of revelation. I will return to this equivalence between prophets and fathers in a moment, but first I want to continue my reading of this passage from Luke. To do so we need to accept Emerson's substitution and trace its implications for Webster in terms of Christ's words to the lawyers.

If we follow Emerson's replacement of "the prophets" by "the fathers," Christ's first two sentences to the lawyers read as: "Woe unto you! Ye build the sepulchres of the fathers; and your fathers killed them." That Webster's fathers killed the fathers whose sepulchres Webster's rhetoric constructs recalls my earlier argument concerning Emerson's reading of Webster and Paine. For Emerson, the same fathers on which Webster wishes to found the authority of an American tradition themselves argued against all forms of patriarchal authority. When Webster forgets the prophetically subversive character of his founding fathers, he betrays their genius. Rather than listening to the words of his fathers, Webster memorializes and monumentalizes his own interpretation of them. We need only recall his prayer at the end of his speech at Bunker Hill. There, Webster turns America itself into a monument. "Let our object be OUR COUNTRY OUR WHOLE COUNTRY AND NOTHING BUT OUR COUNTRY," he says. "And, by the blessing of God, may that country itself become a vast and splendid monument." That this work of monumentalization takes place within language is staged by Webster in his decision to capitalize— to monumentalize—a statement that, inscribing an allusion to the oath on which the legal institution to which he belongs is founded (the oath, that is, through which we affirm that we will speak "THE TRUTH THE WHOLE TRUTH AND NOTHING BUT THE TRUTH"), suggests that he is now speaking the truth of his COUNTRY. Transforming America into a monument for the living, Webster forgets what he had already said earlier in his speech—that "monuments belong to the dead."[51] If America is a monument, then Webster's audience lives within a space which is at the same time a site of death. The shape of the present and its people is determined by those who build the monument or tomb of America. What Emerson suggests is that these builders are not the nation's fathers, but rather those who write in the name of the fathers, those who, like Webster, have assumed the founders' authority. Here, it is Webster's address that builds and inscribes, that freezes and rigidifies the nation, transforming it and its people into a kind of sepulchre. Like the words of the lawyers whom Christ addresses, Webster's words replace those of his revolutionary fathers. In so doing, they entomb the words of these fathers. As Dylan Ford has noted, Webster's speech works to inscribe the American people "into a space of the dead which encloses and determines their identity. The text goes so far as to argue that it has become the duty of the present to kill and bury itself in the name of the past," to become, that is, its own sepulchre.[52] Emerson had already noted the sepulchral quality of Webster's voice in an early journal passage from February 7, 1820. Claiming to be repeating a description of Webster given to him by "Mr. K, a lawyer of Boston," he writes: "Webster is a rather large man . . . he has a long head, very large black eyes, bushy eyebrows, a commanding expression. . . . His voice is sepulchral." He closes the passage by citing Webster. "Contrasting & comparing the worthy and great dead," Webster exclaims, "you may not tell a man 'your neighbor's house is higher than yours' but you may measure gravestones & see which is the tallest" (J, 1: 9).

Emerson's indictment of Webster's effort to arrogate power to himself by claiming to speak in the name of the fathers is later repeated more generally by Douglass in his 1852 address "The Meaning of July Fourth for the Negro." There, in a passage that analyzes the duplicity of rhetoric like that of Webster's, Douglass also includes a reference to the same passage in Luke to which Emerson refers. "My business," he declares, in language that we can fairly recognize as Emersonian:

if I have any here to-day, is with the present. The accepted time with God and His cause is the ever-living now. . . . We have to do with the past only as we can make it useful to the present and to the future. To all inspiring motives, to noble deeds which can be gained from the past, we are welcome. But now is the time, the important time. Your fathers have lived, died, and have done their work, and have done much of it well. You live and must die, and you must do your work. You have no right to enjoy a child's share in the labor of your fathers, unless your children are to be blest by your labors. You have no right to wear out and waste the hard-earned fame of your fathers to cover your indolence. Sydney Smith tells us that men seldom eulogize the wisdom and virtues of their fathers, but to excuse some folly or wickedness of their own. This truth is not a doubtful one. There are illustrations of it near and remote, ancient and modern. It was fashionable, hundreds of years ago, for the children of Jacob to boast, we have "Abraham to our father," when they had long lost Abraham's faith and spirit. That people contented themselves under the shadow of Abraham's great name, while they repudiated the deeds which made his name great. Need I remind you that a similar thing is being done all over this country to-day? Need I tell you that the Jews are not the only people who built the tombs of the prophets, and garnished the sepulchres of the righteous? Washington could not die till he had broken the chains of his slaves. Yet his monument is built up by the price of human blood, and the traders in the bodies and souls of men shout—"We have Washington to *our father*."—Alas! that it should be so; yet so it is.[53]

The relays between Douglass's rhetorical strategy and Emerson's should be read as a measure of the political importance of Emerson's language. If the fact that Douglass's address is directed against slavery can help us understand the ways in which Emerson would later mobilize his own rhetoric for an antislavery position, it also suggests that in *Nature* this rhetoric could already be said to be antislavery. We could even say that Emerson's reading of Webster's speech belongs to his concern with slavery in general. That is to say, his analysis of the way in which Webster's language can be used to enslave his audience, to justify the various forms of slavery that were at work in antebellum America, is inseparable from his efforts to address the institution of slavery more directly and explicitly in the 1840s and 1850s. Or, to put it another way, his later and more recognizably antislavery addresses never abandon his early strategies for reading the relation between language and the realms of history and politics, his earlier efforts, that is, to alter institutions by altering the language that maintains them.

Returning to our reading of the opening of *Nature*, we can note that the various metaphorical exchanges between the passages at hand and between Emerson's and Webster's differing readings of the revolutionary fathers accelerate as Christ's speech continues to unfold in a highly symmetrical fashion: "Truly ye bear witness that ye allow the deeds of your fathers: for they indeed killed them, and ye build their sepulchres." Evoking the words of Christ to suggest that, like the lawyers whom Christ addresses, Webster allows the deeds of "his" fathers, Emerson implies that Webster condones the killing of the fathers as well as that of the prophets. This is not to say that Webster encourages the questioning and undoing of the patriarchal forms that he wishes to perpetuate. Rather, in praising the building of monuments to commemorate the words and deeds of the revolutionary fathers, Webster demonstrates his approval of the betrayal and murder of these very words and deeds. He supports the suppression of the revolutionary fathers' efforts to question the familial authority with which he wishes to justify the emergence of secondary institutions in nineteenth-century America. As the ventriloquism between Emerson, Christ, and Paine suggests, however, such justification is only a rhetorical and historical means of rationalizing the alienating and enslaving capacity of any institution.

The language of Christ's speech links Webster's rhetorical commemoration of the fathers with the building of their sepulchres. Emerson's *Nature* too suggests this connection when it claims that Emerson's age "builds the sepulchres of the fathers" and "writes biographies, histories, and criticisms." More particularly, within the specific rhetoric of the passages from Luke, we can add that this doubled act of building and writing is complicitous with the murder of the fathers and prophets who are being memorialized. Throughout the various passages I have discussed—in Paine, Luke, or Emerson— the emphasis has been on the interpretive violence that occurs when the act of prophetic creation is entombed in speech or writing—in an other's rhetoric. For Emerson, this moment of entombment is the moment of institutionalization, the moment when, as he tells us in "The American Scholar," "the sacredness which attaches to the act of creation, the act of thought, is transferred to the record" (*W*, 1: 88). What this record commemorates, as the monument or tomb of the act of creation, is not the event of creation, but rather its exclusion. It is the historical evidence of an artifact or artifice that defines itself in terms of its relation to an outside—here, to the act of creation or thought—which it simultaneously includes and excludes. The relationship that emerges from this movement between the moment of institutionalization and the process of transference is central to Emerson's historical poetics. This transference must be understood in terms of the various refractions, inflections, appropriations, and transformations that his complex circulation of allusions sets into play. The various ways in which a text entangles itself with other texts, articulates itself in terms of other narratives, or produces articulations with other texts or contexts are for Emerson the means and conditions for the establishment of an institution.[54] There can be no institution or tradition without the possibility of relation in general. That the internal operations of Emerson's texts articulate themselves necessarily in relation to various institutional conditions and forms, which encourage his sentences to move along particular, yet always heterogeneous lines, indicates that his opening remarks in *Nature* serve as a genealogical allegory of the historical process of institutionalization. The structural entanglement between the "inside" of Emerson's text and its "outside" involves the relation between the act of writing and the institutional conditions in which it takes place. Breaking through "the confusion of tradition and the caricature of institutions" (*W*, 2: 27), he suggests that the question of politics must be thought according to this question of relation.

The Emersonian writer, belonging with Christ to "the true race of prophets" (*W*, 1: 128), here performs an active genealogy of the religious, political, social, or literary values which serve to mystify and entomb a historical process of rhetorical and textual appropriation. This solicitation of the values of truth—touching as it does both "material" institutions and significant representations—suggests that the maintenance of an institution or tradition depends on the iterable transmission of a canonical rhetoric. As Emerson writes in his 1838 "Divinity School Address," suggesting the disparity between the "truth" to which Christ refers and that of religious institutions: "The idioms of his language and the figures of his rhetoric have usurped the place of his truth; and churches are not built on his principles, but on his tropes" (*W*, 1: 129). This process of usurpation—as it is performed by Webster and by the lawyers and Pharisees whom Christ attacks—consists of the substitution of one set of textual or historical meanings for another. It enables the imposition of certain forces and forms of authority upon a people. "This is the history of governments," Emerson explains in "Politics," "one man does something which is to bind another" (*W*, 3: 215). That the political question of force and authority corresponds to questions of representation returns us to the obligation to think the ethics of representation. If the power of an institution is the power to impose limits, to enforce demarcations, and in general to maintain, then the realization of this power, as Paine and Christ remind us, depends on a certain dissimulation of its rhetorical or interpretive basis. It requires that we forget Emerson's claim in "The Poet" that "the history of hierarchies serves to show that all religious error . . . [is] at last nothing but an excess of the organ of language" (*W*, 3: 35).[55] Like Christ's accusation of the lawyers, Emerson's claim here is a "provocation" (*W*, 1: 127) to his readers to transform their relation to this "history of hierarchies." He encourages us to recognize that there can be no self-contained, coherent, meaningful system—be it what we call a self, a community, a nation, an idea, a history, a politics, or even a single word—that is not inevitably caught up in a relation to both history and rhetoric.[56]

He makes this point in relation to the concept of an individual, in a passage that anticipates Nietzsche's pronouncement that he was "at bottom all the names of history." "What is our own being," Emerson writes, "but a reproduction, a representation of all the past? I remember the manifold cord—the thousand or the million stranded cord which my being and every man's being is,—that I am an aggregate of infinitesimal parts and that every minutest streamlet that has flowed to me is represented in that man which I am so that if everyone should claim his part in me I should be instantaneously diffused through the creation and individually decease, then I say I am an alms of all and live but by the charity of others. What is a man but a congress of nations?" (*EL*, 3: 251). This passage has wide-ranging consequences for our understanding of the Emersonian self. It tells us that once the self experiences its relation to alterity, once it experiences alterity in others, it experiences the alteration that, "in it," infinitely displaces and delimits its singularity. If the Emersonian self is exposed in this passage, it is because it is posed according to an exteriority that traverses the very intimacy of its being. What Emerson suggests here is that the self that is infused by its relations to others is without self. It no longer has a substantial identity: it in fact deceases. Emerson understands this event as a source of strength rather than of weakness, however. As he explains elsewhere, "we are not strong by our power to penetrate, but by our relatedness. The world is enlarged for us, not by new objects, but by finding more affinities and potencies in those we have" (*W*, 7: 302).

This last point takes a specific turn in terms of Emerson's own history when we recall that Christ's indictment of the lawyers and the Pharisees occurs immediately after Christ neglects to wash his hands before dinner, after his "forgetting" to cleanse his hands of "foreign" bodies. When he is reminded that he has forgotten to participate in this institutionalized cleansing, rather than comply with the Pharisee's request that he now wash his hands, Christ begins his attack by indicting them for building fences around their laws, for instituting boundaries between the "inside" of these laws and their constituted "outside." The reasons behind this indictment can be clarified by a claim that Christ makes elsewhere in another context, a claim which seems in particular to prophesy the coming of the Emersonian writer. He says in Mark 7: 15: "nothing that goes into a man from outside can defile him." If this pronouncement recalls Emerson's insistence that we recognize and accept our inevitable relation to others, then Christ's refusal to participate in the ceremonial and institutional forms of the Pharisee's dinner time recalls Emerson's decision not to participate in the ceremonial and institutional forms of another New Testament dinner; namely, the Last Supper.

Emerson's decision—which eventually led to his leaving the ministry in the fall of 1832—focused on an interpretation of the authority of Christ's Last Supper as a Christian institution. As Gay Wilson Allen has summarized, Emerson's controversy with his church began when he announced "that he could no longer administer the communion service with a clear conscience because he had decided that Christ had not intended it to become a perpetual ritual."[57] Emerson defended this decision in a sermon to his congregation on September 9, 1832: "The Lord's Supper." There, Emerson reminds his listeners that, of the four Evangelists who recorded the event of Christ's Last Supper, only Luke quotes Christ as having said "This do in remembrance of me" (Luke 22: 19). Even if Christ did in fact utter these words, Emerson goes on to say, we need to remember that Christ generally speaks in a figurative and parabolical language. Rather than claiming that his body should actually be eaten—even if only "symbolically"—according to Emerson, Christ reminds us that we should live by his commandments. In suggesting that the Christian interpretation of the "Lord's Supper" has no clear authority in the New Testament, Emerson suggests that Christ wants to provide us with a *living* religion which can question and perhaps displace the empty formalisms of the Jewish religion (and by implication, those of orthodox Christianity). For him, Christ in each instance argues against the institution of interpretive traditions, which can then occult the truth to which he refers. To live by Christ's commandments therefore means to question unceasingly the establishment of all institutional forms. We can trace this equivalence by suggesting some of the significances that Emerson attaches to the Last Supper.[58]

For Emerson, the event of the supper marks a moment of passage or transition that coincides with what he means by Passover. It occurs between an act of eating together out of friendship and a religious act, each of which informs the other. Emerson discusses the supper as a passing-over from an act that produces a sign to one that requires its interpretation.[59] That the event of the supper remains equivocal in itself explains for Emerson why "there has never been any unanimity in the understanding of its nature, nor any uniformity in the mode of celebrating it" (*W*, 11: 3). Nevertheless, for him the supper is divine. The event of the supper does not merely signify; it is. His distinctions here are related directly to his indictment of the various Christian efforts to reduce the supper to a structure of signification. Such a reduction, as I have already argued in terms of Christ's indictment of the lawyers and the Pharisees, is always for Emerson an act of entombment, in this case, a murdering of the sacredness which attaches itself to the event of the supper. Once Emerson characterizes the Last Supper as the pass-over or transition between love and religion, between a meal shared by friends in observation of Passover and the institutionalization of this meal in the forms of religion, the paths to religion can only lead to death, to "the forms of dead oppositions." As his friend Sampson Reed would have it, "it needs no uncommon eye to see that the finger of death has rested on the church."[60] That this metaphorics forms a part of Emerson's decision to leave the ministry is made clear in a journal entry of June 2, 1832. There, in diction that anticipates the metaphorics of his opening remarks in *Nature*, he writes: "I have sometimes thought that in order to be a good minister it was necessary to leave the ministry. The profession is antiquated.

In an altered age, we worship in the dead forms of our forefathers"
(J, 4: 27).[61] That Emerson's "age" worships in the "dead forms" of
its forefathers is an indication to him that it has passed over the significance that Christ gave to the event of the Last Supper. This significance is, for Emerson, the supper's celebration of the process of
transition. We recall that Passover literally marks the moment of
transition between the slavery of the Jews under the Pharoah and
their liberation under God—a transition that occurs before the Mosaic laws are written. For Emerson, if Christ and his disciples observe
Passover, they do so less to repeat it in the form of a ritual than to
repeat it in another and different act of historical and rhetorical transformation. As he suggests, Christ's Last Supper provokes his disciples
to transform their relation to Passover. It should now mark the moment of transition between Passover as "a historical covenant of God
with the Jewish nation" and Passover as "a new covenant" sealed with
the blood of Christ (W, 11: 7).

The divinity of the "Lord's Supper" lies in its performance of
Passover as a moment of transformation. Emerson's reading of the
Last Supper serves him as an allegory of a historical process that
weaves together the moment of the institutionalization of religious
forms and the movement of historical representations. This process,
as I have suggested, is one of textual and material transition, appropriation, and displacement; in terms of Emerson's historical poetics,
it coincides with what he calls "Power." As he explains in "Self-Reliance": "Power ceases in the instant of repose; it resides in the moment of transition from the past to a new state, in the shooting of the
gulf, in the darting to an aim" (W, 2: 69). Or, as he puts it elsewhere,
"the coming only is sacred. Nothing is secure but life, transition, the
energizing spirit. No love can be bound by oath or covenant to secure
it against a higher love. No truth so sublime but it may be trivial to-
morrow in the light of new thoughts. People wish to be settled; only
as far as they are unsettled is there any hope for them" (W, 2: 319–
20). As a historical process of sheer transition and transformation,
power—whether religious, social, political, economic, or literary—
effects an entanglement between old and new, outside and inside,
event and representation, creation and institutionalization, that then
determines its conditions of possibility. This moment of relation
forms the enabling and disrupting basis of any institutional form. As

such, it should not be understood as the activity of an individual, but rather as a complex of diverse historical representations, which are constantly in transition. I have tried to suggest that this rhetorical equivocation leads Emerson to see Christ's Last Supper as "an occasion full of solemn and prophetic interest," but nevertheless one which is not intended "to be the foundation of a perpetual institution" (*W*, 11: 12). More generally, though, the matrix of relational power that Emerson sets into motion in this reading of the "Lord's Supper" is nothing less than that "prodigal power" of which "Prophet," "Poet," "Genius," "Christ," "Nature," "Politics," "History," "America," and even "Emerson" are the names.

This "prodigal power" coincides with the power of figural interpretation and is an essential element in Emerson's questioning of institutional forms of authority. He emphasizes this point in his "Divinity School Address," delivered before the senior class of Harvard's Divinity College on July 15, 1838. The address bears comparison with his sermon "The Lord's Supper" because of the prominence of its higher critical strategies. In the address, Emerson undertakes to persuade students of the Bible that interpretation can either free or enslave them. As in the sermon, he works to encourage his listeners to recognize the historical, rhetorical, and interpretive dimension of any religious institution. This recognition could free his young audience from the conviction that the truths of religion are stable and inviolable and thereby lead them to discover the divinity that exists within themselves. We perhaps can understand why the reception of Emerson's address was characterized by a hostility that justified itself in the name of ethical and moral values. Andrews Norton's review of the address for the August 27, 1838, issue of the *Boston Daily Advertiser* provides us with one of the more provocative examples of such hostility. In particular, Norton seems well aware of the dangers that an Emersonian tradition might imply. He writes:

He would consent to live a lie for the sake of being maintained by those whom he had cheated. It is not, however, to be supposed that his vanity would suffer him long to keep his philosophy wholly to himself. This would break out in obscure intimations, ambiguous words, and false and mischievous speculations. But should such preachers abound, and grow confident in their folly, we can hardly overestimate the disastrous effect upon the religious and moral state of the community.[62]

Norton, who achieved fame for his academic defense of a liberal, rationalist interpretation of the scriptures, as well as for his persistent condemnation of Emerson's "infidelity," was perhaps the chief expositor of the Unitarian view of the Bible in the early nineteenth century. For him, the art of interpreting the Bible derives primarily from what he terms the "intrinsic ambiguities of language." Biblical commentators can overcome this "intrinsic ambiguity and imperfection," he claims, only by "reference to EXTRINSIC CONSIDERATIONS," only by subordinating the scriptural characteristics which he sees as accidental to the "truth" of Christianity, namely, the "historical circumstances surrounding scriptural language, its peculiarities of idiom, and the presuppositions of writer and audience"[63]—all things which Emerson emphasizes in his own writings on biblical exegesis.

That Norton recognizes the "obscure intimations" and "ambiguous words" of Emerson's address or that he suggests such obscurity and ambiguity necessarily lead to "false and mischievous speculations" is therefore scarcely surprising. As Porte notes, "it is hard to see how Emerson's frank appropriation of religious terms and concepts could have failed to offend much of his audience . . . to most of Emerson's listeners, all of this [must have] seemed the sheerest effrontery."[64] But that Norton identifies this obscurity and ambiguity and then in turn relates it to the "disastrous effect" which he believes a succession of Emersonian writers can have on the religious and social institutions of the community is what is really surprising. By suggesting a relation between Emerson's rhetorical performance and an effective questioning of varied institutional forms, Norton's remark touches what I have argued to be the central concern in Emerson's thinking. If we draw out all of its consequences, Norton's condemnation of Emerson leads to an admission of the relationship between questions of representation and the establishment of social and political institutions. His indictment of Emerson is at one level a confirmation of this reading.

Emerson's Cold War

In their invocation of the rhetoric of Webster, Paine, and the Bible, *Nature*'s first few sentences open themselves up to questions of history, politics, religion, and language. What may at first seem a complicated and subtle strategy of allusion and displacement becomes less so when we recall that Webster's Bunker Hill speech had been widely circulated in small-town newspapers and had gone through various editions during the eleven years that separated its delivery from *Nature*'s publication (Emerson himself owned three different copies of the speech). By 1836 Webster's reputation as a powerful political orator was firmly established within the American imagination; Paine's republican rhetoric had been a pervasive cultural resource in America since the mid-1770s; and the Bible had been America's Book since the Puritan settlement in the early seventeenth century. Whatever we might call *Nature*'s political force escapes us as long as we do not recognize the availability of such texts and rhetoric within the America of the 1830s. America's familiarity with these rhetorics defines the conditions of *Nature*'s politics. What may seem abstract and opaque to our modern ears may seem so because we no longer have an ear for the conflictual nature of Emerson's language, the history and politics that this language bears within its movement.

Emerson's *Nature*, the "prodigal power" that infuses all of his writings, works to link language, politics, and history.[65] In each instance, he thinks the names of this power in terms of the questions of representation that enable and disturb their articulation. His first essay propels his thought toward a lifelong concern with rethinking the relationship between representation and the domains that we commonly refer to as domains of real causality—history, politics, and economics. For him, these domains can neither exist nor be thought in isolation from issues of language. The history of political thought is inseparable from a reflection on the history of the politics of representation. As I have suggested, these histories coincide with the meaning and destination of America's own political history. It is because *Nature* offers a succession of citations of other texts, all associated with the same meaning and destination, that it should be read as a self-proliferating recitation of American history. We could even say, as a kind of provocation, that *Nature* is a masterpiece of unoriginality—not because its language reenacts language that already has passed into history, but rather because it speaks its own language as immediately other and thereby makes itself into a language that passes *into* history. *Nature*'s language surrenders itself to an other—be it a Webster, a Paine, a Browne, a Luke, or any of the other voices encrypted within the movement of its sentences—whose language enters its text only fragmentarily. How can we proceed to read this language historically? In the manner in which Emerson reads his precursors—in the first lines of *Nature*, no differently from in the later ones. Webster, Paine, Browne, and Luke are not evoked as names from a positive history and in fact are not evoked as names at all—and yet in Emerson's rewriting they are still legible in their disfigured and transformed linguistic remainders. As we have seen, each of the texts repeats itself in the others, even as their repetition is only the return, the virtually infinite return of what is never the same. It is in the possibility of our being able to read this relation and difference that we can begin to register what Emerson means by history and politics.

To develop the implications of this conclusion would lead to a detailed reading of the rest of *Nature* in conjunction with Emerson's other writings of the period as well as with the history of the various social, political, religious, and literary debates that these writings incorporate and transform within their trajectory. This labor of reading would help us measure further the extent of his engagement with the issues of his day. I have tried to emphasize the importance and the complexity of this task by focusing on the difficult entanglement between politics and nature in these few lines and in Emerson in general. This entanglement operates like a red thread to emphasize the crises of representation that define the domains of history and politics. If in these first two chapters I have used his later writings to recontextualize this entanglement within his earlier texts, I have also hoped to resituate his later texts within the challenges and concerns of his earlier thought. Throughout his career Emerson suggests that, whatever nature and politics may be, they refer to one another according to complex laws. The same laws, with increasing complication, reappear time and time again and underline some of the most famous and thematically suggestive of his statements. What is required is that we recognize the historical force of these laws. This force is inseparable from Emerson's efforts to set in motion a series of statements that reverse the order of associations that usually attend these "entities." We can no more keep out of politics than we can keep out of the frost because their respective domains are inscribed in a system of exchange which is itself structured like a trope. Politics and frost are chiasmic figures for one another.

This analogy is perhaps inescapable for another reason as well, one having to do with the way in which Emerson has generally been read within the last one hundred and fifty years. We all know the story; it is one he both exploited and perpetuated. That is to say, it is a story for which he is not entirely unresponsible. Emerson is the proverbial "cold" man. He remains indifferent to the particularities of history, to the suffering and hardship of particular men and women in particular places and particular times. When we cast our eye over the nineteenth century, the chill we feel comes from the power and influence of his indifference. I have begun to retell the story, but even Emerson recognized the difficulty of altering it. As he writes in the "American Scholar," "the sluggish and perverted mind of the multitude, slow to open to the incursions of Reason, having once so opened, having once received a book, stands upon it, and makes an outcry if it is disparaged" (*W*, 1: 89). The situation is not at all helped by the fact that the writers who appropriated Emerson's rhetoric and then mobilized it for specific social and political reform—the writers who were perhaps in the best position to remind us of Emerson's politicality—were sometimes the very ones who helped to perpetuate the version of Emerson I wish to revise. Theodore Parker, for example, in his 1850 essay on Emerson's writings, after having praised Emerson for being "more American than America," declares that there is always "a certain coldness" in his ethics: "He is a man running alone and would lead others to isolation, not society." He has "the ethics of marble men."[66] Whitman makes the same point when, in his essay "Emerson's Books," he claims that Emerson is dominated by "cold and bloodless intellectuality."[67] And Carlyle speaks for everyone when, on reading Emerson's second collection of essays, he writes to him on November 3, 1844, and says:

We find you a Speaker indeed, but as it were a *Soliloquizer* on the eternal mountain-tops only, in vast solitude where men and their affairs lie all hushed away in a very dim remoteness; and only *the man* and the stars and the earth are visible,—whom, so fine a fellow seems he, we could perpetually punch into, and say, "Why won't you come and help us then? We have terrible need of one man like you down among us! It is cold and vacant up there; nothing paintable but rainbows and emotions; come down and you shall do lifepictures, passions, facts,—which *transcend* all thought, and leave it stilting and stammering.[68]

Whatever we might say about Emerson, we could never say that he was indifferent to the metaphorics of Carlyle's letter. Not only does he himself condemn what he calls the "cold formalism" of certain scholars, New England ministers, and politicians, but he is not unaware of his own reputation as "remote," "withdrawn," "cold," and even "icy." Nevertheless, he responds to Carlyle by exclaiming:

> But of what you say now & heretofore respecting the remoteness of my writing & thinking from real life, though I hear substantially the same criticism made by my countrymen, I do not know what it means. If I can at any time express the law & the ideal right, that should satisfy me without measuring the divergence from it of the last act of Congress. And though I sometimes accept a popular call, & preach on Temperance or the Abolition of slavery, as lately on the First of August, I am sure to feel before I have done with it, what an intrusion it is into another sphere & so much loss of virtue in my own.[69]

Emerson's response to Carlyle would at first seem to reinforce Carlyle's charge rather than answer it. As is often the case when Emerson tries to defend himself—something that occurs only rarely—his insistence on "the law & the ideal right" serves to invite the attack of hostile readers by appearing to offer exactly the evidence they need to convict him. If Emerson claims that his acceptance of popular calls compromises his virtue by forcing him to enter "another sphere," what can we say but that he wishes to distance himself from the concerns of this sphere, that he wishes to retain his virtue by separating himself from the historical domain in which he is being asked to participate? If the multitude for whom Carlyle speaks is left asking "Why won't you come and help us?" it is because Emerson's answer would seem to be "Why won't you help yourselves?"

Emerson did not, however, stop accepting popular calls. If anything, from 1844 on he accepts them with more regularity than before. He had already, in his 1842 essay "The Transcendentalist," distanced himself from those "admirable radicals," those "unsocial worshippers" who "shun general society" (*W*, 1: 342). He writes: "While the good, the illuminated, sit apart from the rest . . . as if they thought that by sitting very grand in their chairs, the very brokers, attorneys, and congressmen would see the errors of their ways, and flock to them . . . the good and wise must learn to act, and carry salvation to the combatants and demagogues in the dusty arena below" (*W*, 1: 350). He makes a similar point in "The American Scholar" (1837) when he claims that it is the scholar's duty "to cheer, to raise, and to guide men by showing them facts amidst appearances" (*W*, 1: 100). Emerson seems to imagine himself doing what Carlyle asks him to do in 1844. It is no wonder that he responds to Carlyle by saying that he does not know what it means for his writings to be accused of "remoteness" from "real life." As Nietzsche would explain later, "it is warmer in the heights than people in the valleys think, especially in the winter. The thinker will know what is meant by this metaphor."[70] Following Nietzsche, we could say that, for Emerson, however theoretical or abstract a thought may seem, however distant a concern with "the law and the ideal right" may seem to be from real life, insofar as it thinks the relationship between thought and experience without subordinating the one to the other, it is inseparable from the real experiences in which it occurs and of which it speaks.

To speak of a separation between idealism and experience in Emerson is to neglect the powerful force of his analysis—to distance oneself from what he means by "life." No thinking of the law and of rights can avoid "the conventional, the local, the perishable," he tells us (*W*, 1: 88). To speak of laws and rights is already to speak of history, is already to address the conditions of any act of Congress, recent or otherwise. To think the law and the ideal right is less an attempt to transcend or neutralize history than to rethink the laws that govern the articulation of laws and rights in history. As he suggests in his 1863 Dartmouth address "The Man of Letters," "the inviolate soul is in perpetual telegraphic communication with the source of events" (*W*, 10: 252). When Emerson declares that his acceptance of a popular call often leaves him feeling compromised, he does not mean to belittle the causes he is being asked to address. Rather, he suggests that these issues are usually thought apart from the principles that provide for their existence and perpetuation in the first place. Men of letters who do not address the social and political issues of the day in terms of these principles display their indifference and "coldness" to real experience. Their "frostiness" toward what Emerson means by "experience" obscures the strength of his social criticism.[71] They tend to simplify historical, economic, religious, or political "realities," presuming that these exist without reference to the thoughts of men and women. Neglecting the role of representation in the constitution of these domains, these "ornamental scholars" (*J*, 11: 380) reduce the efficacy of their pleas for reform.

"The lovers of liberty may with reason tax the coldness and indifferentism of scholars and literary men," Emerson writes in his 1854 address "The Fugitive Slave Law." "Universities have forgotten their allegiance to the Muse, and grown worldly and political" (*W*, 11: 242). The scholar or poet does not need to be "a president, a merchant, or a porter" to be "worldly" or "political." Instead he needs to reveal the ways in which all institutions are "founded on a thought which we have." True action occurs "in a thought which revises our entire manner of life" (*W*, 2: 161). Emerson does not recommend that scholars and literary men refuse to address the political issues of their day; he urges them to think the laws and rights that determine the force of the political. This can be seen in any of the addresses he delivered on the function of the scholar within society, but he expresses the point in the form of a hope in the letter to Cabot of August 1861 to which I have already referred. There he writes, "But one thing I hope,—that 'scholar' and 'hermit' will no longer be exempts, neither by the country's provision nor their own, from the public duty. The functionaries, as you rightly say, have failed. . . . The good heart & mind, out of all private covers, should speak and save" (*L*, 5: 253). Emerson speaks of the distressing consequences that attend the scholar's betrayal of this obligation in his address "The Man of Letters." "The country complains loudly of the inefficiency of the army," he says, "It was badly led. But, before this, it was not the army alone, it was the population that was badly led. The clerisy, the spiritual guides, the scholars, the seers have been false to their trust" (*W*, 10: 254). The man of letters should encourage the populace to recognize its divine capacity for creative social and political reform. This recognition follows that "of the mediate and symbolical character of things" (*EL*, 2: 202). "We are symbols and inhabit symbols," Emerson writes (*W*, 3: 20). It is the scholar's duty to provoke the populace into thinking the relationship between socio-political conditions and questions of representation. This is why, he notes, "Every thing should be treated poetically—law, politics, housekeeping, money. A judge and a banker must drive their craft poetically as well as a dancer or a scribe. That is, they must exert that higher vision which causes the object to become fluid & plastic" (*J*, 7: 329). The scholar who neglects this trust, who neglects the role that language plays within the sociopolitical domain, remains "cold" to the meaning of America and to the urgency of her questions.

"This climate and people are a new test for the wares of a man of letters," Emerson writes in a journal entry of January 1856. "All his thin watery matter freezes" (*J*, 14: 27–28). If he here hints at his own anxieties and fears in the face of a volatile and demanding political climate, he also evokes the scholar's reputation as a person generally unable to meet the challenges of this climate. If "there goes in the world a notion that the scholar should be a recluse, a valetudinarian,—as unfit for any handiwork or public labor as a penknife for an axe" (*W*, 1: 94), this notion results from the habits of the false scholar, the scholar who has betrayed his scholarly obligations. As he suggests elsewhere, "the scholar must be ready for bad weather" (*W*, 10: 286). A follower of "the laws of nature and the experiences of history," "the true scholar grudges every opportunity of action past by, as a loss of power." He knows that it is only through action that thought may "ripen into truth" (*W*, 10: 242; 1: 95). What chills Emerson are the scholars who, in their wish to make a break with idealism, in their desire for practical power, refuse to recognize the inexorable relationship between thought and experience, theory and practice. In the face of such refusals, Emerson becomes the cold man to whom he is so often likened. In a letter of October 1840 to Margaret Fuller, for example, after having been accused of not actively expressing his affection for her, he writes: "tell me that I am cold or unkind, and in my most flowing state I become a cake of ice. I can feel the crystals shoot & the drops solidify. It may do for others but it is not for me to bring the relation to speech" (*L*, 2: 352). His own "thin watery matter freezes." Nevertheless, in a reversal of the connotations we usually associate with ice, he reminds her that "ice has its uses. . . . Being made by chemistry . . . its composition is unerring, and it has a universal value as ice, not as glass or gelatine" (*L*, 2: 351).

It would seem that whatever we might call Emerson's "pragmatism" needs to be thought according to the necessity of this withdrawal, this other kind of engagement. As he writes in his essay "The

Comic," nothing can plead immunity from "the laws of ice" (*W*, 8: 163). In other words, Emerson's political engagement should be read in relation to a disengagement that looks toward a new historical position. It takes the form of a repetition of the common assumptions and connotations of a term or concept—in this case that of "ice"— that is also an active reply, an act that attempts to distance itself from these assumptions and connotations. Emerson would seem to be claiming that *his* ice is warmer than other people's fire. This point is illustrated in his "Divinity School Address," in a passage whose ironic force has been noted many times before.[72] Emerson describes listening to a "formalist" preacher whose "coldness" makes listening to him "hell":

I once heard a preacher who sorely tempted me to say, I would go to church no more. Men go, thought I, where they are wont to go, else had no soul entered the temple in the afternoon. A snowstorm was falling around us. The snowstorm was real; the preacher merely spectral; and the eye felt the sad contrast in looking at him, and then out of the window behind him, into the beautiful meteor of the snow. He had lived in vain. He had no one word intimating that he had laughed or wept, was married or in love, had been commended, or cheated, or chagrined. If he had ever lived and acted, we were none the wiser for it. The capital secret of his profession, namely, to convert life into truth, he had not learned. Not one fact in all his experience, had he yet imported into his doctrine. This man had ploughed, and planted, and talked, and bought, and sold; he had read books; he had eaten and drunken; his head aches; his heart throbs; he smiles and suffers; yet was there not a surmise, a hint, in all the discourse, that he had ever lived at all. Not a line did he draw out of real history. The true preacher can always be known by this, that he deals out to the people his life,—life passed through the fire of thought. (*W*, 1: 137–38)

"Whenever the pulpit is usurped by a formalist," Emerson explains, "then is the worshipper defrauded and disconsolate" (*W*, 1: 137). The preacher he describes here fails to draw his eloquence from either nature or real history. In the passage, history, the movement of life as it passes "through the fire of thought," resides more in nature than in the rhetorical force of this particular spiritual guide. Unlike the true preacher, he does not resound with experience; he does not translate the experiences of history into the minds and hearts of his audience. In this, he commits violence upon his listeners. He goes against "the truth" it is his duty to impart. Refusing to link his discourse to the life he lives, neglecting to suggest the relationship between language and experience, he demonstrates his lack of vitality. What is perhaps most striking in all of this, however, is the figure with which Emerson chooses to compare him. Dramatizing his role as exemplary listener, his attention—which the preacher's rhetoric is unable to hold—shifts to the snowstorm outside the window. The preacher competes with the snowstorm for his auditor's attention and loses. The irony of the passage, as Porte has noted, lies in Emerson's suggestion that the preacher seems spectral even when compared to the cold and "ghostly reality" of the snow.[73] The struggle between the preacher's passion (or lack of it) and the relative warmth of the snow is made only more evident when we recall that the preacher to whom Emerson refers is the Reverend Barzillai Frost, who had been ordained in Concord in February 1837 and installed as a colleague to the aging Ezra Ripley. Frost had quickly gained a reputation for the inflexibility of his voice—a "ragged half screaming bass," as Emerson describes it—and he exemplified, for Emerson, the dead and formal preaching of the day.[74] O. W. Firkins recognizes the force of Emerson's playfulness when he observes that "Emerson's discourse drew its matter and coloring largely from private experience, and the bitter hours which he had passed under the ministrations of Mr. Frost of Concord—a preacher who seems to have justified his name in the congealing effect he produced upon the most distinguished of auditors—and other clergymen of the glacial type spoke out in these biting and restive paragraphs."[75] Frost's "corpse-cold" sermons make the snow seem to burn. Nevertheless, as Emerson suggests in his address, "the remedy is already declared in the ground of our complaint" (*W*, 1: 144). The passage insists on an entanglement between what goes on inside the church and what exists and occurs outside its walls. Emerson suggests that the skillful preacher brings together the spiritual and the material, thought and experience, rhetoric and passion. Evoking the laws of nature, he once again declares the indissociable relation between representation and our historical and political existence.

I have tried to suggest that whatever we might call Emerson's politics has everything to do with the insistence of this declaration. For him, the foundation of political history corresponds to a process of rhetorical and historical conceptualization that is neither materialistic nor idealistic, neither worldly nor unworldly, neither political nor apolitical. It takes its point of departure neither from what we call the external world nor from what we refer to as consciousness. The political in Emerson involves this provocation: a challenge to rethink the categories with which we generally have tried to measure the politicality of such and such an act or thought, to rethink, that is, the status of the oppositions between active and passive, engagement and retreat, passion and indifference, heat and coldness, to name only a few of the more prominent. This labor of thinking involves a thinking of the historicity at work in each of these concepts. That Emerson commits himself to this labor reveals his conviction of the tie between thought and history. The obligations that attach to this commitment coincide with his attempt to think the major social and political issues of his day, to think the meaning of America. At a time when one senses a growing desire among literary critics to return to either history or politics, we may do well to remember Emerson's insistence that we do not really need to return to either of these domains because we have never really left them. We are involved with them from the very moment that we think, write, speak, or act. We are perhaps never more under the sway of history than when we think we have denied or repressed it. This is the truth that Emerson gives us to understand. This is the truth that, for him, requires us to think our relation to history, politics, and language. If "we are incompetent to solve the times" (*W*, 6: 3), it is because we remain entirely unprovided for in a world whose legacy is that the historical and the political traverse our very being. We are left with the incalculable dimensions of a hope that, for Emerson, corresponds to what he calls the chances of our future. "When we pass into some new infinitude out of this Iceland of negations," he explains, it may "please us to reflect that though we had few virtues or consolation, we bore with our indigence, nor once strove to repair it with hypocrisy or false heat of any kind" (*W*, 1: 354). We may recall here that the Indo-European root for the word "frost"—*preus*—means both "to freeze" and "to burn"—or, as Emerson tells us in his poem "Uriel," that "ice will burn" (*W*, 9: 14).

Chapter Three

❧ The Rhetoric of Slavery and War

> Who, following in War's bloody trail,
> Shall every lingering wrong assail;
> All chains from limb and spirit strike,
> Uplift the black and white alike;
> Scatter before their swift advance
> The darkness and the ignorance . . .
> The cruel lie of Caste refute,
> Old forms recast, and substitute
> For Slavery's lash the freeman's will . . .
> Till North and South together brought
> Shall own the same electric thought,
> In peace a common flag salute,
> And, side by side in labor's free
> And unresentful rivalry,
> Harvest the fields wherein they fought.
> —Whittier, "Snow-Bound" (1866)

Less than five years before the outbreak of the Civil War, in a speech on the consequences of the Kansas-Nebraska Act, Emerson announces a crisis in the structures of representation, a crisis provoked by the historico-political events of the day: "Language has lost its meaning in the universal cant. *Representative Government* is misrepresentative; *Union* is a conspiracy against the Northern States which the Northern States are to have the privilege of paying for; the *adding of Cuba and Central America* to the slave marts is *enlarging the area of Freedom. Manifest Destiny, Democracy, Freedom,* fine names for a ugly thing" (*AS,* 113–14). The Kansas-Nebraska Act repealed the Missouri Compromise, claiming that it no longer had jurisdiction in either Kansas or Nebraska. It legislated that the question of slavery be determined by individual state constitutions rather than by a national policy of exclusion. For Emerson, that slavery is to be preserved and extended signals a contradiction in the meaning of America, a contradiction that is dissimulated within a rhetoric of representation, democracy, and freedom. Declaring the rhetorical and historical basis of the virtues on which America was to be founded, he here predicts the crisis of representation that would define the issues over which the coming war would be fought.[1] These issues included debates over who could claim the right to representation, over the respective powers of state and federal governments within the system of representation. The crisis to which Emerson refers is therefore a crisis written into the history of America, insofar as America was itself conceived in various efforts to rethink and define the nature and concept of representation.

As Emerson suggests, however, this crisis in political representation is inseparable from the acts of representation that would soon render, and sometimes justify, the suffering and death brought on by the war. What interests him are the various rhetorical means whereby the war or its ideological implications are legitimated. Throughout the war, his lectures, essays, poems, and journal entries persistently challenge the tendencies of contemporary representations of the war to, in the words of Timothy Sweet, "aestheticize the effects of violence and to evade questions about the historical contingency of politics."[2] We should not be surprised if, within this arena of representation, Emerson's attention focuses on the recourse to a rhetoric of nature. Both Union and Confederate soldiers and civilians often used nature to legitimize their respective causes and the war's violence. Moreover, as we have already seen, the rhetoric of nature was central to the constitution of a nationalist ideology in the antebellum period. Insofar as this rhetoric attempts to dissimulate the violence that has been effected in its name, the historical issues and questions that have led to the civil crisis, or the death and violence of the war, Emerson positions himself against it.

Nevertheless, amidst the brutality and terror of the Civil War, Emerson's appeal to the virtues of liberty and justice converges with an appeal to a rhetoric of nature. Aroused by the dangers of the war, by the danger that the ethical dimension of the war might be attenuated by the colossal carnage and suffering that are the struggle's most visible effects, he consistently mobilizes his efforts to stir up enthusiasm for the war and its moral benefits. Nothing characterizes these efforts more than his use of natural imagery. Men and women need to be moved to act, he argues. They need to be persuaded to make sacrifices in the name of justice and freedom. And nothing moves or persuades people better than the evocation of nature. The idiom of nature is everywhere in Emerson. "In the broil of politics," he had written twenty-five years earlier, the poet never speaks without measuring what he says or what he refers to against the movement and laws of nature. Time and time again Emerson announces that the activities of men ought to accord with the activity and rectitude of nature. If he seems to use the same recuperative topoi used by others to justify the war, he uses them both to explore the meaning of the war and to criticize such strategies, even as he tries to mobilize them in another direction. Only in this way, he says, can we take a step in the direction of justice.

The war itself is, of course, such a step, but Emerson suggests at least two more such steps in his poetry written during this time, each in their own way a turning point for the war—Lincoln's Emancipation Proclamation and the recruitment of black soldiers into the Union army. In his "Boston Hymn" he celebrates the occasion and significance of the Proclamation, and in "Voluntaries" he eulogizes the heroism of the Massachusetts 54th Regiment, perhaps the most renowned black regiment of the war. Emerson was not alone in granting such importance to these two steps. In a public letter of August 26, 1863, attacking opponents of emancipation, Lincoln himself proclaimed that "some of the commanders of our armies in the field who have given us our most important successes, believe the emancipation policy, and the use of colored troops, constitute the heaviest blow yet dealt to the rebellion."[3] In both poems, Emerson names the revolutionary forces of emancipation with natural metaphors. In the first, he turns to the natural phenomena of snow, a close relative of frost, to figure the gathering momentum of the northern drive toward freedom. In the second, he joins this same climatic metaphor to a meteorological one, the aurora borealis, in order to emphasize the moral center around which the North, having welcomed black soldiers into its army, is now magnetized. In the process, the metaphors of snow and the aurora take on specific historical, political, theologi-

cal, and literary connotations that, in the long run, will require us to
return to the relationship between these domains and questions of
language. Always, in Emerson, the urgency that we align ourselves
with the laws of nature—or, as he would have it, with the laws of a
"vast trope" (W, 8: 15) whose signature is rapid transformation—corresponds to the necessity that we be attentive to the rhetorical dimension of our historical and political existence. In what follows, I wish
to trace the link between nature and politics as it manifests itself in
these two poems. If their political agendas sometimes seem to support Unionism, they at the same time work to criticize the political
and rhetorical assumptions that might ground such support. This
work of criticism can again be read more easily in the practice of
Emerson's writing, this time in its staging and treatment of the rhetoric of slavery and war, than in any explicit and straightforward arguments. This is again why much of what follows will involve tracking
the history sealed within the language of his poems.

The Rhetoric of Emancipation

Emerson delivered his "Boston Hymn" on January 1, 1863, the
effective date of the Emancipation Proclamation, at a "Jubilee Con-
cert" in the Boston Music Hall. He praises the Proclamation for having inaugurated the dawning of a new day in the meaning of America
and challenges his audience to meet the responsibilities this new day
and meaning entail. For him, the Proclamation revises America's legacy and thereby renews the legacy's power and promise. It declares a
promise that is also a rethinking of the promise of America's settlement, America's revolution, and America's future. This is to say, however, that the Proclamation draws its social and political force from
the history it wishes to overcome. If the Proclamation is not to repeat
the sins of this history, if it is to realize its promise of political and
social change, it must convey the promise of its own truth to all
peoples. But this can only happen if the declaration encourages
people to take responsibility for their own history. Men and women
must risk thinking the history that has made this declaration necessary. Only in this way can they be prepared to respond to the demands of emancipation. What is at stake for Emerson as he writes his
poem is the possibility of translating the truth of the Proclamation

into the minds and hearts of his audience. The hymn rehearses the history of the proclamation, of its terms and conditions—in its present form as well as in its Puritan form—and encourages its audience to commit itself to realizing the proclamation within history. Such commitment is necessary because the mere declaration of a promise can never be its realization. The revolutionary emancipation of the slave can only begin with this act and can only take place if it is continually renewed by every individual who receives the force of its truth. "Every revolution," he explains in his essay "History," is "first a thought in one man's mind, and when the same thought occurs to another man, it is the key to that era" (*W*, 2: 3). The Proclamation attests to this necessity. Abolitionists had called for emancipation as a war policy, since the outbreak of the war, but it was not until the conflict intensified that the exigencies of war began to persuade northerners that emancipation was the only means to victory.[4] In Emerson's words, "the War does not recommend slavery to anybody" (*J*, 15: 273). Coming as a powerful means of persuasion, the war itself declared what was necessary.

The task of abolitionists and antislavery republicans was, in a fundamental and essential way, a rhetorical one: the North had to be convinced that slavery was the issue of the war. "The negro is the key of the situation," Douglass pronounced in September 1861, "the pivot upon which the whole rebellion turns. . . . To fight against slaveholders, without fighting against slavery, is but a half-hearted business, and paralyzes the hands engaged in it."[5] Emancipation was presented as a "military necessity." This phrase soon became the watchword for abolitionists and was eventually cited by Lincoln as the primary reason for his Proclamation. Despite opposition to emancipation within the administration, there was a dramatic increase of emancipationist sentiment in the weeks following the North's defeat at Bull Run. Even the *New York Tribune* and the *New York Times* revised their earlier stances and began to foresee emancipation. Still discouraged by Lincoln's reluctance to forward a resolution for emancipation and by conservative hostility toward their cause, however, abolitionists began a broad program of popular education aimed at moving public opinion toward the abolition of slavery. This new organization, tentatively called the Boston Emancipation League, was to distribute articles and editorials by prominent abolitionists to newspapers throughout the North. Although the campaign was initially kept quiet because of the prevailing prejudice against abolitionists, this battle of words was supplemented by well-advertised speeches by Sumner, Garrison, Phillips and others from October through November. The campaign was successful and, on December 16, because of the growing support of emancipation and the increasing influence of abolitionists, the Emancipation League formally announced its organization. In the winter and spring of 1861–62 the number of emancipation organizations and lecture associations grew rapidly.[6] Pressured by the continued defeats of the North and the growing forces of the abolitionist movement, Lincoln finally issued a preliminary Emancipation Proclamation on September 22, 1862.

Although the terms of the Proclamation provoked disappointment and suspicion among the abolitionists, most believed that the determination with which Lincoln had finally announced his decision indicated that he had every intention of putting his promise into effect. Garrison and Phillips encouraged abolitionists to use their forces to influence public opinion in favor of emancipation rather than to denounce the weakness of the administration's announcement. Garrison, for example, after having expressed his concern that the emancipation would not be immediate, that it was only confined to the rebelling states, and that it was to be a gradual, compensated emancipation, publicly rejoiced in the Proclamation as "an important step in the right direction, and an act of immense historic consequence."[7] Within a few days, abolitionists arranged a rally in Boston at which Emerson was asked to speak. Emerson's speech is traversed by the political and rhetorical exigencies of the moment. Linking the Proclamation to such acts as "the plantation of America . . . the Declaration of Independence in 1776, and the British emancipation of slaves in the West Indies," he calls the act "poetic" and encourages his audience to recognize its "great scope." In his famous opening sentences, he writes:

In so many arid forms which states incrust themselves with,—once in a century, if so often, a poetic act and record occur. These are the jets of thought into affairs, when roused by danger or inspired by genius, the political leaders of the day break the else insurmountable routine of class and local legislation, and take a step forward in the direction of catholic and universal interests.

Every step in the history of political liberty is a sally of the human mind into the untried Future. . . . [This act] makes a victory of our defeats. Our hurts are healed; the health of the nation is repaired. With a victory like this, we can stand many disasters. . . . We have recovered ourselves from our false position and planted ourselves on a law of nature. (*AS*, 129, 131–32)

Emphasizing the poetic and moral force of an act of thought that follows the laws of nature—the laws of transformation and change— Emerson points to the Proclamation's revolutionary character. The Proclamation is in fact revolutionary *because* it aligns itself with the forces of nature. The very act of its declaration propels the country beyond the prejudice and legislation that until now so forcefully had determined national sentiment against emancipation. But now "the cause of disunion and war has been reached and begun to be removed" (*AS*, 133). Lincoln's edict reveals its force, its transformative power, by committing the country to justice. In so doing, it promises political and social changes that call forth "a new public . . . to greet the new event" (*AS*, 130). Clearing the way for an "untried Future," the Proclamation recalls the American people to their true founding in nature. Both a promise and a memory, it indicates the nation's health. "In the light of this event," Emerson says, "the public distress begins to be removed" (*AS*, 132). Whatever we might have thought to be Lincoln's shortcomings, "every mistake, every delay," may now be called "endurance, wisdom, magnanimity." "Liberty is a slow fruit," Emerson explains, "It comes, like religion, for short periods, and in rare conditions. . . . We are beginning to think that we have underestimated the capacity and virtue which the Divine Providence has made an instrument of benefit so vast" (*AS*, 129–30).[8]

Emerson's invocation of organic and religious imagery is more than a spontaneous response to an act whose moral aspect seems unquestionable. Or rather, if it is "spontaneous," it is spontaneous only in the sense that Emerson gives this word—that is to say, only as a "blending of experience with the present action of the mind" (*W*, 1: 31). In joining an act of great political and national significance with the movement of religious history, Emerson's rhetoric exploits the pervasive sense among many northerners that God's hand could be recognized in Lincoln's edict.[9] In this edict, religious and political mission are brought together through the promise of their ultimate realization. January 1, 1863, marks a new era in the history of America—an era in which injustice and oppression would be forced to flee before the divine principles of justice and freedom. The Proclamation bears witness to the sacred cause of the war. The justice of the northern cause turns the Civil War from a crisis of national legitimacy into a conflict with eschatological significance.

For Emerson, the Emancipation Proclamation plays a decisive role in the history of this transformation. This role and this history are the subjects of his "Boston Hymn." Written for the specific purpose of celebrating the moral and historical importance of the Proclamation, the poem opened the festivities at the Music Hall. It was read to a wildly enthusiastic audience, which included many former slaves.[10] In the poem, Emerson dramatizes the importance of this act by inscribing its declaration within the form of a jeremiad that presents in small the history of America as "the great charity of God to the human race" (*AS*, 152). Choosing to frame his poem in the jeremiad form enables him to respond to the heterogeneity of his audience. The jeremiad had frequently been adapted by abolitionist and black political writing in order to reproach a country that had been unfaithful to its sacred beginnings and to recall the promise on which America was founded.[11] Providing a lesson in national genealogy, Emerson's sermon sets out the sacred history of the New World and describes the typology of the American mission. By situating the significance of the Proclamation within a history that claims to reveal the nation's divine mission, Emerson emphasizes the historical significance of the Proclamation and the political and cultural significance of this Puritan history. He also entwines this history with the motifs of black emancipation and national regeneration at work within antebellum black rhetoric. The joining of the history of recent events with the history of the meaning of America requires that we read every line of the poem in a double register. For Emerson, whatever significance we may attribute to the force of Lincoln's pronouncement, this significance can only be read through the history of similar pronouncements, each of which, in their own way, have worked to link the destinies of America's peoples.

Within the movement of the poem, the pronouncement to which Lincoln's is compared is that of God to his chosen people. In both cases, the pronouncement takes the form of a promise, the promise of freedom. If the Emancipation Proclamation has the force of God's edict, it is because it is the promised realization of God's will. What is most striking about this particular jeremiad, however, is that both it, and by implication, the Proclamation, are spoken by God himself. It is God who laments the tyranny and the selfishness of the Old World and who reveals the terms of his promise to his listeners—the Pilgrims mentioned in the poem, but also their descendants, including all Americans of the year 1863:

> The word of the Lord by night
> To the watching Pilgrims came,
> As they sat by the seaside,
> And filled their hearts with flame.
>
> God said, I am tired of kings,
> I suffer them no more;
> Up to my ear the morning brings
> The outrage of the poor.
>
> Think ye I made this ball
> A field of havoc and war,
> Where tyrants great and tyrants small
> Might harry the weak and poor?
>
> My angel,—his name is Freedom,—
> Choose him to be your king;
> He shall cut pathways east and west
> And fend you with his wing.
>
> Lo! I uncover the land
> Which I hid of old time in the West
> As the sculptor uncovers the statue
> When he has wrought his best.
>
> (stanzas 1–5; *W*, 9: 201)

Emerson's sources for this emergent allegory of the history of America are the writings of the early colonists.[12] These opening stanzas identify what Philip Gura has singled out as the most important factor in the development of the colonists' collective identity: their typological reading of history, a reading that both presumes and accounts for "their strong identification with the covenanted people of Israel." The New England Puritans defined their community, he notes, "not so much through its political or territorial integrity as through a common ideology: specifically, their incessant rhetorical justification of what they regarded as their divinely ordained purpose."[13] For the Puritans, the typological relationship that existed between the New Testament and the Old linked the progressive unfolding of history to the possibility of redemption in this world.[14] At the same time, since the New Testament speaks of the future still to come, when events in England transformed the New England Puritans' relation to their homeland, they came to believe that they alone were left to fulfill biblical prophecy. It is no accident, then, that the model for the Great Migration to which Emerson alludes here is the biblical exodus. Guided by the hand of Providence, the Pilgrims, like the Hebrews, abandon an oppressive monarchy for a new Promised Land. The Puritan God delivers the Pilgrims from the rod of tyranny and oppression and leads them to America.[15] Although this country is the latest found, it is also the earliest. Both the New Canaan and the New Jerusalem, this Columbia "of clouds and the boreal fleece" (*W*, 9: 202) is integral to God's sacred design. In giving the Pilgrims a new opportunity, He calls on His people to renew their covenant with Him. This renewal will seal the new covenant and guarantee Puritan independence. The Puritan migration unveils the promise of the New World, given to the Pilgrims as their everlasting inheritance.

The poem's next six stanzas outline the conditions of the covenant, the rules for this alliance between God and His chosen people. He promises to divide his goods. He promises expansion and growth for all of humanity. He offers to all without distinction of color or creed the infinite variety of America's natural resources. In return, He asks that the people build schools and churches in His name, govern the land and sea with just laws, not give way to selfish or proud rulers, refuse to swerve away from what is right, and, most of all, never bind another man or woman into their service. For Emerson, the measure of the degree to which the Puritans and their descendants have lived up to their end of the promise, have followed the laws of the covenant, is nothing less than the entire history of America—from the settlement of New England up to the pronouncement he now celebrates. Emerson's judgment here is decisive. Rather than suggest in any explicit fashion what this history has been, he brings his audience to the moment within which they are listening to him deliver his poem:

Lo, now! if these poor men
Can govern the land and sea
And make just laws below the sun,
As planets faithful be.

And ye shall succor men;
'T is nobleness to serve;
Help them who cannot help again:
Beware from right to swerve.

I break your bonds and masterships,
And I unchain the slave: .
Free be his heart and hand henceforth
As wind and wandering wave.
(stanzas 12–14; *W*, 9: 203)

Fusing the legacy of the Puritan founders with the present—according to a law of reading that recalls the law that governs the Pilgrims' reading of their own special place within history—Emerson implies a typological relationship between the promise of the Puritan settlement of America and its fulfillment in the enactment of the Emancipation Proclamation. If the first half of his poem evokes the "birth" of this legacy, the second half will serve to call on his audience, or rather to have God call on his audience, to recognize that it is within its support of the Proclamation that the renewal of His promise will take place. But if God's "Lo, now!" calls attention to the present, it at the same time expresses a kind of surprise at what God sees, almost as though He had, in growing even wearier than before in the face of continued disappointment, come to wonder whether or not men could ever "govern the land and sea" with justice. Nevertheless, the Proclamation is presented as a profound indication that "these poor men" can "make just laws."

The directness with which both Emerson and God turn to this act as the fulfillment of the alliance between God and the Pilgrims, however, makes it difficult not to notice their silence upon the years that intervene between these two "events." This silence is hardly an omission. Rather, it is a quiet condemnation of everything that, within the history of America, has betrayed or breached this special alliance. It is especially an indictment of the transgressions that occurred in the name of this promise, that justified themselves by the rhetoric and claim of God's grace. If Emerson begins his poem by having God give voice to the terms and conditions of the covenant, he does so not only to draw a link between the covenant and its realization in Lincoln's edict, but also to draw attention to the rhetoric with which the Puritan founders attempted to conquer and transform the New World in God's name. In giving voice to the story of the covenant, God tells the story of the Puritans as well. That is to say, He tells the Puritans their own story, the story that they told in order to rationalize the often violent means whereby they settled their new home. The America whose history goes unspoken in Emerson's poem, like the Old World the Pilgrims sought to leave, has been "a field of havoc and war," a place where "tyrants great and small" have consistently oppressed "the weak and poor." The Puritan understanding of the nation's eschatological significance installed an understanding of the sanctity of the national union that in turn enabled the Pilgrims to justify westward expansion, slavery, the extermination of the native population, the marginalization of cultural diversity in general, and the idea of manifest destiny. In carrying the notion of America as God's chosen westward, the Puritans and their descendants felt obliged to subdue, transform, and overcome nature. The strong sense of their place within this sacred history gave them license to "cut down trees in the forest / And trim the straightest boughs" (*W*, 9: 202). The settlement of America, while it may have at one time promised a beneficent reunion with Nature, now revealed the more selfish and material impulses that the vision of a "free" and "prosperous" land promoted. In 1823, Emerson had already registered his understanding of these impulses. "The vast rapidity with which the deserts & forests of the interior of this country are peopled here led patriots to fear lest the nation grow *too fast* for its virtue & its peace. . . . At this day, the axe is laid to the root of the forest; the Indian is driven from his hut & the bison from the plains. . . . Good men desire, & the great Cause of human nature demands that this abundant & overflowing richness wherewith God has blessed this country be not misapplied & made a curse of" (*J*, 2: 115–16). For the steady Pilgrims of his poem, however, such impulses were instead central to a community that saw in material prosperity signs of God's favor. As he explains elsewhere, "it was the human race, under Divine leading, going forth to receive and inhabit their patrimony."

For Emerson, the Puritans' capacity to appropriate anything be-

fore them within the rhetoric of the covenant indicates the power of
this rhetoric as well as the Puritan will to authority. The legitimacy
accorded to their rhetoric, for example—sometimes both within and
without their community—enabled them to determine in advance
what belonged to the chosen community and what did not. This
rhetoric demanded the marginalization or assimilation of immigrants
and other groups who did not belong to their conception of American
nationality. In addition to excluding other cultures, this nationalistic
dimension of Puritan thought worked to bring the wide range of
theological opinion in the colonies within the boundaries of what
Gura has called "the internal development of American Puritan
doctrine."[16] Although there was no unified community of Puritan
thought, the unity of purpose and mission claimed by the New England Puritans was not only essential to their social and political organization but also defended by recourse to the covenant.[17] This
unity was then used to require submission to the founding fathers and
their laws, conformity to convention, and reverence for the sacred
moral purpose of whatever this community might deem necessary to
further its special mission—even if such purpose might in truth go
against every one of the terms of the covenant. For Emerson, such
respect, conformity, and reverence works against the virtue of independence in the name of which the New World was founded. If Emerson and God turn from the terms and conditions of the covenant
directly to the effective date of the Emancipation Proclamation, it is
in part because each wishes to suggest that, until this day, the rhetoric
of God's promise has been used primarily to promote interests that
betray the letter of this promise. That is to say: since the plantation
of America there have been no truly just laws. There have been no
laws which protect the divine rights of all men. Only with this Proclamation does America redeem itself; only with this act does it meet
the conditions of God's promise.[18] This act works to purify the covenant as it has been passed down from generation to generation, to
recover the promise of an America without slavery. Within the terms
of Emerson's poem, the emancipation of the slaves works to revise
older concepts of manifest destiny, concepts which, emerging from
the Puritan rhetoric of mission and errand, were advanced, at least
implicitly, by the expansion of the southern slaveholding system.[19]

    If the powerful ethical force of the Proclamation corresponds with the justice of divine law, it is also because, as Emerson states, in pronouncing this law men have planted themselves on "a law of Nature." God himself seconds this point when he claims that as long as men "make just laws" they remain as faithful to the divine order of nature as do the planets.[20] Such claims are by no means surprising, however. For over two hundred years eschatological and prophetic images within Puritan rhetoric had been inseparable from natural metaphors. One could now find figurations of divine order not only through the figurative expressions that appear in the Bible but also through the seemingly more direct revelation of the divine principle in the activities of the natural world. "Every natural fact," Emerson writes, "is a symbol of some spiritual fact" (*W*, 1: 26). What is surprising, though, is the recognition that the words that God speaks are already echoes of Emerson's own language. The matter becomes immediately more complicated when we begin to realize that nearly every stanza in the second half of the poem alludes in some way to the various speeches, lectures, essays, and even poems that Emerson had written on the theme or question of freedom, that is, on the theme or question of emancipation. Drawing in particular from Emerson's speeches "The Emancipation Proclamation" (1862), "American Civilization" (1861), "American Slavery" (1855), and "The Emancipation in the British West Indies" (1844), Emerson's God speaks Emerson's language.[21] The power of God's voice relies in an essential way on the force of Emerson's own rhetoric. The "Lo, now!" of January 1, 1863, merges the voice of the Puritan God with the voice of Emerson's God, with the voice of men who speak in the name of "just laws." "If a man is at heart just," Emerson proclaims in his "Divinity School Address," "then in so far is he God; the safety of God, the immortality of God, the majesty of God do enter that man with justice" (*W*, 1: 122). The Puritan God is not the God of To-day. The God of To-day is man himself. The God of To-day is the man who, refusing to swerve from right, has proclaimed this act of emancipation and so revealed the divinity that lies within his heart and his hands. Breaking away from the God of Puritan tradition and rhetoric, this man finds the presence of God within his own soul.[22] This man is not only Lincoln; rather, he is any man who recognizes the divinity of Lincoln's edict and chooses to serve its cause of universal freedom. If the Emancipation Proclamation is the fulfillment of God's promise, the Proclamation is itself a promise requiring fulfillment. This act will not accomplish the work of its promise all alone. Emerson well knows that this measure will not "be suddenly marked by any signal results" (*AS*, 131) vis-à-vis the slaves or their rebel masters. Rather, this declaration—if it is not to be "a paper proclamation"—will require that men "succor" each other. Not only will Lincoln have to "repeat and follow up his stroke," but the nation will be asked to "add its inevitable strength." "If the ruler has duties," Emerson says, "so has the citizen. . . . What right has any one to read in the journals tidings of victories, if he has not bought them with his own valor, treasure, personal sacrifice, or by service as good in his own department?" (*AS*, 132).

The Snowflake as Freedom Fighter

The realization of the Proclamation within history depends on the acts and thoughts of men and women who every day and every hour renew their alliance with the declaration's revolutionary truth. This Proclamation is in fact a declaration of independence truer to the spirit of the revolution than that of the revolutionary fathers because it remembers a people whom they forgot. If the edict fulfills the promise of God's covenant, it also realizes the promise of the revolutionary struggle for freedom. From the beginning of the war, abolitionists and others had evoked the rhetoric of the revolution in order to further their cause. By the early 1860s the revolution, as a singular and powerful event within the history of American freedom, had become a trope of persuasion within the war's new crusade for freedom. In an editorial entitled "The Second American Revolution," written less than three weeks after the attack on Fort Sumter, William Goodell pronounced: "It has begun. It is in progress. . . . The Revolution must go on, to its completion—*A National Abolition of Slavery*. . . . What . . . can long delay the proclamation, inviting the slave to a share in *the glorious second American Revolution*."[23] The virtue of this second revolution was that it revealed what had always been the nation's "fatal weakness." In *The Rejected Stone*, a book which went through three editions in 1861–62, Moncure Conway argued that when the founding fathers imagined the edifice of the Union they threw aside one essential "foundation stone." That stone, he suggested, was "essentially, *Justice*." "The form in which it stands for us," he went on to say, "is THE AFRICAN SLAVE."[24]

On the basis of such arguments, abolitionists refused to recognize the southern rebellion as a revolution. Only the North was in a position to fight a revolution of freedom. "The revolution is on our side," Conway argued, "and as soon as the nation feels that, and acts upon it, the strength of the South is gone. . . . WE ARE THE REVOLUTIONISTS."[25] But if "we are the revolutionists" because we break the "bonds and masterships" of all Americans, including those of the slave, for Emerson we are also the revolutionists because we break these bonds and chains before God does. By the time that God declares His own emancipation proclamation in stanza 14, He has already acknowledged in stanza 12 that men have preceded Him in this act. If the hand of God is really at work within Lincoln's proclamation, it is because the proclamation, as an image of our creativity and freedom, is already divine. If God is preceded in this act, it is because He has also been preceded in other, perhaps more fundamental, ways. From the moment that His voice merges with the voice through which He speaks on January 1, 1863, He speaks in this other voice rather than in His own—in the same way that He had earlier spoken in the voice attributed to Him by the Puritan pilgrims. This is to say at least two things: (1) the God of To-day speaks in a voice that is different from the voice in which He spoke to the Pilgrims; and (2) the 1863 Emancipation Proclamation precedes the proclamation of To-day's God by fulfilling the promise of the Puritan God, but in a way that questions the Puritan conception of God. To be more precise, from the moment that Emerson recalls God to the present, has God address the present, God's voice is one with Emerson's.

This is not to say that God speaks the words that Emerson has Him speak solely because He is a persona within Emerson's poem. Emerson does not speak for God; he speaks *as* God. The force of Emerson's rhetoric lies in its assumption of divinity. Emerson's thought is "ejaculated as Logos, or Word" (*W*, 3: 40). Whenever God says "I," Emerson says "I." Whenever God speaks, He quotes Emerson. Emerson's God is an emanation of Emerson's own rhetoric, a figure for Emerson's ambitions as a powerful political orator. Moreover, in having God speak within his language, Emerson sets up a typological relationship between the revolutionary promise of his earlier writings and the Proclamation as the promised fulfillment of this promise. In a certain sense, God's voice makes the potentiality within Emerson's language real. If God's rhetoric depends on Emerson's, Emerson's is in turn enhanced through being spoken by God. Emerson subsumes his own voice, his own rhetoric, within the voice of God in order to lend it more authority, in order to better persuade his audience of the virtues of the Proclamation as well as of the necessity constantly to renew one's commitment to its promise of justice. In the passage from which God derives the sentence He speaks in stanza 13, Emerson claims that "God is God because he is the servant of all" (*W*, 11: 298). God has served the Puritan founders. Now, in this poem, God *serves* Emerson as a figure of persuasion. If He can do so, it is because, as Emerson states in "Circles," the "words of God" are "as fugitive as other words" (*W*, 2: 314). They can be turned from one significance to another depending on how they are heard or read. This is why we can only imagine the impact that Emerson's rhetoric would have had on his audience. Having been recalled to their present moment by the "Lo, now!" of stanza 12, his listeners could not have overlooked the powerful fusion of God's "I" with Emerson's.

We will never know the tone or force with which Emerson read this poem—a poem whose themes had been his for over thirty years—but anyone with the least familiarity with Emerson's writings would have certainly heard his voice within the following four stanzas:

> I cause from every creature
> His proper good to flow:
> As much as he is and doeth,
> So much he shall bestow.
>
> But, laying hands on another
> To coin his labor and sweat,
> He goes in pawn to his victim
> For eternal years in debt.
>
> To-day unbind the captive,
> So only are ye unbound;
> Lift up a people from the dust,
> Trump of their rescue, sound!
>
> Pay ransom to the owner
> And fill the bag to the brim.
> Who is the owner? The slave is owner,
> And ever was. Pay him.
>
> (stanzas 15–18; *W*, 9: 203–4)

God speaks here in the voice of the Emersonian Poet, whose task is to liberate all men. Like the Poet, God breaks the chains that prevent men from recognizing and realizing their divine potential—the "proper good" that determines who man is and what he does.[26] He takes on the Poet's "office of announcement and affirming" (*W*, 3: 13) and declares the necessity and rectitude of emancipation. Relying on the language of Emerson's essay "American Civilization," He explains that the moment a man lays his hands on another person and tries to transform this person's "labor and sweat" into "coin," into money, he reverses the "natural sentiments of mankind" (*W*, 11: 297). In the opening paragraph to this essay, Emerson had already argued that, in accordance with the laws of nature, "man coins himself into his labor; turns his day, his strength, his thought, his affection into some product which remains as the visible sign of his power" (*W*, 11: 297). To secure this labor for the laborer, this should be "the object of all government." Insofar as the slaveholder presumes that "the well-being of a man" consists "in eating the fruit of other men's labor," however, he not only prevents the establishment of a just government, but he also goes against nature (*W*, 11: 297). Betraying nature, he betrays himself. In exploiting the slave's labor he becomes eternally indebted to him, eternally subjected to the institution of slavery. Emerson had delineated this argument almost twenty years earlier in his address "The Emancipation in the British West Indies," suggesting that it had in fact played an important role in the history and events contributing to that emancipation. "It was shown to the planters," he explains, "that they, as well as the negroes, were slaves. . . . The oppression of the slave recoiled on them. . . . Many planters have said, since the emancipation, that, before that day, they were the greatest slaves on the estates" (*AS*, 21).

This argument both follows and anticipates those made by Phillips and Sumner as they tried to persuade both the North and the South of the insidiousness of slavery. Slaveholding, they argued, corrupted the manners and morals of white southerners, since it presented their children with examples of brutal violence and despotism.[27] Phillips, in his speech "The Right of Petition" (1837), one of his earliest addresses before an antislavery gathering, had emphasized national complicity in the issue of slavery. "Our fate is bound up with that of the South," he said, "so that they cannot be corrupt and we sound; they cannot fail and we stand."[28] In his own speech, Emerson hints at the planters' exaggeration of their own suffering in relation to that of the slave and then links Phillips's point to an older, more philosophical issue: "the civility of no race can be perfect whilst another race is degraded. It is a doctrine alike of the oldest, and of the newest philosophy, that, man is one, and that you cannot injure any member, without a sympathetic injury to all the members. America is not civil, whilst Africa is barbarous" (*AS*, 32).[29] Since "every man is an inlet to the same and to all of the same" (*W*, 2: 3), no man can commit a violence upon another without committing a similar violence upon himself. "You cannot use a man as an instrument," he declares in 1855, "without being used by him as an instrument" (*AS*, 99). In other words, if any man is a slave, every man is a slave. Emerson already had reversed the direction of indebtedness between a slave and his owner when he claims in "Man the Reformer" that "the abolitionist has shown us our dreadful debt to the southern negro. In the island of Cuba, in addition to the ordinary abominations of slavery, it appears, only men are bought for the plantations, and one dies in ten every year, of these miserable bachelors, to yield us sugar" (*W*, 1: 232). For him, this consideration leaves no choice for the country's conscience. In the name of respect, for both ourselves and others, we must rid ourselves of slavery. As he states in his 1851 address on the Fugitive Slave Act, "every thing invites to emancipation" (*AS*, 69).

Emerson's God invites emancipation as well. But if His invitation is made in Emerson's language, this language takes a turn in stanza 18 against Emerson's earlier statements—in his addresses on the West Indies, the Fugitive Slave Law, and especially his 1855 speech "American Slavery"—about the necessity of compensating slaveholders for their losses upon emancipation. Following the example of the British emancipation of the West Indies, Emerson argues in these speeches that southern slaveholders ought to be paid a kind of "ransom" for their slaves. In his 1851 address against the Fugitive Slave Law, for example, he proclaims: "Why not end this dangerous dispute on some ground of fair compensation on one side, and satisfaction on the other to the conscience of the free states? It is really the great task fit for this country to accomplish, to buy that property of the planters, as the British nation bought the West Indian slaves. I say buy,—never conceding the right of the planter to own, but that we may acknowledge the calamity of his position, and bear a countryman's share in relieving him; and because it is the only practicable course, and is innocent" (W, 11: 208).[30] Such claims were prevalent in the North in the late 1840s and 1850s and generally were made either in the name of preserving the Union or, in what amounted to the same thing, in the name of admitting some shared responsibility in the matter. Nevertheless, even if Emerson argues for disunion on the basis of the Union's passing of the Fugitive Slave Act, we should still question his willingness to risk reinforcing the claim that slaves were property owned by the slaveholders. Most abolitionists had been consistently hostile to compensation for just this reason. We should not neglect, however, that after the outbreak of the war, even though Lincoln and others were still making similar arguments in the interest of effecting some kind of wartime compromise, such a suggestion was for Emerson no longer either "practicable" or "innocent." The "Boston Hymn" is the record of this turn of mind. For if stanza 18 begins by referring to Emerson's earlier appeals to his countrymen to "Pay ransom to the owner / And fill the bag to the brim," it ends by questioning the appeal's assumption that the slave could be considered as property. "Who is the owner?" God asks. "The slave is owner, / And ever was," comes the answer. "Pay him."[31] These lines implicate an earlier Emerson in the outrages the Proclamation wishes to overcome. The poem is at this point a moving confession of Emerson's shared guilt, a renunciation of his earlier position, and an impassioned reminder that no one ever forget again that the slave has always owned his or her own labor.[32]

This admonishment and appeal are particularly pertinent at a time when many abolitionists were wondering whether the Proclamation had itself been purchased at too great a cost. What disturbed them most was the sense that Lincoln's edict was based on the argument of "military necessity"—an argument in which earlier they themselves had had a hand—rather than on a concern for the rights of the black man as a person. Although he later changed his position, even Sumner had claimed that abolition was not "the object of the war, but simply one of its agencies." He repeated this point in a letter to John Jay of November 10, 1861, arguing that emancipation "is to be presented strictly as a measure of military necessity, and the argument is to be thus supported rather than on grounds of philanthropy."[33] For both Sumner and Jay, the argument for emancipation based on "military necessity" was a strategic, that is to say, rhetorical one. They, like many others, assumed that the administration would respond more quickly to this argument than to the moral issues they had been promoting for over thirty years. Other abolitionists questioned these tactics, however. Emancipation would mean very little, they argued, if it did not spring from a strong commitment to justice and human rights. As Lydia Maria Child solemnly proclaimed: "This entire absence of a moral sense on the subject, has disheartened me more than anything else. Even should they be emancipated, merely as a 'war necessity,' everything *must* go wrong, if there is no heart or conscience on the subject. . . . It is evident that a great moral work still needs to be done."[34] Douglass expressed the same fear in a speech delivered at Cooper Union on February 6, 1863, five weeks after the enactment of the Proclamation. "Much as I value the present apparent hostility to Slavery at the North," he said, "I plainly see that it is less the outgrowth of high and intelligent moral conviction against Slavery, as such, than because of the trouble its friends have brought upon the country. I would have Slavery hated for that and more. A man that hates Slavery for what it does to the white man, stands ready to embrace it the moment its injuries are confined to the black man, and he ceases to feel those injuries in his own person."[35]

These arguments would have had special force for the Emerson who insists that everything be thought according to first principles. He might have been particularly moved by Douglass's remarks, since he had opened his 1854 speech on the Fugitive Slave Law by admitting that until this law was passed he had lived all his life "without suffering any known inconvenience from American Slavery." "I never saw it," he says, "I never heard the whip; I never felt the check on my free speech and action; until the other day when Mr. Webster by his personal influence brought the Fugitive Slave Law on the country" (*AS*, 74). Or, as he notes three years earlier, in his 1851 address, he had never experienced any personal inconvenience because of unjust laws: "They never came near me to my discomfort before. I find the like sensibility in my neighbors. And in that class who take no interest in the ordinary questions of party politics. There are men who are assure indexes of the equity of legislation and of the sane state of public feeling, as the barometer is of the weight of the air; and it is a bad sign when these are discontented" (*AS*, 53). Presenting himself as one of these indexes, himself a kind of barometer, Emerson here takes advantage of his sense that he is often understood as someone who keeps his distance from public questions. Although these sentences would need to be read as part of the rhetorical pose he assumes in both of his Fugitive Slave Law speeches—posing as a figure who does not like to address contemporary political issues (something we have seen him do ever since his earliest writings), he lends more force to the impression that even he has come out of hiding to speak on the issue of slavery—we can say that they at least dramatize his awareness of the ease with which we can neglect suffering that does not touch our own person. In drawing attention to these arguments in his poem, Emerson expresses his sympathy with Child and Douglass. He reveals his shared concern over the possibility that the Proclamation might become a dead letter if it is not taken up into the hearts and minds of individuals willing to commit themselves to the difficult struggle of genuine emancipation. His insistence that the slave be treated as a person rather than as property serves as a powerful reminder of the tremendous moral stakes involved in this struggle. They are nothing less than the integrity of the self-reliant individual. If compensation should go to anyone, it should therefore go to the slave. But this compensation can only take the form of true emancipation. This is to say that the slave can only be truly compensated through a task of thinking: a thinking whose task it is to think the slave as a person rather than as a thing.

This task will involve a confrontation with the painful and distressing history that has led to the necessity of this moral reevaluation. Emerson encourages his listeners to begin this task by offering his own sense of this history. Racing against time, because going against the embattled history of America, emancipation must be immediate, but genuine.[36] Emerson's God commands the slaves to arise and run to meet the challenge of their newly pronounced freedom. In the poem's final two stanzas, He calls on peoples of all races to help in this challenge, to carry His purpose forth into the world. He then ends his speech by turning, in a properly Emersonian fashion, to the force and efficacy of His own rhetoric:

> Come, East and West and North,
> By races, as snow-flakes,
> And carry my purpose forth,
> Which neither halts nor shakes.
>
> My will fulfilled shall be,
> For, in daylight or in dark,
> My thunderbolt has eyes to see
> His way home to the mark.
>   (stanzas 21–22; *W*, 9: 204)

God's Word works as a force of provocation and gathering. He calls forth men and women of all races to come together and carry his declaration of emancipation into the slaveholding South—as snow-flakes. Coming according to the laws of nature, these peoples come as snowflakes—that is to say, in one of the figure's many connotations, *in numbers*—to realize the will of God. "Every spark of intellect," Emerson tells us in his speech on the Proclamation, "every virtuous feeling, every religious heart, every man of honor, every poet, every philosopher, the generosity of the cities, the health of the country, the strong arms of the mechanics, the endurance of farmers, the passionate conscience of women, the sympathy of distant nations" (*AS*, 132)—all rally to the support of this edict. A host of different peoples and sentiments shall draw together in this "great and good work" of emancipation.

But what exactly does it mean for them to draw together *as* snow-flakes? In what way are people like snowflakes? What could it mean for Emerson's God to associate men and women of different colors to an element of nature known by its single color—especially when, within the context of questions of slavery and race, this color is hardly an innocent one? Could it be that God's will may only be realized if ethnic minorities come to be white? In calling for men and women from different races rather than from a single race, God suggests that these questions may not be as black and white as they seem. To begin with, the figural connotations of snowflakes within such a context are multiple and in no way simple. Even if this conjunction between races and snowflakes may at first seem a strange one, we should remember that within the biblical and theological traditions to which both God and Emerson belong snow and snowflakes have borne a broad range of rhetorical significances—all of which have some figural relationship to God's will. For example, in H. W. Beecher's "Teachings of Snow," the movement of snowflakes is seen as a figure for the movement of God's hosts in battle.[37] Wafting down from the sky like the thoughts of God, snowflakes fight to realize the will of God. They conceal in their beauty a great power of annihilation and in their color a means of purification. Covering the land and thereby changing the whole aspect of nature, they represent a powerful force of conversion. As the article "Snow" in the February 1862 issue of the *Atlantic Monthly* describes them, they are "laborious warriors of the air."[38] This force is not always destructive, however. Like frost, snow plays an important role in nature's economy. It "tends to mitigate the severity of winter" (*EL*, 1: 59) and, when it melts, it serves as a powerful force of regeneration. As a figure for the will of God, it can also figure the Word of God itself. In Isaiah 55: 10–11, for example, God says: "as the rain cometh down, and the snow from heaven, and returneth not thither, but watereth the earth, and maketh it bring forth and bud, that it may give seed to the sower, and bread to the eater: So shall my word be that goeth forth out of my mouth: it shall not return unto me void, but it shall accomplish that which I please, and it shall prosper *in the thing* whereto I sent it."

When God demands that the men and women of all races come together as snowflakes for the purpose of enacting his will, He means to invoke each and all of these connotations. He may also be relying on what was by this time common scientific speculation: that "the color of snow is white because it is composed of an infinite variety of crystals, which reflect all the colors of light, absorbing none, and these, uniting before they reach the eye, appear white, which is the combination of the colors."[39] In other words, suggesting that all races join together as snowflakes, He means less to erase the specific color of each race in the name of whiteness and more to figure a community that, consisting of all the races, gathers together not only in His name but in the name of abolition. We could say that He expects us to be, as readers, like the man who is "raised to a platform whence he sees beyond sense to moral and spiritual truths; when he no longer sees snow as snow . . . but only sees or names it representatively, for those interior facts" which it signifies (*W*, 10: 548). He wishes us to understand that, coming to battle slavery in the name of God, these peoples will purify the sin that has beset America from its beginning. "Announced by all the trumpets of the sky" (*W*, 9: 41), like the snow in Emerson's poem "The Snow-Storm," they will be architects of a new union, fierce artificers of a new revolution. Rebuilding the edifice of America according to the principles of nature—again, according to the principles of linguistic transformation—and in realization of the divine potential of man's creative capacity for reform, these snow-flakes shall inaugurate a new era.

The snowflake is, as Emerson says elsewhere, "Freedom's star" (*J*, 15: 250). Led by the light of this star, God's hosts will fulfill simulta-neously the Emancipation Proclamation, the Word of God, the Words of Emerson's God, and the words of Lincoln, who, in 1854, had already pronounced the necessity that would lead to his 1863 Proclamation. "Our republican robe is soiled, and trailed in the dust," he said. "Let us repurify it. Let us turn and wash it white, in the spirit, if not the blood, of the Revolution. . . . Let us re-adopt the Declara-tion of Independence, and with it, the practices and policies which harmonize with it. Let north and south—let all Americans—let all lovers of liberty everywhere—join in the great and good work." [40] The snow falling downward from the heavens—like the races which, coming from the East and the West and the North according to God's directive, move southward—represents the descent of the thought which will become the ground for a new declaration of in-dependence. This thought works to trigger the conversion of the en-tire country. Transforming the landscape of American history, the snowflake brings men and women to rethink their relation to both nature and history. As Emerson states in his epigraph to "Quotation and Originality," "old and new put their stamp to everything in Na-ture. The snowflake that is now falling is marked by both. The pres-ent moment gives the motion and the color of the flake, Antiquity its form and properties. All things wear a lustre which is the gift of the present, and a tarnish of time" (*W*, 8: 175). Bringing together the promise of America's beginning and the present effort to realize this promise, the work of the snowflake is "the great and good work" of emancipation. The snowflake comes like a poem of freedom. The snowflake is a freedom fighter.

Like the God whose word it figures, the snowflake is a force of provocation and emancipation. It gains its force as a trope through the religious and literary associations attributed to it by the very men and women it now wishes to mobilize. God's analogy between snow-flakes and races is a powerful means of persuasion, an effective means of bringing people and nature together in the common work of emancipation. If history has as its goal the process of moral justice and freedom, that process can only be achieved by the forces of na-ture; similarly, if nature is the means to human justice and freedom, its end is to be found in human action and human history. The Eman-cipation Proclamation depends on the cooperation between nature and people. If the Proclamation is a poetic act, that is because it joins human history with natural history. As Emerson writes in *Nature*, "Natural history by itself has no value; it is like a single sex. But marry it to human history, & it is poetry" (*W*, 1: 28; *J*, 4: 311). God's poetry works to define the grounds and necessity of this cooperation. Em-erson had proclaimed this necessity in the final sentence of his 1854 speech on the Fugitive Slave Act. There, forcefully encouraging his audience to believe in the amelioration that "will not save us but through our own co-operation," Emerson prophesies the end of slav-ery (*AS*, 89). No matter how much he may evoke the necessity of self-reliant deeds, free men are bound together in a community whose votes must cooperate with the work of emancipation if they are not to impede its victory—or, as Gertrude Hughes would have it, for Emerson, the burden of self-reliance is the burden of cooperation.[41] The difficulty of taking on this responsibility, however, is not due to any contradiction. Emerson's doctrine of "self-reliance" is insepa-rable from its commitment to social and political reform. The self-reliant individual is from the very beginning "related and engaged" with others (*AS*, 73). In the very act of delivering this poem, Emerson himself keeps this engagement and fulfills this relation. As he had already explained in 1855, "whilst I insist on the doctrine of the in-dependence and inspiration of the individual, I do not cripple but exalt social action. It is so delicious to act with great masses to great aims" (*AS*, 103). Engaging his audience through the force of his rhetoric, Emerson transforms his exhortation into a commitment—his as well as his audience's—to emancipation. Emerson and his God pronounce the virtues and necessity of having everyone support Lin-coln's edict. This edict breaks "bonds" and "masterships" and un-chains the slave by binding "lovers of liberty" into a community that can cooperate in revolt against the institution of slavery as well as against its own guilt in this institution—for who among us, Emerson seems to suggest, has not at one time or another relied on an idea of America that includes the possibility of slavery within its language? Even now, he warns, even now, "in the midst of a great Revolution," we are "still enacting the sentiment of the Puritans, and the dreams of young people 30 years ago" (*J*, 15: 404). What is necessary, he argues, is a renewal of the community of the covenant that remains vigilant to the various ways in which the covenant can become a means of enslavement. Rather than flee before the demands of the revolution, we should become "guides, redeemers, and benefactors," who, "obeying the Almighty effort and advancing on Chaos and the Dark," do not fear to enter the struggle for emancipation (*W*, 2: 47).

We should all race to become snowflakes—agents of cooperation and regeneration. To say this is to admit the role of rhetoric in the process of emancipation. God uses the trope of the snowflake precisely to persuade His listeners to meet the challenges of freedom. Like Emerson, He knows that "nothing so works on the human mind . . . as a trope" (*W*, 7: 90). He condenses the urgency and necessity of His message of freedom into the figure of the snowflake and, in so doing, expects to electrify all men and women, to spur them toward this freedom. As Emerson tells us in "The Poet," the use of tropes "has a certain power of emancipation and exhilaration for all" (*W*, 3: 30). It is within this context that we should understand Lincoln's Proclamation as a powerful act of language. Like the acts of God and Emerson, it too takes the form of a promise whose force is nothing if not rhetorical. The necessarily rhetorical dimension of any such Proclamation answers to the demand that men and women of all races be persuaded to act in the name of this act. Emerson's entire poem ought to be read within the context of this demand, within the requirements of this hope.

The importance of the rhetorical dimension of the poem is highlighted in a striking and unmistakable fashion in its final sentence, as Emerson's God announces the irresistible force of His rhetoric:

> My will fulfilled shall be,
> For, in daylight or in dark,
> My thunderbolt has eyes to see
> His way home to the mark.

God's unerring flash of lightning recalls the Puritan use of thunder and lightning as signals of God's voice. This topos is pervasive in biblical literature and commentary and is quite common in Massachusetts literature from the seventeenth century on. In Michael Wigglesworth's *God's Controversy with New England*, for example, thunder is the voice of God reprimanding the sins of the Puritan pilgrims:

> The Air became tempestuous;
> The wilderness gan quake:
> And from above with awfull voice
> Th' Almighty thundring spake.[42]

The image also recurs in sermons such as Cotton Mather's "Brontologia Sacra," included in the *Magnalia Christi Americana*, and Jonathan Edwards's *Personal Narrative*. As Mitchell Breitwieser reminds us, Mather's sermon was given "extemporaneously upon the occasion of a thunderstorm in September 1694."[43] "The omnipotent God in the thunder," Mather explained to his audience, "speaks to those hardy Typhons, that are found fighting against him." In Edwards's narrative, the association between thunder and God's voice is made within a discussion of his present understanding of the thunder's significance. "Before," he writes, "I used to be uncommonly terrified with thunder, and to be struck with terror when I saw a thunder storm rising; but now, on the contrary, it rejoiced me. I felt God, so to speak, at the first appearance of a thunder storm; and used to take the opportunity to . . . hear the majestic and awful voice of God's thunder."[44] God's claim for the inevitable power of His rhetoric in the poem's last sentence should be read against the background of this Puritan rhetoric. This is to say that the poem ends where it began—by recalling the rhetoric of the Puritan God. It is framed by the burning words of the God that earlier filled the Pilgrims' hearts with flame and that now wishes to enflame men and women of all races for the difficult but necessary work of emancipation.

But the apocalyptic language of the God of 1863 takes a form different from that of the God of the early seventeenth century. The meaning of His covenant has been altered to meet the challenges of the Civil War and of the slave's emancipation. Now the voice of the Puritan God merges with the voice of Emerson's God, and together their target is at least fourfold. The primary target is, of course, emancipation for the slave, but this emancipation can occur only through the threefold cooperation of the audience listening to Emerson and God within the walls of the Music Hall, the men and women called together in stanza 21 to fulfill the terms of God's covenant, and finally the slave himself—although this last target is implied in each of the preceding three. That the slave is a mark internal to the others is made clear in the internal rhyme of lines two and four in the poem's last stanza—in the rhyme, that is, between "dark" and mark." The slave is the "dark mark" of God's word. God's word shall reach the ears of the black man and pronounce his freedom. As in stanza 20, God encourages the slave to take part in his own emancipation.[45] In this instance, however, He in the same stroke condemns the interpretations of the biblical curse of Canaan and of the exile of Cain sometimes used to justify the black man's color and enslavement.[46] He distinguishes the dark mark to which His voice is now directed from the "dark mark" which, according to these interpretations, His voice had earlier condemned. In the biblical account, when the drunken Noah realizes that his son Ham has been staring at his naked body, he curses Ham's son Canaan. He condemns Canaan to servitude and, according to Talmudic and Midrashic sources, tells Ham that his seed will from then on "be ugly and dark skinned." As David Brion Davis suggests, these explanations for the black man's enslavement were probably intensified by religious cosmologies that "envisioned spiritual progress as the triumph of the children of light over the pagan or infidel children of darkness."[47] For Emerson, however, the difficulty that the issue of slavery poses for people who understand America's mission as furthering the cause of divine truth and enlightenment is precisely that of distinguishing between the forces of light and those of darkness. The rhetoric of this mission has too often been used to reinforce rather than to undo patterns of enslavement among both blacks and whites for such a distinction to be clear. The conditions of genuine emancipation ought to include a reconsideration of the implications of this color symbolism. As Emerson declares in his speech "The Emancipation in the British West Indies," at the moment of emancipation, all "disqualifications and distinctions of color" cease and "men of all colors have equal rights in law. . . . If you have man, black or white is an insignificance" (AS, 19, 31). "The fixity or incontrovertibleness of races as we see them," he says some years later in *English Traits*, "is a weak argument for the eternity of these frail boundaries" (*W*, 5: 49). In these two passages, Emerson becomes the Lockean philosopher who, questioning the distinction between black and white (and thereby dismantling the traditional hierarchy between them), questions the means of knowledge in general. "Unlearned men well enough understood the words white and black," Locke writes, but "there were philosophers found who had learning and subtlety enough to prove that snow was black; i.e. to prove that white was black" and, as a result, "they had the advantage to destroy the instruments and means of discourse, conversation, instruction, and society."[48] Both Locke and Emerson point to the relation between critical thought and revolution. To be more precise, we could say that Emerson's political gesture—like all political gestures—can be read in its transformation of language. In marking a man or a woman in terms of the single color of their race, he suggests, one paves the way for slavery. The purpose both of these passages from 1844 and of Emerson's poem, then, is to inspire independence from all "disqualifications and distinctions of color," an independence that is revolutionary because it promotes as its declaration of independence "the philosophical doctrine of the identity of all minds" (*W*, 1: 92).

While this position would at times make it difficult for him to accept the idea that race and nationality are essential to human development, it is also why he can claim that there is something within the mark of the black man that marks his relationship with other men and that, because of this relationship, ought to prevent him from being enslaved. Whether "in daylight or in dark," the truth of Emerson's God will find its way home to the mark, will find its way to men and women of all races. Rather than curse the black man for any original sin, God prophesies his redemption and emancipation from the sins committed against him in the name of a justice determined by color. If the black man is still marked, he is marked for freedom rather than punishment. He is marked for inclusion within the family of man.[49] Like the snowflake—whose angles "are invariable" but whose forms exhibit "the greatest variety and beauty" (*EL*, 1: 64)—the black man has a share in what is universal in man's nature, even as he maintains the singularity of his existence. God's rhetoric displays its force by re-marking the marks of Cain and Canaan in the direction of a more just understanding of the divinity that the black man shares with all men.

In this, God also questions the rhetoric within which both the North and the South described the Civil War as a fratricidal conflict. Each tried to mark the other with the brand of Cain. Each claimed that it was the righteous brother—trying to defend the legacy bequeathed to the nation by the founding fathers.[50] Within the context of the poem's last sentence, such branding coincides with the rhetoric and logic of exclusion that has justified and thereby maintained the institution of slavery. If God's thunderbolt does indeed see its way home to the mark, it does so by striking against any rhetoric and logic that would privilege any single mark over another.

The authority of God's Word therefore cannot be separated from His vision of emancipation. His thunderbolt has eyes that enable it to see its way home to its mark—however various and complex that mark might be—and His voice has eyes that enable it to see its way to express His Will. God's speech is visionary and His vision can be communicated. The Word of God and the vision of God are, as Emerson writes in a journal entry of 1835, "not two acts but one. The sight commands, the command sees" (J, 5: 272). The poem's last stanza can be read as a tribute to the inexorable force of God's visionary rhetoric, to the marksmanship of His signature. But to stop here would be to miss what has by now come to be the poem's trademark: God's Word and vision gain their power from the force of Emerson's own visionary rhetoric. God and Emerson steal each other's thunder. This is to say that the poem's last stanza is also a tribute to Emerson's marksmanship, not only because God continues to evoke arguments that Emerson has already made, but also because He cites Emerson speaking eloquently on the importance and power of eloquence. God takes his final sentence from a passage in Emerson's "The Celebration of Intellect," an address that Emerson delivered before the students of Tufts College on July 10, 1861, less than four months after the firing on Fort Sumter. In the address, Emerson encourages his audience not to be swayed away from the urgent tasks of thinking that the present times of "arraignment," "trial," and "judgment" require. Rather than be taken in by the "fracas of politics" and the "brute noise of the cannon," we should instead think the principles that motivate both politics and cannons. Even though the "brute noise of the cannon" has "a most poetic echo in these days when it is an instrument of freedom and the primal sentiments of humanity . . . it is but representative and a far-off means" (*W*, 12: 113). We should think the creative cause of the war's fracas and brute noise, the "sanctity and omnipotence of Intellectual Law." "The whole battle is fought in a few heads" (*W*, 12: 121), he says.

To think the relationship between the laws of the intellect and the laws of politics, however, requires us to think the place of rhetoric within these laws. As we have seen, nothing moves the minds of men and women or effects the direction of politics more than rhetoric does. But to say this is to say as well that nothing moves people or effects politics more than history does, since, for Emerson, rhetoric is essentially historical. What gives force to a trope like that of the snow-flake, for example, are the myriad associations that have been attributed to the crystal within history. If there is, and Emerson says there is, a relationship among questions of politics, history, and language, the issue becomes how to direct one's rhetoric toward accomplishing moral effects. It becomes how our rhetoric can see its way home to the mark when the figures we use may include, within their history, con-notations that lead our argument away from its intended end. How, in other words, can we be at the same time both eloquent and just? Within this context, Emerson declares the passage from which God will draw His final sentence. "I wish you to be eloquent," he says:

to grasp the bolt and to hurl it home to the mark. I wish to see that Mirabeau who knows how to seize the heart-strings of the people and drive their hands and feet in the way he wishes them to go, to fill them with himself, to enchant men so that their will and purpose is in abeyance and they serve him with a million hands just as implicitly as his own members obey him. But I value it more when it is legitimate, when the talent is in true order, subject to genius, subject to the total and native sentiment of the man, and therefore in har-mony with the public sentiment of mankind. Such is the patriotism of De-mosthenes, of Patrick Henry and of what was best in Cicero and Burke; not an ingenious special pleading, not the making of a plausible case, but strong by the strength of the facts themselves. Then the orator is still one of the audience, persuaded by the same reasons which persuade them, not a ven-triloquist, not a juggler, not a wire-puller paid to manage the lobby and cau-cus. (*W*, 12: 119–20)

Emerson encourages his audience to become eloquent by provid-ing them with examples of the power a skilled orator can have over his listeners. The orator who knows his art well knows how to seduce and direct the hearts and minds of the people. Giving free reign to his creative and transformative power, the orator thereby claims his rightful identity. Whether this orator is a Mirabeau, a Demosthenes, a Henry, a Cicero, a Burke, or even God, he has the capacity to direct people to the fulfillment of his will rather than theirs. He has the power "to grasp the bolt" of rhetoric and "hurl it home to the mark." But the orator's singular power may quickly become despotic if it is not "legitimate." The orator risks tyrannizing over his audience whenever he simply effects "an ingenious special pleading," or constructs "a plausible case," in order to realize his personal aims. To say that an orator's eloquence is legitimate, however, is not to say that he may do just about anything with language, as long as he remains fully aware of the misleading power of his rhetoric. Rather, his rhetoric is legitimate only under certain conditions. (1) It must be in true order, that is to say, in accord with the laws of nature. In other words, the orator's rhetoric must remain faithful to the transformative power of language and therefore to a thinking of the rhetoricity of nature. (2) It must be subject to genius, that is to say, subject to the particularity of the orator's own history as well as to all of history. The orator must think his relationship to history in order to confront the chances of the future. (3) It must be subject to the native sentiment of man. The orator must, as Emerson explains in the opening paragraph of "American Civilization," think, speak, and act in a way that respects the self-reliance of each of his listeners. Only by meeting these conditions can an orator remain "in harmony with the public sentiment of mankind." Only in this way are "the spells of persuasion, the keys of power . . . put into his hands" (*W*, 1: 32).

These are the directives that guide Emerson's hand as he writes the "Boston Hymn." He wishes to celebrate the Emancipation Proclamation, to encourage his listeners to pledge their support for emancipation, but without imposing his own particular will upon them. Directing his efforts toward emancipation and self-reliance rather than enslavement and dependence, he remains "one of the audience." He too must promise to keep the promise of the Proclamation. Although the Proclamation comes, as the Fugitive Slave Law did, like "a sheet of lightning at midnight" to strike the truth of emancipation into the hearts and minds of the populace, although it affects the country with the suddenness and revelatory force of God's Word, as Emerson well knows, "the habit of oppression was not destroyed by a law and a day of jubilee" (*AS*, 17). We must rethink the meaning of emancipation, while remaining vigilant to the ways in which the promise of freedom can easily become a means to enslavement. We should also consider the habits of thinking that determine our "habit of oppression," habits that include the rhetoric of nationalism, cultural difference, and racial superiority. As the Puritan God set out the conditions and terms of His promise, the Emersonian Poet must set out the terms and conditions of the task of thinking his audience must meet if the Proclamation is to be fulfilled. The Poet must also provide his listeners with courage, with faith in their own divine potential to realize the promise of the Proclamation. This is a difficult task, but the Poet can find help by drawing on a source of energy that is larger than he is. He can abandon himself to "the nature of things" (*W*, 3: 26). "Besides his privacy of power as an individual man," Emerson explains, "there is a great public power on which he can draw, but unlocking, at all risks, his human doors, and suffering the ethereal tides to roll up into the life of the universe, his speech is thunder, his thought is law" (*W*, 3: 26–27).[51] If Emerson chooses to subsume his voice within the authority and "ethereal tides" of God's voice, he does so because he knows that, within the nature of things, God has "a great public power," a great power over the public. He knows that when God speaks, people listen. He speaks as God not only because he wishes to indicate the divine creative potential he believes exists within us all but also because he may then appropriate God's "public power" as his own—by surrendering himself to its effects. Using God as a powerful trope of persuasion, Emerson mobilizes God's "public power" for emancipation. Abandoning himself to this trope of power, Emerson transforms his voice into thunder and his thought into law. He becomes "the mere tongue of the occasion and the hour, and says what cannot but be said." He surrenders himself to "the principle on which he is horsed, the great connection and crisis of events, thunder in the ear of the crowd" (*W*, 7: 49).

The power of Emerson's strategy becomes evident when we recognize that the force of his poem remains intact regardless of who his audience thinks is speaking—God or Emerson as God. In either case, God's thunder reaches its mark: once it enters the ears of the crowd, it matters little whose thunder it was; it becomes the listener's responsibility. But in order to realize the work of emancipation, the listener must come to recognize the thunder of this responsibility as his own. Lincoln's edict can only be realized if men and women of all races take on the challenge of self-reliance—a reliance on the self that, as we know from Emerson's second Fugitive Slave Law Address, is a reliance on God (*AS*, 84). To rely on the "public power" of God is to rely on one's self—because one's self is already infused with the power that is God. This is the recognition on which emancipation depends. Emerson writes the "Boston Hymn" to proclaim the conditions for realizing the promise of emancipation, to signal the divinity that defines our potential for freedom. Like the voice of God, which calls men and women to realize His will as snowflakes, the poem creates the audience that is to hear it by speaking to that audience as if it could already hear. The thunderbolt that is the poem sees its way home to the mark insofar as it articulates a rapport in the possibility of a future. This future lies in the hands of the races who, coming like snowflakes, commit themselves to its chances. If the "Hymn" celebrates an emancipation that does not yet exist but is occurring in the form of a promise, "Voluntaries" figures the enactment of this promise in the acts of the 54th Regiment. Fighting under the banner of the snowflake and the aurora borealis, Colonel Robert Shaw and his black troops give their lives over to the force of this promise—a promise that has always magnetized American desire.

Northern Lights

Emerson wrote "Voluntaries" late in the summer of 1863, in commemoration of the heroism the 54th Massachusetts Regiment had displayed in its attack on Fort Wagner in mid-July. The poem is nearly contemporaneous with the analogy between politics and frost with which I began and is never far from demonstrating the analogy's pertinence to an understanding of the political conflicts that define the crises of the war during this time. Traversed by the conflictual history of black soldiers within the Union Army, the poem identifies the regiment's heroism as an important turning point within this history. This heroism became a powerful means of persuasion for abolitionists and antislavery Republicans who wished the North to recognize the virtues of including black soldiers within the northern army. The recruitment of black soldiers into the army had begun late in 1862, just before the announcement of Lincoln's Preliminary Emancipation, and since then had been one of the most revolutionary features of the Civil War. As James McPherson notes, "Black men had fought in the American Army during the Revolution, and New Orleans blacks had helped Andrew Jackson defend the city against the British in 1815, but since 1792 blacks had been prohibited by federal law from the state militias and there were no blacks in the regular United States Army."[52] After the firing on Fort Sumter, however, many blacks and abolitionists believed that the national crisis would force the North to overlook its prejudices and recruit black volunteers. If the black man exhibited his patriotism and courage in the battlefield, they argued, the nation would be morally obliged to grant him citizenship and equality. As Douglass declared: "Once let the black man get upon his person the brass letters, U.S.; let him get an eagle on his button, and a musket on his shoulder and bullets in his pocket, and there is no power on earth which can deny that he has earned the right to citizenship in the United States."[53] But the North was not yet ready to admit that it needed black soldiers to win its war. Abolitionists reacted strongly against the government's refusal to recruit black troops. "This is no time to fight only with your white hand, and allow your black hand to remain tied," Douglass exclaimed. Referring to the courage black soldiers had demonstrated during the revolution and the praise that Jackson had bestowed on them for their help in defeating the British in 1815, he added, "They were good enough to help win American independence, but they are not good enough to help preserve that independence against treason and rebellion."[54]

Despite the administration's reluctance to recruit black troops, the North's continued losses, especially at Bull Run and Richmond, led more and more northerners to accept the idea of black soldiers—again under the exigencies of "military necessity." Under what McPherson has summarized as "pressure from Republicans and abolitionists, declining white manpower, continuing lack of success of Union arms, and increasing sentiment in the army itself favoring use of black troops,"[55] Lincoln finally changed his mind late in the summer of 1862. Volunteers came slowly at first, but by November the first black regiment to be officially recognized by Washington, the First South Carolina Volunteers, led by Thomas Wentworth Higginson, was formed. In January 1863, John Andrew, governor of Massachusetts, obtained permission to recruit a black regiment in his state, on the condition that commissioned officers be white. Andrew wrote to his friend, abolitionist Francis G. Shaw of New York, to seek advice and finally settled on Shaw's son Robert to lead the 54th Massachusetts volunteers. Blacks were by this time less eager to join than they had been earlier. There were many reasons for this, including a prosperous war economy that had created jobs for blacks throughout the North, rumors that black volunteers would receive less pay than white soldiers and that, if captured, they would not be treated as ordinary prisoners, and resentment that black men were not eligible to become officers in the new regiments.[56] Because of these factors, recruiters had to call on all their eloquence to persuade blacks to join the army. As Douglass proclaimed in March 1863, in his widely circulated monthly:

Shall colored men enlist notwithstanding this unjust and ungenerous barrier raised against them? We answer yes. Go into the army and go with a will and a determination to blot out this and all other mean discriminations against us. To say we won't be soldiers because we cannot be colonels is like saying we won't go into the water till we have learned to swim. A half a loaf is better than no bread—and to go into the army is the speediest and best way to overcome the prejudice which has dictated unjust laws against us. To allow us in the army at all, is a great concession. Let us take this little the better to get more. By showing that we deserve the little is the best way to gain much.[57]

Like many other abolitionists, Douglass argued that if blacks refused to enlist they would only reinforce public opinion against them, whereas if they joined and fought courageously they could win equal rights for themselves. Moreover, he added, in joining the northern cause they would be fighting against slavery. Emerson was asked by Thomas Russell to speak at a meeting to raise funds for Robert Shaw's regiment and to encourage volunteers. "If the war means liberty to you, you should enlist," Emerson writes in his notes for the speech, delivered on March 20, "I speak for the forces above us those issues which are made for us over our heads, under our feet, paramount to our wills. If you will not fight for your liberty who will? We go not to restore those falsehearted usurpers of the power of Union or the like of them to their places . . . but to restore the spirit of the American constitution & not its forced & falsely construed letter . . . not to maintain slavery but to maintain freedom" (*J*, 15: 210–11). Although response from New York blacks was slow, response from the rest of the North was sufficient to form an additional regiment by the end of April. On May 1, the *New York Tribune* stated that most northerners now believed in the need to recruit blacks, but that there was still doubt about whether they would make good soldiers. Higginson's regiment had performed well in minor confrontations, but no black troops had yet fought in a major battle.

In May and June 1863, however, black regiments displayed their courage in two major engagements at Port Hudson and Milliken's Bend in the Mississippi Valley. Their performance in these battles encouraged many northerners to support arming black soldiers. Even more important in turning northern opinion, however, was the assault of the 54th Massachusetts Regiment on Fort Wagner, a Confederate outpost guarding the entrance to Charleston Harbor, on July 18, 1863. The regiment fought their way into the fort, but was eventually forced to retreat when their white reinforcements did not arrive in time. The attack was therefore turned away with heavy loss to the regiment, including the death of Colonel Shaw, but the heroic conduct of the regiment during the battle was celebrated throughout the North. As McPherson notes, "The Fifty-fourth's assault on Fort Wagner was in a narrow sense a failure. But in a broader sense it was a significant triumph. In the face of heavy odds, black troops had proved . . . their courage, determination, and willingness to die for the freedom of their race."[58] Shaw and the black soldiers who died alongside him were "virtually canonized by the abolitionists and by a large segment of northern public opinion." The northern press publicized the battle as a moral victory for the black soldiers. The first black regiment to be raised in the free states, the 54th was part of a "holy crusade." Fort Wagner was a "holy sepulchre" to the black race, wrote the *Anti-Slavery Standard*. The battle "made Fort Wagner such a name to the colored race as Bunker Hill had been for ninety years to the white Yankees," the *New York Tribune* later noted. In a letter of July 28, abolitionist Angelina Grimké Weld asked Gerrit Smith, "Do you not rejoice & exult in all that praise that is lavished upon our brave colored troops even by Pro-Slavery papers? I have no tears to shed over their graves, because I see that their heroism is working a great change in public opinion, forcing all men to see the sin & shame of enslaving such men."[59] Emerson's celebration of Shaw and his black troops in "Voluntaries" belongs to a large degree to the fervor of this enthusiasm. The poem was printed in the October issue of the *Atlantic Monthly* as well as in a Memorial for Shaw, and quickly gained a certain popularity. Parts two and three of the *Atlantic* version were printed separately as broadsides by the New England Loyal Publication Society of Boston and part of the poem was also reprinted in *Cloud-Crystals: A Snowflake Album*, a collection of poems and articles devoted to the virtues of the snowflake. Emerson had also prepared a copy of the poem for Francis Shaw and sent it to him on September 10, along with a note in which he cites the heroism of Shaw's son as an important inspiration for the poem.[60]

The poem opens where Emerson's speech on the Emancipation Proclamation leaves off—with an evocation of the suffering and hardship that the "ill-fated" black race has been forced to endure in the name of selfish and economic interests. While the speech ends with the hope that the Proclamation will help to relieve "the dejection sculptured for ages" in the black man's countenance, the opening stanza of "Voluntaries" dwells on the slave's legacy—a legacy which, from generation to generation, has consisted in the "low and mournful strain" of his "plaintive music" and the irons that have held him captive. The stanza follows with a condensed history of the slave's plight in the days and years prior to 1863. This history includes his being displaced, injured, stripped of family, home, and property, and his being prey to the "vulture's beak" and the "thirsty spear" of both northerners and southerners. This history and legacy are unhelped by the "Great men in the Senate" who, favoring the Union over freedom, until recently had refused to emancipate him:

> They forebore to break the chain
> Which bound the dusky tribe,
> Checked by the owner's fierce disdain,
> Lured by "Union" as a bribe.

Nevertheless, the irresistible force of Destiny will not be stopped. She intervenes in history and proclaims that she will hold these "Great men" accountable for their "false peace" and "coward head," for the violence they have committed against the black race. She will "bring round the harvest day" and the measure of the irresponsibility of this false peace will be the degree to which the black race demonstrates itself worthy of freedom.

As if in response to Destiny's decree, the poem turns in its second stanza to a history of Freedom's progress, a history that moves to include the black race within its horizon. Shaw's black troops have

shown themselves willing to "hazard all in Freedom's fight." Freedom exhibits her appreciation by taking the race under her wing. The
stanza figures the specific role that Shaw and his regiment have played
in effecting this historical and political revolution, this extension of
Freedom's realm, by inscribing this role within an allegorical vision
of the consequences of their acts for the meaning of America. As the
stanza develops, the allegory draws together a series of relationships
between the progress of Freedom—a progress that the poem sees as
coincidental with the black race's own progress toward emancipation—and the reversal and displacement of the various myths of climate, character, and racial inferiority that have worked to keep the
black man in chains. This redefinition of the place of the black man
within America corresponds to a revolution that moves America forward by returning her to her founding in Nature. I quote the stanza
in its entirety:

> FREEDOM all winged expands,
> Nor perches in a narrow place;
> Her broad van seeks unplanted lands;
> She loves a poor and virtuous race.
> Clinging to a colder Zone
> Whose dark sky sheds the snowflake down,
> The snowflake is her banner's star,
> Her stripes the boreal streamers are.
> Long she loved the Northman well;
> Now the iron age is done,
> She will not refuse to dwell
> With the offspring of the Sun;
> Foundling of the desert far,
> Where palms plume, siroccos blaze,
> He roves unhurt the burning ways
> In climates of the summer star.
> He has avenues to God
> Hid from men of Northern brain,
> Far beholding, without cloud,
> What these with slowest steps attain.
> If once the generous chief arrive
> To lead him willing to be led,
> For freedom he will strike and strive,
> And drain his heart till he be dead.
>
> (*W*, 9: 206–7)

Freedom advances, it would seem, according to her own laws of expansion. Refusing to be restricted, "her broad van seeks unplanted lands." Her van is expansive not only because it spans the breadth of her reach but also because it includes people of all races, who, themselves moving forward, have joined in her work of emancipation. Like the men and women in the "Boston Hymn" who come, as snowflakes, to help realize the promise of freedom pronounced by the Proclamation, Freedom's van—moving under the banner of the snowflake and the borealis—seeks to extend freedom from the cold zone to the hot zone, from the North to the South. But this van also takes its energy from the hot zone, as its foremost division, Freedom's military wing, is the 54th Massachusetts Regiment. As Emerson had noted in his address on the emancipation of the British West Indies, "The emancipation is observed . . . to have wrought for the negro a benefit as sudden as when a thermometer is brought out of the shade into the sun" (*AS*, 30). Offspring of the sun, Freedom's black troops seek to help found lands which are not stricken by the plantations that have required and supported her restriction. Not yet set in the ground, not yet colonized, these lands will be flexible and open to the future.

Wherever these lands may be, "now that the iron age is done," Freedom may extend herself across boundaries of geography, race, color, and even temperature. Now that the last and worst era of the world is past—we recall that, according to Greek and Roman mythology, the Iron Age succeeds the Golden, Silver, and Brazen Ages and is characterized by wickedness, cruelty, oppression, and debasement—the slave's iron shackles are broken. In this new age, inaugurated by the Emancipation Proclamation and furthered by the recruitment of black soldiers into the Union Army, Freedom "will not refuse to dwell / With the offspring of the Sun." If Emerson here recalls arguments concerning the black man's physical traits—he was well read in the racial science of the day[61]—he does so in order to turn such myths against themselves. According to classical authorities, the black man's color is due to climatic and environmental forces, most often the result of the action of the sun. Whether the sun is assumed to have burned and scorched the skin or blackened the blood, the sun's action is seen as a curse. Emerson's poem suggests, however, that precisely the black man's color and ancestry, his familiarity with hot climes, enable him to rove "unhurt the burning ways / In climates of the summer star," to win a moral victory in the warm climes of the South. In struggling for his freedom, this "Foundling of the desert far" transforms his "curse" into a blessing. Child of the sun, he salutes the snowflake.

Emerson had earlier articulated the conditions for this reversal of the climatic explanation of the black man's color in his essay "Civilization." Considering the effects of climate on man's progress toward civilization, he writes: "Climate has much to do with this melioration. The highest civility has never loved the hot zones. Wherever snow falls there is usually civil freedom. Where the banana grows the animal system is indolent and pampered at the cost of higher qualities: the man is sensual and cruel." He adds, however, that "this scale is not invariable. High degrees of moral sentiment control the unfavorable influences of climate; and some of our grandest examples of men and of races come from the equatorial regions. . . . These feats are measures or traits of civility; and temperate climate is an important influence, though not quite indispensable, for there have been learning, philosophy and art in Iceland, and in the tropics. But one condition is essential to the social education of man, namely, morality. There can be no high civility without a deep morality" (*W*, 7: 25–26). What determines the character of a race, of the individuals who comprise that race, is morality, not climate.[62] Fighting for freedom on July 18, 1863, the 54th demonstrates its courage, its commitment to the rights of men, under the summer star. It reveals its divine and moral capacity for reform. This capacity has until now gone mostly unappreciated—hidden as it has been "from men of Northern brain." But the 54th attains with their "slow" steps what the "great men of the Senate" could never accomplish with their even "slower" steps. No longer wishing to wait for these men to act on their behalf, the men of the 54th take charge of their own destiny. They gain their freedom by fighting for it, belying myths of the black man's laziness and passivity. Their acts bring about a revolution in the meaning of America. In his speech "The Emancipation in the British West Indies," Emerson predicts their role in this transformation. The black man, he writes, "carries in his bosom an indispensable element of a new and coming civilization." "In the great anthem which we call history, a piece of many parts and vast compass, after playing a long time a very low and subdued accompaniment," the black race will "perceive the time arrived" when it can "strike in with effect" and take a central part in that music (*AS*, 31). "Stealing away the memory of sorrows new and old," this music unfolds its wings and diffuses its revolutionary tune beyond Freedom's present realm. Fighting for his freedom, the black man exchanges his "wailing song" for a song that "Lauds the Eternal Rights." Emerson refers to this account of black agency in his poem's title, "Voluntaries," which emphasizes the unconstrained freedom of will with which many blacks decided to fight for their rights. The lines that close the poem's second stanza—"If once the generous chief arrive / To lead him willing to be led, / For freedom he will strike and strive, / And drain his heart till he be dead"—should therefore not be read as a suggestion that these black soldiers could not have achieved what they did without their white leader. Written as part of Emerson's effort to praise Shaw's heroism— a heroism that had already been read in relation to Shaw's decision to lead the black regiment in the first place—these lines also have their origin in the fact that blacks were not permitted to be officers in the Union Army. If they wished to contribute to their liberation, they— like every other union soldier—had to be willing to serve a white officer. Emerson himself warns us against a reading that would diminish the role of the black soldier's effort to earn his own freedom. "The negro has saved himself," he tells us, "and the white man very patronizingly says I have saved you" (*J*, 9: 126).

The stanza can therefore be read as effectuating a series of reversals within the repeated polarities between black and white, light and dark, freedom and slavery, North and South, and cold and hot. It becomes impossible to say, even if we weigh the terms' more usual associations against their opposite connotations, how the polarities of light and dark match up with those of white and black, how hot and cold correspond to either freedom and slavery or North and South. If Freedom's forces inaugurate a new revolution within the nation's social and political configuration, this revolution corresponds to a transformation of the network of concepts figured within the poem. The signal of this conceptual revolution is the melting of oppositions in the formation of a new union. This reconciliation will not so much erase the differences between these terms as provoke a consideration of their shared historical and figural status.

This is why the new union requires a new emblem. The nation's

new flag will represent America's return to the laws and forces of Nature—to the laws of writing and transfiguration. Emerson anticipates
the new configuration he envisions and presents in the poem in a sequence of journal entries from 1862. "Wherever snow falls," he says,
"man is free." "You alone with all your six feet of experience are the
fool of the cold of the present moment, & cannot see the southing of
the sun," he says elsewhere. "Besides the snowflake is freedom's star."
And finally, in an entry that introduces the auroras, he writes, "Freedom does not love the hot zone. The snow-flakes are the right stars
of our flag, and the Northern streamers the stripes" (*J*, 15: 178, 249-
50, 246). This association between the snow and stars of the flag
could have one of its many sources in the *Atlantic Monthly* article
"Snow," also written in 1862, cited above. There, the author not only
suggests that "the white surface of the snow glitters in the sunlight
with stars" but he also refers to the work of recent philosophers who,
with the help of the microscope, "have observed the wonderful Wisdom of God in the Figure of the Snow; each flake is usually of a *Stel-
late* Form, and of six Angles of exact length from the Center. It is *like
a little Star*." [63] Whatever their origin in Emerson's imagination, however, both the snow and the auroras enter into a system of relationships that integrates the phenomenal with the spiritual. In this,
Emerson's imaginative flag is only one in a series of flags that have
attempted to represent the meaning of America. The history of the
American flag, like the history of the nation it is to represent, is an
inchoate one. The flag as we know it today was not standardized until
1912. Much could be said about the relationship between nature and
the political history of America in an investigation into the represen-
tions of this history within the various flags that have, throughout it,
sought to figure America's natural founding—one need only recall
the number of birds, animals, trees, leaves, stars, moons, suns, clouds,
and mottoes that have dotted the fabric of the nation's history. [64]
Emerson's flag too tries to represent the slow fusing of separate and
discordant political communities into one natural whole. The symbol
of a people united in the common cause of freedom, the banner in
this poem has been completely naturalized. Righting itself, America
has, as Emerson suggests in his speech "The Emancipation Proclamation," planted itself on a law of nature—whose signature is the
process of reading and writing, without which there would be no
Proclamation.

As we have already seen, however, natural metaphors within Emerson are not merely tropes but also principles of articulation among language, politics, and history.[65] These principles not only account for the force of tropes on whatever we might call the "reality" of history or politics, but also for the essential figurality at work within the movement and constitution of either history or politics. Emerson's flag is a figure for the figurality at work *within* and *as* history and politics. The specular structure of the banner as a fabric of snow and aurora figures a more general structure that involves natural metaphors as historically and politically marked articulations of knowledge. The snowflake and the aurora, each figures for the aesthetic imagination as well, are primarily social and political indexes, ethically grounded in Emerson's notion of freedom. Inscribing an entire network of references to images and debates over the meaning of snow within the American experience—in addition to the figures already mentioned, we might include here the image of General George Washington and his troops crossing the icy Delaware River in 1776 and camping in the snow at Valley Forge, Crevecoeur's suggestion that snow teaches us foresight and improves communication, and Noah Webster's famous claim that the experience of snow defines what it means to be American[66]—the figure of snow becomes a figure for America in general. The America of which this flag is the emblem or figure, then, is not just a landscape of the mind or of the soul, but a principle of political value and authority that has claims on the form and limits of our freedom. Emerson's flag, although utterly naturalized, is not naturally given or produced but posited through an act of language. This act is not Emerson's alone, however; it bears an entire network of historical relations within it. The force of the act depends on this history. I have already suggested something of the historical and metaphorical chain that links snow to the forces of purity, divinity, and freedom—all actively connoted in the flag's significance. Before reading the implications that follow the joining of this figure to that of the auroras, I want briefly to sketch some of the connotations that Emerson wishes to set into motion with this reference to the Northern Lights—lights which, during the war, were a popular figure for the northern cause.

We might begin with Emerson's lifelong interest in the aurora as a figure for the arrival of the new. Emerson more than once mentions his enthusiasm and fascination with Jakob Böhme's *Aurora*—a book he read in the mid-1830s, which he claims is full of the "morning knowledge" of truth. Böhme, Emerson writes, "is all imagination" (*J*, 5: 75). In 1839, Carlyle sent Emerson a print of Guido Reni's *Aurora* as a token of the bond between them. Emerson thanked Carlyle by letter, writing that the print "is a right morning thought, full of health and flowing genius" (*L*, 1: 375).[67] Moreover, in his essay "The Poet" Emerson uses the figure of the aurora as a figure for the arrival of a new poet. Sitting "in the aurora of a sunrise which was to put out all the stars" (*W*, 3: 10), Emerson links the poet's imaginative powers to the light, fire, and oracular nature of the aurora. In each instance, the aurora becomes associated with an act of the imagination that inaugurates a new dawn of meaning. This act is inseparable from the various efforts in the eighteenth and nineteenth century to explain the phenomenon of the aurora. In 1779, for example, Benjamin Franklin delivered a paper at the Royal Academy of Sciences in Paris entitled "Aurora Borealis: Suppositions and Conjectures Towards Forming an Hypothesis for its Explanation."[68] In the essay he claims that auroras result from the release of electricity that has been accumulated in snow and ice, especially during the winter. In 1815, Charles Hutton published a *Philosophical and Mathematical Dictionary* in which he writes that the aurora borealis is "a kind of meteor appearing in the northern part of the heavens, mostly in the winter season and in frosty weather."[69] Although both of these theories are erroneous, they suggest the terms that were available to Emerson as he imagined a connection among the figures of the auroras, snow, and frost.

But in Emerson's mind these lights would also have had more explicitly conflictual, even militaristic connotations.[70] In terms of their mythological associations, auroras have been read historically as signs of battles and fires in the sky: their flashing rays as the reflection of light on steel weapons, the movement of burning lances, their rapid and shifting motion as the shifts and reversals of war, their red streamers as showers and pools of blood. Omens of calamities to come, they figure the approaching battle of celestial lights. In an article in the December 1859 issue of the *Atlantic Monthly* entitled "The Northern Lights and the Stars," a poem describes the auroras as "embattled meteors" that "scale the arch. / And toss their lurid banners wide; / Heaven reels with their tempestuous march. / And quivers in the flashing tide."[71] Nearly thirty years earlier, in 1831, Whittier published a collection entitled *Legends of New England*, which includes a poetic tribute to the force of the aurora. The poem, entitled "Aerial Omens," is preceded by a short paragraph in which Whittier summarizes the significance of the lights for New Englanders in the late eighteenth and early nineteenth century:

It was supposed that an army of fiery warriors were seen in the sky, with banners floating, and plumes tossing, and horsemen hurrying to and fro. . . . The strange changes of the Borealis were considered by many as ominous of approaching war; and consequently excited no little apprehension. The breaking out of war soon after, completely confirmed this supposition; and many an aged Revolutionist will yet tell of the wonderful Northern Lights, and that he saw the battles of Saratoga and Bennington, pictured distinctly on the sky, long before their actual occurrence.[72]

Associated with the coming of war, with the coming of the American Revolution, with battle and civil strife, the aurora borealis became an inescapable figure during the Civil War. Literally the northern dawn, the aurora was used by northerners to figure both the variable fortunes of the war and the essential role of the northern army in the inauguration of a new dawn for the Union. In the May 25, 1861, issue of *Harper's Weekly*, just over five weeks after the firing on Fort Sumter, Emerson could have seen a cartoon on Union mobilization which depicted "A Rebel General startled in his Camp by the Beautiful and Unexpected Display of Northern Light."[73] He may also have heard of a widely reported display of the auroras which occurred near Fredericksburg, Virginia, in mid-December 1862, just after the Confederate victory there. This particular occurrence is of interest because the Confederate Army later appropriated the lights as their own, as an omen of their imminent victory. Many contemporary accounts of the display survive. A Union staff officer recorded in a journal entry of December 14 that a "fine auroral display took place at night—one of the finest I have ever seen here," and a Confederate veteran recalled how his comrades "felt that the heavens were hanging out banners and streamers and setting off fireworks in honor of our victory."[74] The North and the South both wish to figure themselves as a natural community whose achievements and destiny are written in the heavens. They each suggest that nature celebrates their victories. The aurora borealis portends a new dawn to which each side wants to lay claim. Reappropriating the auroras for the northern cause, Emerson aligns himself within the horizon of these efforts. Insofar as the poem articulates the conditions of a new union in which the North and the South cannot be distinguished, he works to reveal the necessarily historical and political dimension of any effort—including his own—to naturalize our community and destiny. This necessity is perhaps clearest at a time of rapid, even extreme change. With its constant shifts and reversals, the war encourages both sides to use nature either to explain or to justify their victories and defeats. We can perhaps measure the degree of this necessity by looking at the rhetoric within which the North and the South described the events of the battle at Fort Wagner. For the sake of economy, I here rely on the accounts provided by historians George Washington Williams and Benjamin Quarles.

The 54th was to participate in an assault on Fort Wagner, in the hope of eventually gaining access to Charleston Harbor—for many northerners, "the heart of the rebellion." According to Williams, himself a soldier during the war, the regiment left for Morris Island on the morning of July 16, marching all day "under the exhausting heat of a July sun in Carolina" and all night "through darkness and rain, amid thunder and lightning, over swollen streams, broken dikes, and feeble, shuddering, narrow causeways." Continuing in this way, the troops finally reached the island on July 18 at six in the morning. As Williams explains, the regiment "was intended to open a preliminary bombardment at daylight on the 18th, and having by heavy ordnance tranquillized Wagner, to effect its reduction by the bayonet. But a tempest came on suddenly and delayed the cruel ingenuity of war. The thunder roared, the lightning flashed, and the rain fell in torrents. The military operations were suspended in the presence of Nature's awful spectacle."[75] The naval bombardment did not begin until early in the afternoon, but once initiated the "storm of fire" was kept up all afternoon. Toward evening the fort seemed "practically dismantled" and the 54th prepared for their assault. The troops were by this time exhausted, but Shaw's "burning words of eloquent patriotic sentiment" urged them on to battle. Williams summarizes the ensuing events:

The ramparts of Wagner flashed with small-arms, and all the large shotted guns roared with defiance. Sumter and Cumming's Point delivered a destructive cross-fire, while the howitzers in the bastions raked the ditch; but the gallant Negro regiment swept across it and gained the parapet. Here the flag of this regiment was planted; here General Strong fell mortally wounded; and here the brave, beautiful, and heroic Colonel Shaw was saluted by death and kissed by immortality. The regiment lost heavily, but held its ground under the most discouraging circumstances. The men had actually gained the inside of the fort, where they bravely contended with a desperate and determined enemy. The contest endured for about an hour, when the regiment, shattered and torn, with nearly all of its officers dead or wounded, was withdrawn under the command of Captain Luis F. Emilio.[76]

"From a purely military standpoint the assault upon Fort Wagner was a failure," Williams concludes, "but it furnished the severest test of Negro valor and soldiership. . . . The Negro soldier had seen his red-letter day, and his title to patriotic courage was written in his own blood."[77]

Quarles's retelling of the same events in 1953 is no less dramatic and theatrical than Williams's, but it presents some essential differences. According to Quarles, the Union command, impressed "by the great strength of Wagner," "decided to erect counterbatteries on the island . . . with the co-operation of the guns of the Federal fleet, it might be possible to tranquilize Wagner's armament, demoralize her defenders, and thus mount a successful attack." In Quarles's account, however, nature's intervention in the implementation of this plan is strikingly absent—or at least present to different effect. He declares that "the morning of July 18 broke bright and beautiful." Citing Confederate officer Robert C. Gilchrist as saying that "the God of day rising to the splendor of his midsummer glory flung his red flame into the swelling sea, and again performed the miracle of turning water into wine," he concludes that "the Federal forces made the most of the perfect weather. Their land batteries opened up the cannonading from the south side, and were soon joined by six ironclads. . . . From a distance of a few hundred feet these Union vessels poured a remorseless stream of shells into Wagner's east side. . . . The tempest of iron hail rained against Wagner was perhaps unparalleled in history. . . . The whole Confederate-held end of the island emitted smoke like a furnace, and the horizon was fitfully illumined by the flashes of flame belching from the monster guns on land and sea."[78] Quarles summarizes the assault as follows:

The signal was given . . . and the metallic tones of the bugle sounded the advance. . . . As the Fifty-fourth broke ranks while passing the defile, Battery Wagner, miraculously it seemed, lit up with a withering sheet of flame and fire from bastion to bastion. Wagner had become a volcanic hell, vomiting shot and shell with deafening explosions. . . . The darkness proved a distinct disadvantage to the storming Union forces, who were in unfamiliar surroundings with no visibility. . . . Despite all obstacles, Shaw and some of his men reached the top of the parapet, and for a few moments there was a bitter hand-to-hand struggle. . . . Standing on the parapet, Shaw waved his sword and shouted to his troops, "Rally! Rally!" A moment later a bullet pierced his heart and he fell forward into the fort. "I saw his face," said a survivor. "It was white as snow, but in every line was that courage which led his men to the very crest of that wall of death." . . . The desperate struggle could not be long protracted. The outnumbered Union troops were etched against the horizon, furnishing an easy target. The supporting regiments had not moved rapidly enough to take advantage of the first fierce onslaught. . . . Checkmated, the colored regiment fell back, firing at the shadowy figures above as a parting gesture.[79]

Like Williams, Quarles ends by claiming that "from a purely military point of view the assault was a costly failure, but Wagner was an event which could not be measured in terms of immediate success. Wagner was not simply another of the Civil War's 2400 recorded military engagements. The storming of that slaughterhouse furnished the severest test of valor and soldiership. . . . In the dread twilight on that barren Carolina shore the Fifty-fourth fixed beyond recall the Negro's right to the title of citizen-soldier. . . . The valor . . . of the Fifty-fourth opened the floodgates for the fresh army of more than 180,000 Negro soldiers who would infuse new spirit into a war-weary North. The brave black regiment thus blazed a path which would wind its way to Appomattox."[80]

I will not analyze these two accounts here. I wish only to underline the pervasiveness in both of metaphors drawn from nature and the weather. To speak of either nature or the weather, I have suggested, is to speak of the relationship among politics, history, and language. This relationship is indissociable from what, within these passages, thinks history and politics according to a rhetoric of the laws of nature. Both the North and the South attempt to account for the violence, the bloodshed, and the defeats of the war in a language that links these with the volatile and sometimes violent storms of nature itself. Rendering the battle in natural or climatic terms, each attempts to naturalize the war, as well as its own place within the history of that war, within a destiny that is both natural and providential. Each evokes the idiom of nature to justify killing and dying for its respective cause. That this is so is evident in the contradictory weather claims that emerge in these two descriptions of the battle at Fort Wagner.

It would be one thing if each account of the struggle claimed that the morning of July 18 broke with rain, and then one of the accounts went on to exaggerate the extent and effects of this rain. But the two accounts could not be more diverse. In the first, the weather meets the 54th regiment with an "awful spectacle" of its violent power and prevents the assault from taking place as planned. In the second— which is based on documents written by southern soldiers and officers—the weather is "perfect," and, because of this, it actually helps further the assault by enabling the Union navy to enter the harbor. If the North wishes to rationalize its defeat in terms of all the obstacles it had to overcome simply to enter the fort, the South needs to account for why a black regiment could enter its fort in the first place. If in one account nature helps the South and hurts the North, in the other it helps the North and harms the South. The local weather attending the struggle becomes nationalized, as it begins to coincide with the hopes and fears of the parties involved. The weather must take sides; it must be made to express its preference. Rather than attempt to discover what the weather was really like on that fateful morning in order to measure the veracity of the accounts against this "weather fact"—a task that is perhaps as impossible as it is uninteresting—what is essential is to recognize the extent to which both the North and the South try to explain their defeats in terms of the weather rather than in terms of their own acts. The events of the battle are presented as the result of natural rather than human or social causes. Even gunshot becomes naturalized as "a tempest of iron hail" that rains against the fort. Whatever nature may be within these passages, it belongs to the political, historical, and rhetorical motivations that help determine what it is.

Emerson's poem "Voluntaries" allegorizes the heroic struggle of Shaw and his regiment against the Confederate army at Fort Wagner. It commemorates the struggle as a force of persuasion, as a means of turning the "men of Northern brain" who, until this battle, had expressed suspicion concerning the black man's courage and morality. In demonstrating their courage, the soldiers of the 54th provoke a revolution in the meaning of America that proceeds under a flag whose stars are snowflakes and whose stripes are the streamers of the northern lights. If Emerson evokes the rhetoric of nature here, he does so to suggest that America now aligns itself with nature's forces. This alignment coincides with an effort to think the history and rhetoric that define our relationship to what Emerson means by nature. Emerson's reconfiguration of the American flag gathers its force from this history and rhetoric. More than once, Emerson reminds us of "the power of badges and emblems," and in particular "of the power of national emblems" (*W*, 3: 16). Men of every class, he tells us, are driven to the "use of emblems." "The schools of poets, and philosophers," he goes on to say:

are not more intoxicated with their symbols, than the populace with theirs. In our political parties, compute the power of badges and emblems. See the great ball which they roll from Baltimore to Bunker Hill! In the political processions, Lowell goes in a loom, and Lynn in a shoe, and Salem in a ship. Witness the cider-barrel, the log-cabin, the hickory-stick, the palmetto, and all the cognizances of party. See the power of national emblems. Some stars, lilies, leopards, a crescent, a lion, an eagle, or other figure, which came into credit God knows how, on an old rag of bunting, blowing in the wind, on a fort, at the ends of the earth, shall make the blood tingle under the rudest, or the most conventional exterior. The people fancy they hate poetry, and they are all poets and mystics! (*W*, 3: 16–17)

Rather than distance themselves aesthetically from the war, Emerson's "Boston Hymn" and "Voluntaries" register poetically the traces that the Civil War has left on them. The concern that each expresses over its own status as an act of representation is one and the same with its analysis of the varied cultural and political attempts to invent and enforce a particular image of America. Linking its language to the events of its time, evoking their various contexts and enacting the way in which history informs its own movement, each poem also suggests the way in which texts inform the practices of history. If these poems—with their figures, emblems, and symbols— are linked to the state's capacity to constitute, within a general network of representation, the political experience of its citizens, Emerson wishes them to reflect critically on efforts to evade the historical issues that had led to the civil crisis and to legitimize the war and its violence by recourse to the rhetoric against which the war is being fought.[81] In recalling these issues and this history, in evoking the genealogy of the rhetorics within which his listeners thought about their place within this history, these two poems encourage a rethinking of our relation to the meaning of America, to an America that would realize its founding promise of emancipation. In so doing, they take their place within a corpus of writing whose entire trajectory can be read as an insistent exploration of the conditions necessary for an experience of freedom that is also a praxis of thought. If these writings bequeath to us an inheritance that belongs to what we still call our future, they demonstrate that there can be no thought of the future which is not at the same time an engagement with the question "How shall we conduct our life?" We can only begin to answer this question, Emerson suggests, by learning to read historically, by exposing ourselves to the climates of a history to which we remain responsible because it is we who are at stake.

Reference Matter

❧ Notes

Preface

1. Robert D. Richardson, Jr., *Emerson*, 43.
2. Poirier makes this point in *Poetry and Pragmatism*, 17.

Chapter 1

1. For a brief overview and bibliography of the various myths of climate—esp. in relationship to the issue of political organization—see Johnson, "Of Differing Ages and Climes."

2. For discussions of the role that environmentalist views on racial differences played in questions of slavery and equality, see Frederickson, *The Black Image in the White Mind*, esp. chaps. 1 and 4; Horsman, *Race and Manifest Destiny*, esp. chap. 7; Jordan, *White Over Black*; Anne Norton, *Alternative Americas*, esp. chap. 6; and Stanton, *The Leopard's Spots*.

3. I am indebted here to Kevin Newmark's discussion of the relation between language and history in his *Beyond Symbolism*, 21.

4. Although they seriously consider the economic and political registers of "materialism" in Transcendentalist discourse, Parrington and Rose neglect the questions of style and forms of representation that for Emerson determine his particular form of idealism as an agency of cultural criticism. See Parrington, *The Romantic Revolution in America*, and Rose, *Transcendentalism as a Social Movement*. Although more thorough in its description of Emerson's involvement in the issues of his day, Gonnaud's *An Uneasy Solitude* also neglects the force of questions of writing within Emerson's social criticism. An exception to these readings is Bell's "The Hard Currency of Words." For a discussion of these issues in terms

of Parrington's reading of Transcendentalism, see Jay, "Hegel and the Dialectics of American Literary Historiography."

5. This is, of course, an old etymology and was well known during Emerson's time. Noah Webster, for example, tells us that "in most languages, as far as my information extends, the terms used to signify *spirit*, or the intellectual principle, are primarily the names of *breath, air, wind*." See his *Selected Works*, 183–84.

6. The origin of the wind was a serious philosophical consideration in Emerson's day. The author of the essay "Meteorology" in the July 1860 issue of *Atlantic Monthly* writes: "The origin of wind, its direction and its force, its influence on the health of man, his business, his dwelling-place, and the climate where he perpetuates his race, have attracted the profound attention of the greatest philosophers" (8).

7. Although this line is absent in the final version of the "Fortune of the Republic," which Len Gougeon and Joel Myerson include in their new, corrected edition of Emerson's antislavery writings, its inclusion in the version reprinted in the 1904 edition of Emerson's essays not only situates it in relation to the historico-political issues addressed by the lecture but also places it within the same period as the journal entry with which we are concerned.

8. See Frederickson, *The Inner Civil War*, 79.

9. See Maizlish, "Race and Politics in the Northern Democracy."

10. This point is stated again in Emerson's analogy between frost and politics. That is to say, to the extent that we go inside our homes, or inside in general, to "avoid the frost," the analogy suggests that politics, the domain of politics, can no longer be restricted to the public sphere: politics has always already touched even our most private and intimate spaces. That we go "inside" in order to avoid the frost is in fact perhaps the best indication of the frost's continued influence, of its force over us, at the very moment we would escape it. This is why, for Emerson, the person who would retreat from both the frost and the realm of politics, this person is the truly "frosty" person. Registering the inescapable influence of the frost—evoked in militaristic terms and in relation to "glaring days of pitiless cold"—the article "Snow" in the February 1862 issue of the *Atlantic Monthly* states that: "On such days life becomes a battle to all householders. . . . In innumerable armies the frost besieges the portal, creeps in beneath it and above it, and on every latch and key-handle lodges an advanced guard of white rime. . . . The sensations of such days almost make us associate their clearness and whiteness with something malignant and evil" (193). To think through the consequences of Emerson's analogy therefore requires not only a rigorous deconstruction of the

opposition between the public and the private but also a reconsideration of the notion of democracy.

11. This last worry reappears in another form in the spring of 1865 when, after reading General Grant's terms of surrender, Emerson writes in his journal: "General Grant's terms certainly look a little too easy, as foreclosing any action hereafter to convict Lee of treason, and I fear that the high tragic historic justice which the nation with severest consideration should execute, will be softened and dissipated and toasted away at dinner-tables" (*J*, 15: 459). See Allen, *Waldo Emerson*, 626–28.

12. Sundquist, "Slavery, Revolution, and the American Renaissance," 2. The literature on the issue of slavery in America is vast. Useful summaries related to the issues I discuss here can be found in: Davis, *The Problem of Slavery in the Age of Revolution*, 164–212 and 255–84, and *Slavery and Human Progress*, 231–73; Jordan, *White Over Black*; Macleod, *Slavery, Race, and the American Revolution*; Morgan, *American Slavery, American Freedom*, 293–387; and Potter, *The Impending Crisis*, 40–48. For an excellent discussion of the controversies over the constitutional basis for slavery, see Cover, *Justice Accused*. For an excellent discussion of Emerson's own complicated and diverse relation to the question of slavery, see Gougeon's comprehensive *Virtue's Hero*. See also Moody, "The Evolution of Emerson as an Abolitionist."

13. Potter, *The Impending Crisis*, 43.

14. "I have no purpose, directly or indirectly," Lincoln said in his First Inaugural Address on March 4, 1861, "to interfere with the institution of slavery in the States where it exists." See his *Collected Works*, 4: 250. Lincoln here quotes himself from his 1858 debates with Stephen Douglas.

15. Ibid., 2: 461–69. For a detailed reading of the House Divided Speech, see Fehrenbacher, *Prelude to Greatness*, 70–95. See also Sundquist, *Faulkner*, 102–5.

16. See Potter, *The Impending Crisis*, 48–49 and 51–62.

17. Lincoln, *Collected Works*, 4: 14.

18. Ibid., 4: 331–32.

19. *New York Times*, April 15, 1861; quoted in Perkins, ed., *Northern Editorials on Secession*, 2: 735. Such rhetoric concerning the northern reaction to Sumter was widespread and readily taken up by the abolitionist cause. Dr. Henry Bowditch, a Boston abolitionist, wrote, for example: "Ye gods, what a change has come over the spirit of our people since that occurrence. We had been lying as in a state of apparent listlessness. . . . Now . . . the whole North is a unit. . . . The times are ripening for a march of a liberating army into the Confederate States. If slavery is to be

the cornerstone of treason, slavery will, must be, undermined" (quoted in McPherson, *The Struggle for Equality*, 47). See also Stampp, *And the War Came*. Phillips later emphasizes the rhetorical basis of such claims when he writes, just three weeks after the Emancipation Proclamation is put into effect: "There never was a time since the commencement of the struggle when, if the North had been a unity, the war might not have been ended in three months. . . . But the North has never been a unit. With the North as a unit, democratic, intelligent, resolved, in earnest, the South never would have risked the struggle." See "The State of the Country" in his *Speeches, Lectures, and Letters* (1864), 527–28.

20. Quoted in Cabot's *A Memoir of Ralph Waldo Emerson*, 605.

21. Perkins, ed., *Northern Editorials on Secession*, 2: 796, 1065, and 771.

22. Brownson, *Works*, 17: 121; Whitman, *Complete Poetry and Collected Prose*, 428–29.

23. Cabot, *A Memoir of Ralph Waldo Emerson*, 605.

24. Ibid., 559.

25. Quoted in ibid., 600–1.

26. See Perkins, ed., *Northern Editorials on Secession*, 2: 1068.

27. The war makes man's divinity manifest: "There are scriptures written invisibly in men's hearts whose letters do not come out until they are enraged. They can be read by the light of war fires by eyes in peril" (*W*, 11: 303, and *J*, 15: 180).

28. "The Public Feeling," *Philadelphia Press*, April 16, 1861, cited in Perkins, ed., *Northern Editorials on Secession*, 2: 742.

29. See Foner, *Free Soil, Free Labor, Free Men*, esp. chaps. 3 and 4.

30. Lincoln echoes Emerson's sentiments in his House Divided Speech. There he states: "'A house divided against itself cannot stand.' I believe this government cannot endure, permanently half *slave* and half *free*. I do not expect the Union to be *dissolved*—I do not expect the house to *fall*—but I *do* expect it will cease to be divided. It will become *all* one thing, or *all* the other" (*Collected Works*, 2: 461).

31. The 1793 act provided for the enforcement of the Fugitive Slave clause of the federal Constitution (in Article IV). On the history of the Fugitive Slave Law from 1793 to the 1850s, see Cover, *Justice Accused*, 159–91. Emerson's sensitivity to the Constitution's contradictions qualifies statements he makes elsewhere concerning the revolutionary generation's commitment to liberty and freedom and raises questions about the status of his various allusions to the "authority" of the founding fathers' act of social revolution. He may admire the revolutionary efforts to free the colonies from their sense of enslavement under British rule, he may read in these efforts a figure of every attempt to proclaim the rights of

man, but he respects the legacy of revolution enough to turn it against the documents, individuals, and institutions that claim to be its guardians. What is at stake for Emerson is the possibility of what has never yet belonged to our inheritance: liberty for everyone.

32. Cover, *Justice Accused*, 210. For discussions of the slave power conspiracy, see: Phillips, *The Constitution, a Proslavery Compact*; Theodore Parker, *The Slave Power*; Davis, *The Slave Power Conspiracy and the Paranoid Style*; and Gienapp, "The Republican Party and the Slave Power." For discussions of the rhetoric of conspiracy during the American Revolution, see: Bailyn, *The Ideological Origins of the American Revolution*, esp. chap. 4; and Wood, *The Creation of the American Republic*. For a provocative reading of the place of conspiracy within American politics in general, see Rogin, *Ronald Reagan, the Movie, and Other Episodes in Political Demonology*, esp. chap. 9.

33. Douglass, *Life and Writings*, 2: 192.

34. Cf. the following journal passage on the Nebraska question: "What effrontery it required to fly in the face of what was supposed settled law & how it shows that we have no guards whatever, that there is no proposition whatever, that is too audacious to be offered us by the Southerner" (*J*, 13: 283).

35. Robinson, *Emerson and the Conduct of Life*, 124.

36. See Foner, *Free Soil, Free Labor, Free Men*, chap. 4.

37. Allen, *Waldo Emerson*, 606.

38. See Potter, *The Impending Crisis*, 517–21.

39. Quoted in ibid., 520n.

40. Lincoln's announced policies were not that different from those of the Buchanan administration. Buchanan himself carefully analyzed Lincoln's inaugural address and found in it many parallels with his own. See Buchanan's remarkable history (and defense) of his own administration in his *Mr. Buchanan's Administration on the Eve of the Rebellion*, 229–30. In retrospect, the difference between the two is, as Potter explains, "partly one of context. Buchanan's policy during his final weeks in office has been judged against the background of his proslavery behavior in the preceding four years; Lincoln's conduct during his first weeks in office has been judged against the background of all that followed in the next four years" (*The Impending Crisis*, 569).

41. Ibid., 526.

42. Quoted in McPherson, *The Struggle for Equality*, 23.

43. See Phillips's address "Lincoln's Election," in *Speeches, Lectures, and Letters* (1864), 295.

44. Allen, *Waldo Emerson*, 606.

45. Phillips, *Speeches, Lectures, and Letters* (1864), 526.

46. McPherson, *The Struggle for Equality*, 54.

47. Quoted in McPherson, *The Struggle for Equality*, 35 and 55. Although Emerson's writings of this period are often saturated with the rhetoric of the abolitionist cause and although abolitionists often cite him as an authority for their claims (e.g., see Phillips, "Progress," in *Speeches, Lectures, and Letters* [1864], 378), Emerson's relation to the abolitionist movement in general is characterized—as are his relations to any of the formal reform movements of the period—by distrust on his part. As he writes in a journal entry from his notebook "Liberty," "the friends of freedom fall out: the Abolitionists are waspish egotistical Ishmaelites" (*J*, 14: 405). See also *W*, 1: 276–81.

48. Phillips, *Speeches, Lectures, and Letters* (1864), 383.

49. Cited in Gonnaud, *An Uneasy Solitude*, 437.

50. Quoted in McPherson, *The Struggle for Equality*, 52.

51. Ibid., 123.

52. See also Emerson's statements in *J*, 15: 64, 179–80, 434, and *W*, 11: 345.

53. In "Apathy and Enthusiasm," a poem about the ambiguities of northern sentiment during the winter of 1860–61, Melville uses the figure of frost to different effect. Melville's "frost" gives voice to the fear that attends the sensed approach of the Civil War. As he writes in stanza 1: "O the clammy cold November, / And the winter white and dead, / And the terror dumb with stupor, / And the sky a sheet of lead; / And the events that came resounding / With the cry that *All was lost*, / Like the thunder-cracks of massy ice / In intensity of frost— / Bursting one upon another / Through the horror of the calm." See his *Battle-Pieces and Aspects of the War*, 41.

54. Perkins, ed., *Northern Editorials on Secession*, 2: 1070. See, in the same volume, "The Benefits of War," *Boston Saturday Evening Gazette*, May 4, 1861; "Worth All It Costs," *Albany Evening Journal*, June 1, 1861; and "A Blessing in Disguise?" *Newark Daily Mercury*, June 15, 1861 (1072, 1090, 1093).

55. *EL*, 1: 24. See also *W*, 1: 32–33.

56. That Emerson's philosophy of nature is, in essential ways, also a philosophy of war, that is, a philosophy of antagonism, conflict, or resistance, has been noted by Lopez in his "Emerson's Rhetoric of War." The potential danger of Emerson's recourse to natural metaphors in his discussions of war—the danger of naturalizing or poeticizing the progress of war or violence—needs to be evaluated in relation to the shifting status of nature in his writings: the strength of his analysis of war may in fact lie in his attempt to think the relation between the war as a reality and the

war as a figure. I will return to this point later in "Nature's Ethics" and in Chapter 3.

57. For a brief summary of Emerson's readings in natural history and natural science in the early 1830s, see *EL*, 1: 1–4.

58. On this division and on the figuration of winter landscapes in the early Republic, see Mergen, "Winter Landscape in the Early Republic." On the perceived dangers of hot climates during the colonial period, see Kupperman, "Fear of Hot Climates in the Anglo-American Colonial Experience." On environmental theories of racial and moral differences, see note 2 above.

59. Emerson insists on this complicity between the North and the slave system. "Under the Union," he writes, "I suppose the fact to be that there are really two nations, the north and the south. It is not slavery that severs them, it is climate and temperament. The south does not like the north, slavery or no slavery, and never did. The north likes the south well enough, for it knows its own advantages" (*AS*, 67).

60. See *Les bases de la météorologie dynamique*, 1: 45; cited in Middleton, *A History of the Theories of Rain*, 152.

61. *Atlantic Monthly* (January 1858), 272–73 and 279. Whitman opens his *Democratic Vistas* by associating the weather with freedom and democracy. "As the greatest lessons of Nature through the universe are perhaps the lessons of variety and freedom," he writes, "the same present the greatest lessons also in New World politics and progress." The issue of "a truly grand nationality," he goes on to say, "seems to be for general humanity much like the influences that make up, in their limitless field, that perennial health-action of the air we call the weather—an infinite number of currents and forces, and contributions, and temperatures, and cross purposes, whose ceaseless play of counterpart upon counterpart brings constant restoration and vitality" (*Complete Poetry and Collected Prose*, 929).

62. This tradition was, as Ross has argued, "established and religiously observed by Washington, Jefferson, Franklin, and thousands of other unsung weather diarists," but would also certainly reach back to the Puritan tendency to read providential omens and hints of the future in the signs of nature ("Forecasting Ideology," 117).

63. See C. C. Hazewell's "Weather in War," *Atlantic Monthly* (May 1862), 593.

64. Ross, "Forecasting Ideology," 116. See also Espy, *The Philosophy of Storms*.

65. Emerson also mentions Espy in a letter to Sumner dated January 19, 1858. See *L*, 5: 97.

66. On this point, see Ross, "Forecasting Ideology," 117 and 123; see

also Middleton, *A History of the Theories of Rain*, 160. Middleton excerpts the following passage from Espy's proposal to Congress: "Now, if masses of timber, to the amount of forty acres for every twenty miles, should be prepared and fired simultaneously every seven days in the summer, on the west of the United States, in a line of six or seven hundred miles long from north to south, then it appears highly probable from the theory, though not certain until the experiments are made, that a rain of great length, north and south, will commence on or near the line of fires; that the rain will travel towards the east side-foremost; that it will not break up until it reaches far into the Atlantic Ocean; that it will rain over the whole country east of the place of beginning; that it will rain only for a few hours at any one place, . . . that it will rain enough and not too much at any one place." Espy also claimed that the benefits provided by such a plan would cost each citizen less than one cent per year.

67. See Whitman, *Complete Poetry and Collected Prose*, 758–60.

68. *Encyclopedia Americana*, ed. Francis Leiber (Philadelphia: Carey, Lea and Carey, 1829–33), 5: 325.

69. *The Horticulturalist*, 2.2 (August 1847): 75.

70. Herman Melville, for example, brings together the philanthropic and agricultural aspects of frost in his 1854 short story "Poor Man's Pudding and Rich Man's Crumbs." In the story, the poet Blandmour—whose name already betrays the irony with which Melville regards his worn-out platitudes—explains to the story's narrator: "So, you see, the winter's snow *itself* is beneficent; under the pretense of frost—a sort of gruff philanthropist—actually warming the earth, which afterward is to be fertilizingly moistened by these gentle flakes of March" (*Great Short Works*, 167). That Melville could ironize the trope of frost in this way is evidence of its currency in the period. I am grateful to Krista Walter for having directed me to this passage.

71. See Playfair, *Illustrations of the Huttonian Theory of the Earth*, 98–101. Playfair's text is a summary of and commentary on Dr. James Hutton's two-volume *Theory of the Earth*, which appeared in 1795. Hutton's text is a study of the laws that determine the composition, dissolution, and restoration of the earth.

72. This identification between a population and the way it thinks is reinforced if we note that, in an earlier version of the journal passage with which we are concerned, Emerson had stated that the war would come to "restore intellectual and moral power" not "to these languid and dissipated populations" but "to these languid and dissipated minds" (see *J*, 15: 379–80).

73. Phillips, *Speeches, Lectures, and Letters* (1864), 543.

74. Ibid., 137.

75. In his essay "The Method of Nature," Emerson reinforces the connection he sees between thought and crystallization. He writes: "The crystal sphere of thought is as concentrical as the geological structure of the globe. As all our soils and rocks lie in strata, concentric strata, so do all men's thinking run laterally, never vertically" (*W*, 1: 195–96).

76. Although Emerson claims that in his addresses and writings, in his own acts of persuasion, he is fighting his "own campaign," he at the same time claims that "this revolution is the work of no man, but the (eternal) effervescence of nature" (*J*, 15: 415 and 405). In so doing, he figures the contradiction of the anonymous individual that characterizes the structure of American democracy. For a discussion of this issue, see Cheyfitz's analysis of the Emersonian "hero" in *The Trans-Parent*, esp. 21–35. See also Kateb's analysis of Emerson and democratic individuality in *Emerson and Self-Reliance*.

77. "Salmagundi," no. 7 (April 4, 1807), in Irving, *History, Tales, and Sketches*, 144. For a reading of America as a nation of Scripture, see Bercovitch, "The Biblical Basis of the American Myth"; see also his *The Puritan Origins of the American Self* and *The American Jeremiad*. A recent revision of Bercovitch's argument is provided by Anne Norton's *Alternative Americas* (see esp. chap. 1). Norton claims that Bercovitch slights the sectional and economic character of such scripturalism and goes on to argue against his acceptance of what she calls "the Whig account of the nation's origins" (27). The virtue of her reading lies in her remaining sensitive to the rhetorical aspect of such cultural myths of origin.

78. See: Edward G. Parker, *The Golden Age of American Oratory*; Brigance, ed., *A History and Criticism of American Public Address*; Shaw, *History of American Oratory*; Buell, *New England Literary Culture*, esp. chap. 6; Daniel Walker Howe, *The Political Culture of the American Whigs*, esp. chap. 2; and Gustafson, *Representative Words*.

79. Gustafson, *Representative Words*, 3.

80. John Quincy Adams, *Lectures on Rhetoric and Oratory*, 1: 72.

81. Howe, *The Political Culture of the American Whigs*, 27. This last point may help to explain why the study of rhetoric was generally linked in antebellum America to the study of moral philosophy and ethics.

82. Madison et al., *Federalist Papers*, 360.

83. Emerson expresses a similar sentiment in a journal entry from November 1833. There he proclaims: "Let a man under the influence of strong passion go into the fields and see how readily every thought clothes itself with a material garment" (*J*, 4: 95).

84. This passage not only seals a reference to Emerson's ambivalence

toward his older contemporary, William Wordsworth, but to Wordsworth's own efforts in "Tintern Abbey" to introduce language into nature as the "language of sense." It therefore registers the revolution in Wordsworth's development that accounts for the poet's stance toward political and social history in the aftermath of the French Revolution. For a discussion of the relation between *Nature* and "Tintern Abbey," see Michael, "Emerson's Chagrin."

85. John Adams, *Earliest Diary*, 74.

86. On the relationship between the natural law tradition and the issues of both slavery and the American Revolution, see: Cover, *Justice Accused*; Benjamin Fletcher Wright, Jr., *American Interpretations of Natural Law*; White, *The Philosophy of the American Revolution*; and Mullett, *Fundamental Law and the American Revolution*.

87. Phillips, *A Review of Lysander Spooner's Unconstitutionality of Slavery*, 3–4.

88. Cover, *Justice Accused*, 9.

89. Garrison, *Selections*, 149.

90. Gerrit Smith, letter to Henry Clay, 1839, quoted in Benjamin Fletcher Wright, Jr., *American Interpretations of Natural Law*, 214; Mann, *Slavery*, 59; Sumner, "Freedom National, Slavery Sectional," in his *Complete Works*, 276.

91. Bailyn, Introduction to *Pamphlets of the American Revolution*, 74–75.

92. Paine, *Complete Writings*, 2: 16 and 18.

93. Pease, *Visionary Compacts*, 117.

94. John Adams, *A Defense of the Constitutions of the Government of the United States of America*, excerpted in his *Political Writings*, 117. For interpretations of America as "Nature's Nation," see: Miller, *Nature's Nation*; Henry Nash Smith, *Virgin Land*; Slotkin, *Regeneration Through Violence*.

95. Calhoun, quoted in Benjamin Fletcher Wright, Jr., *American Interpretations of Natural Law*, 229.

96. Ibid.

97. On this point, see Faust, *A Sacred Circle* and *The Ideology of Slavery*.

98. Pease, *Visionary Compacts*, 118.

99. For a discussion of this passage in relation to Emerson's addresses on the Fugitive Slave Law, see Cavell, "Emerson's Constitutional Amending: Reading 'Fate.'"

100. Emerson, *Emerson in His Journals*, 38.

101. See esp. West, *The American Evasion of Philosophy*, 28–35, and Nicoloff, *Emerson on Race and History*.

102. In a journal entry entitled "The Sad Side of the Negro Question," for example, Emerson points to the racism that can be found even in the abolition movement. He writes: "The abolitionist (theoretical) wishes to abolish Slavery, but because he wishes to abolish the black man. He considers that it is violence, brute force, which, counter to intellectual rule, holds property in man; but he thinks the negro himself the very representative & exponent of that brute base force; that it is the negro in the white man which holds slaves" (*Selected Writings*, 158–59).

103. The courage to assume this risk is what helps to characterize Emerson's doctrine of self-reliance. In a famous formulation, he writes: "A foolish consistency is the hobgoblin of little minds, adored by little statesmen and philosophers and divines. With consistency a great soul has simply nothing to do. He may as well concern himself with his shadow on the wall. Speak what you think now in hard words and to-morrow speak what to-morrow thinks in hard words again, though it contradict every thing you said to-day.—'Ah, so you shall be sure to be misunderstood.'—Is it so bad then to be misunderstood? Pythagoras was misunderstood, and Socrates, and Jesus, and Luther, and Copernicus, and Galileo, and Newton, and every pure and wise spirit that ever took flesh. To be great is to be misunderstood" (*W*, 2: 57–58).

104. I am indebted in my formulation here to Jacques Derrida's analysis of the issues of complicity and collaboration in his *Of Spirit*, 39–40.

105. Hume, *A Treatise of Human Nature*, 542–43. On Emerson's relation to Hume, see: Michael, *Emerson and Skepticism*, esp. chap. 2; Whicher, *Freedom and Fate*, esp. chap. 1; and Packer, *Emerson's Fall*, esp. chap. 4.

106. On this point, see Cover, *Justice Accused*, 29–30.

107. Emerson recirculates a variant of this passage in his 1854 address on the Fugitive Slave Law. This variant is not included in the Centenary Edition of his works. For the full text see *AS*, 82.

108. For a discussion of the colonial use of the metaphors of "the heart and the head, emotions and ideas, passions and politics" in pamphlets on the "beauties of liberty," see Gustafson, *Representative Words*, 222.

109. Cf. on this point Thomas, *Cross-Examinations of Law and Literature*, 236.

110. For a clear and forceful elaboration of this point, see Derrida's Afterword to the republication of *Limited Inc*. There Derrida explains: "This *particular* undecidable opens the field of decision or of decidability. It calls for decision in the order of ethical-political responsibility. It is even its necessary condition. A decision can only come into being in a

space that exceeds the calculable program that would destroy all responsibility by transforming it into a programmable effect of determinate
causes. There can be no moral or political responsibility without this trial
and this passage by way of the undecidable" (116).

111. See Robinson, *Emerson and the Conduct of Life*, 156.

112. In his *Aesthetics*, Hegel, perhaps the greatest Romantic philosopher, associates frost with allegory. He writes: "It is therefore rightly said
of allegory that it is frosty and cold [*frostig und kahl*]" (1: 399).

113. That Emerson was thinking about Coleridge's *Ancient Mariner*
at this time is made clear in a letter to Frederick Henry Hedge, dated
June 25, 1835, approximately one month before the journal entry in
question. There Emerson tells Hedge that he has begun working on a
lecture for the American Institute of Instruction "on the means of inspiring taste for English Literature" (*L*, 1: 447). The final version of this
lecture, delivered on August 20, refers explicitly to Coleridge's poem. "A
good book," Emerson writes, "is like the Ancient Mariner who can tell
his tale only to a few men destined to hear it" (*EL*, 1: 214).

114. For the description of Life-in-Death, see Coleridge, *Poetical
Works*, 194. For the citations from Reed, see his *Romantic Weather*, 155.
The chapter from which these citations are taken has been adapted and
published as Reed, "The Mariner Rimed."

115. In his "Immortality Ode," for example—a poem that would
play a central role in Emerson's *Nature*—Wordsworth writes "custom
lies upon thee with a weight,/Heavy as frost, and deep almost as life!"
(*Poetical Works*, 1: 23). This association between frost and different forms
of slavery extends to the American Romantics as well. I think in particular of John Whittier's "Snow-Bound" (itself indebted to Emerson's
"Snow-Storm"), Thoreau's "Pond in Winter," and Hawthorne's "The
Snow-Image."

116. See, for example *J*, 1: 68–69, 305; 3: 14, 104; 15: 175–76.
Although Emerson early on dismissed Shelley as "stiff and academical,"
he continued to read him on Margaret Fuller's insistence. In a journal
entry from 1841, Emerson suggests that, even though he is still unaf-
fected by Shelley, Shelley's "power is so manifest over a large class of the
best persons, that he is not to be overlooked" (*J*, 8: 61). Six years later, in
1847, Emerson claims that it is Shelley's "merit of timeliness" (*J*, 10: 75)
that accounts for his popularity. This comment takes on special significance when we recall that "Hellas" is one of the few poems Shelley wrote
that explicitly addresses contemporary events. Moreover, Aeschylus' *The
Persians*, the play whose stagecraft served as a model for Shelley's drama,
is perhaps unique among the extant Greek tragedies because it drama-

tizes nearly contemporary history instead of old legends. It is not unlikely that the "merit" Emerson finally came to see in Shelley's work may have had something to do with Shelley's capacity to transpose his doctrines of spirit and nature into a specific historical context.

117. Cited in Edward Everett's review of A. Coray's edition of *The Ethics of Aristotle*, *North American Review* 41 (October 1823): 415.

118. Ibid., 417 and 422.

119. See "The Revolution in Greece" in Daniel Webster, *Works*, 3: 62–63, 76, and 84. For a discussion of the events that led up to this speech, see Baxter, *One and Inseparable*, 99–104.

120. See Shelley, *Poetry and Prose*, 407. Subsequent references to Shelley's "Hellas" are to this edition unless otherwise noted and will be accompanied in the text by line numbers.

121. Wasserman, *Shelley*, 375 and 403.

122. Locke, *Two Treatises of Government*, 145; Paine, *Common Sense*, 120; Whitman, "Starting from Paumanok," in *Complete Poetry and Collected Prose*, 187.

123. Anne Norton, *Alternative Americas*, 1.

124. Shelley, *Poetry and Prose*, 409.

125. Shelley, "A Discourse on the Manners of the Ancients, Relative to the Subject of Love," in *Complete Works*, 7: 226. I am grateful to Jerrold Hogle for referring me to this essay, as well as for various conversations we have shared about Shelley.

126. See Webster, "The Revolution in Greece," in *Works*, 3: 61; and Everett, review of A. Coray's edition of *The Ethics of Aristotle*, *North American Review* 41 (October 1823): 422. Emerson's recognition of America's debt to Greek thought and forms is evident throughout his writings. A passage that is particularly pertinent to Shelley's poem can be found in his essay "History." He writes: "What is the foundation of that interest all men feel in Greek history, letters, art and poetry, in all its periods, from the heroic or Homeric age, down to the domestic life of the Athenians and Spartans, four or five centuries later? What but this, that every man passes personally through a Grecian period. The attraction of these manners is, that they belong to man, and are known to every man in virtue of his being once a child; besides that there are always individuals who retain these characteristics. A person of childlike genius and inborn energy is still a Greek, and revives our love of the muse of Hellas" (*W*, 2: 23–24 and 26). Although this essay was not published until 1841, these passages had already appeared in his earlier lecture "Manners" (see *EL*, 2: 134–46).

127. See Davis, *Slavery and Human Progress*, 23–26.

128. Aristotle's famous defense of slavery as a natural institution indispensable for the well-being of the household and the polis can be found in his *Politics*, 1253bl–1255bl.

129. Quoted in Davis, *Slavery and Human Progress*, 111. Emerson was familiar with Heeren's writings and owned his *Reflections on the Politics of Ancient Greece*. See Harding, *Emerson's Library*, 130. See also *L*, 2: 154, 158, 174–175, and 4: 185.

130. Shelley, *Complete Works*, 7: 10.

131. Ibid., 225.

132. Ibid., 227.

133. I am indebted in my reading of this declaration to Derrida's reading of the performative nature of America's Declaration of Independence in "Déclarations d'Indépendance."

134. Shelley, *Complete Works*, 7: 227.

135. Ibid., 11. For Paine's anticipation of this point, see his *Rights of Man*, 207: "One of the greatest improvements that has been made for the perpetual security and progress of constitutional liberty, is the provision which the new constitutions make for occasionally revising, altering, and amending them."

136. Cf. on this point Warner's discussion of the American innovations in written constitutions in *The Letters of the Republic*, esp. chap. 4.

137. Paine, *Rights of Man*, 187.

138. This is particularly true for Paine, who sees the creative potential of language in its capacity to define and perpetuate political relations. John Quincy Adams seems to recognize this understanding of the revolutionary character of language when he writes, discussing Paine's claim that England had no constitution: "Of course there never was a people that had a constitution, previous to the year 1776. But the word with an idea affixed to it, had been in use, and commonly understood, for centuries before that period, and therefore Mr. Pain must, to suit his purpose, alter its acceptations, and in the warmth of his zeal for revolutions, endeavor to bring about a revolution in language also" (John Quincy Adams, *Answer to Pain's Rights of Man*, 10; cited in Olivia Smith, *The Politics of Language*, 45). I will discuss Emerson's relation to Paine in greater detail in Chapter 2, in relation to the opening of *Nature*.

139. Noah Webster, "Government," 139; cited in Wood, *The Creation of the American Republic*, 379.

140. Shelley, "A Discourse on the Manners of the Ancients," *Complete Works*, 7: 226.

141. Gustafson, *Representative Words*, 7.

142. See: Bailyn, *The Ideological Origins of the American Revolution*, 1–

21 and 175–98; Wood, *The Creation of the American Republic*, 128–32; and Gustafson, *Representative Words*, esp. parts I and II.

143. Cited in Simpson, *The Politics of American English*, 30.

144. Madison, *Letters and Other Writings*, 3: 442.

145. "The Union and the State," *North American Review* (1833), 245.

146. Several recent studies of the theories and practices of American language have focused on the history of this relation between language and politics. The most comprehensive of these is Gustafson, *Representative Words*, from which I have drawn some of my examples. In addition, see: Gura, *The Wisdom of Words*; Simpson, *The Politics of American English*; Cmiel, *Democratic Eloquence*; and Kramer, *Imagining Language in America*.

147. Wood, *The Creation of the American Republic*, 185.

148. Samuel Williams, *History of Vermont*, 342; cited in ibid., 596.

149. Paine, *Rights of Man*, 178.

150. Wood, *Representation in the American Revolution*, 1.

151. Madison et al., *The Federalist Papers*, 386.

152. The phrase "spirit of *locality*" is Madison's. See Wood, *The Creation of the American Republic*, 195.

153. Madison et al., *The Federalist Papers*, 78–79.

154. For Madison's definition, see *The Federalist Papers*, 78: "By a faction I understand a number of citizens, whether amounting to a majority or minority of the whole, who are united and actuated by some common impulse of passion, or of interest, adverse to the rights of other citizens, or to the permanent and aggregate interests of the community."

155. Rousseau, *The Social Contract*, 101.

156. Noah Webster, "Government," 141; cited in Wood, *The Creation of the American Republic*, 377.

157. *The Farmer Refuted: or, A More Impartial and Comprehensive View of the Dispute Between Great Britain and the Colonies, Intended as a Further Vindication of the Congress* (New York: James Rivington, 1775), 7; cited in Gustafson, *Representative Words*, 141.

158. Gustafson, *Representative Words*, 24–25.

Chapter 2

1. Nietzsche, "On Truth and Lie in an Extra-Moral Sense," 84.

2. On this point, see Kronick, *American Poetics of History*, 1.

3. Theodore Parker, "The Writings of Ralph Waldo Emerson," 28–29 and 34.

4. Fuller, "Emerson's Essays," 194.

5. The phrase "hymn to power" is Holland's. See his "Authority, Power, and Form," 5.

6. Pease, *Visionary Compacts*, 207.

7. Ibid., 222.

8. Marx, *The Eighteenth Brumaire of Louis Bonaparte*, 103–4. I am indebted in the following comments to Derrida's recent reading of this passage in *Specters of Marx*, 108–11.

9. I am indebted here to Riddel's discussion of a similar point in "Emerson and the 'American' Signature," 55.

10. Anne Norton, *Alternative Americas*, 27.

11. See: Middlekauff, *The Mathers*; Bercovitch, *The Puritan Origins of the American Self* and *The American Jeremiad*; Miller, *The New England Mind* and *Errand into the Wilderness*.

12. See Bercovitch, *The American Jeremiad*, 9 and 16.

13. For analyses of the contradictions in the Puritan errand—contradictions between New England as a new place and as an extension of the old country, between the elect community as church and as nation, between the Calvinist call for purity and the Calvinist expectation of worldly responsibility—see Miller, *The New England Mind* and "Errand into the Wilderness," in *Errand into the Wilderness*, 1–15; see also Morgan, *The Puritan Dilemma* and *Visible Saints*.

14. See Scobey, "Revising the Errand," 24.

15. For a discussion of some of these appropriations, see Gustafson, *Representative Words*, 351–52; and Pease, *Visionary Compacts*, 213–16. As Gustafson rightly notes, "to compose his theory of language in *Nature* Emerson creates abstractions from concrete references to the practice of American political oratory" (352). Much of what follows in this chapter will be an effort to demonstrate this claim.

16. Daniel Webster, "The Bunker Hill Monument," in *Works*, 1: 59–62 and 77–78. Webster had long had an interest in the battle of Bunker Hill and had in fact already expressed many of his views on its significance to American society and government in a review of Henry Dearborn's *Account of the Battle of Bunker Hill*, written for the July 1818 issue of the *North American Review*, 225–58.

17. On this point, see Porter, *Seeing and Being*, 72.

18. I am indebted here to Dylan Ford's discussion of Webster's speech in his unpublished essay "Body Politics and the Nation's Insinuations."

19. Rogin, *Subversive Genealogy*, 34. For an excellent discussion of Emerson's relation to Webster, particularly in terms of their respective views on economic issues of the period, see Porter, *Seeing and Being*, 74–90.

20. Daniel Webster, "The First Settlement of New England," *Works*, 1: 23. This is one of Webster's best-known orations. In the speech, he explores the foundations of Puritanism in the New World, the history of its expansion, and its effects on American society and government. As in his Bunker Hill speech, he encourages us to revere the past. Emerson's library included both speeches in a single, bound volume published by Cummings, Hilliard. See Harding, *Emerson's Library*, 294.

21. On the way in which familial rhetoric was assimilated into various efforts to justify the emergence of "impersonal" institutions in nineteenth-century America, see: Rogin, *Fathers and Children*, esp. chaps. 1 and 8; Rothman, *The Discovery of the Asylum*; and Anne Norton, *Alternative Americas*, 39–45. "The family image in asylums, factories, and plantations," Rogin claims, "suggested patriarchy; it did not describe a complexly related, fraternal extended family. The new paternalism disguised exploitation" (*Fathers and Children*, 273).

22. Rogin, *Subversive Genealogy*, 35.

23. Porter, *Seeing and Being*, 79. In what follows, I am indebted to Porter's account of "Emerson's America" in her third chapter.

24. On this point, see Pease, *Visionary Compacts*, 214. Emerson's admiration for the power of Webster's rhetoric is well known, but early on Emerson worried about the effects of this rhetoric, about its capacity to overinfluence us. As he writes in a journal entry from December 21, 1834: "Who says we are not chained? He lies. See how greedily you accept the verse of Homer or Shakspear; the outline of M. Angelo; the strain of Handel; the word of Webster; how thoroughly you understand and make them your own; and are well assured, too, that they are only units from an infinite store of the same kinds. Well, now put out your own hands and take one more unit thence. I say you are chained" (*J*, 4: 365). He makes the same point in September 1836, the month of *Nature*'s publication. "I dislike the gruff jacobin manners of our village politicians," he states, "but I reconcile myself to them by the reflection that Genius hurts us by its excessive influence, hurts the freedom & inborn faculty of the individual: &, if Webster, Everett, Channing, yea Plato & Shakspear, found such cordial adorers in the populace as in the scholars, no more Platos & Shakspears could arise" (*J*, 5: 216–17).

25. Gilmore makes this point more generally when he suggests that Emerson and his contemporaries worked "to liberate the rhetoric of the Revolution from its current function of reinforcing political loyalty" ("Eulogy as Symbolic Biography," 155).

26. As Emerson writes in a journal entry of 1834: "What is a man but a Congress of nations? Just suppose for one moment to appear before

him the whole host of his ancestors. All have vanished; he—the insulated result of all that character, activity, sympathy, antagonism working for ages in all corners of the earth—alone remains. Such is his origin; well was his nurture less compound. Who and what has not contributed something to make him that he is? Art, science, institutions, black men, white men, the vices and the virtues of all people, the gallows, the church, the shop, poets, nature, joy, and fear, all help all teach him" (*J*, 4: 351–52). He makes this point more succinctly elsewhere when he tells us: "Pray don't read American. Thought is of no country" (*J*, 12: 40).

27. Paine, *Complete Writings*, 2: 1480.

28. Emerson's use of Paine against Webster here has its cinematic version in Woody Allen's *Annie Hall*. While Allen and Diane Keaton wait in line for a movie, Allen overhears a New York University professor of communication explain the theories of Marshall McLuhan. Unable to listen without irritation, he confronts the professor and tells him that he doesn't understand McLuhan at all. As the professor insists on his qualifications, Allen steps away and brings back McLuhan, who has been waiting in the wings and who tells the professor that he knows nothing about his theories. Like Allen, Emerson evokes Paine in order to tell Webster that, in arguing for dependence and obedience, he really knows nothing about the value of independence for which the founding fathers fought.

29. Paine, *Rights of Man*, 196.

30. On this point, see Thompson, *The Making of the English Working Class*, 90–95.

31. Foner, *Tom Paine and Revolutionary America*, 264.

32. Emerson's half-uncle, Samuel Ripley, had once warned Emerson of just this attraction. After Emerson delivered his "Divinity School Address," Ripley asked him not to publish the address, for fear that he might then be associated with "the notorious atheist" Paine. See Allen, *Waldo Emerson*, 320.

33. Porter, *Seeing and Being*, 59.

34. Porte, *Representative Man*, 77. For an extended reading of Emerson's reading of the Fall, see Packer, *Emerson's Fall*.

35. For an excellent summary and analysis of Emerson's relation to German biblical criticism, see Packer, "Origin and Authority," 67–92. See also: Grusin, *Transcendental Hermeneutics*, esp. chaps. 1 and 2; Kalinevitch, "Turning from the Orthodox"; and Ellison, *Emerson's Romantic Style*, 61–66 and 104–13.

36. For the influence of German biblical studies in New England, see Jerry Wayne Brown, *The Rise of Biblical Criticism in America*, esp. chaps. 1 and 2. For discussions of the relation of biblical criticism to Ro-

manticism in general, see Shaffer, *Coleridge, "Kubla Khan," and the Fall of Jerusalem*.

37. For discussions of the deist movement in America, as well as of its European backgrounds, see: Morais, *Deism in Eighteenth-Century America*; May, *The Enlightenment in America*; and Reventlow, *The Authority of the Bible and the Rise of the Modern World*. For discussions of Paine's, Franklin's, and Jefferson's relationship to this tradition, see Philip S. Foner's biographical introduction to Paine, *The Age of Reason*, 7–42; Aldridge, *Benjamin Franklin and Nature's God*; Breitwieser, *Cotton Mather and Benjamin Franklin*, esp. 171–204; and Eugene R. Sheridan's Introduction to Jefferson, *Extracts from the Gospels*, 3–42.

38. See Foner, *Tom Paine and Revolutionary America*, 256.

39. Paine, *Complete Writings*, 2: 727. This passage opens Paine's famous letter to Thomas Erskine, who had in 1792 defended Paine's right to publish his *Rights of Man* but who in 1797 led the prosecution of Thomas Williams, a London publisher and bookseller accused by the Society for the Suppression of Vice and Immorality with printing a copy of *The Age of Reason*.

40. For discussions of Paine's thought during this time, see: Foner, *Tom Paine and Revolutionary America*, esp. chap. 7; Conway, *The Life of Thomas Paine*, 2: 181–222; and Aldridge, *Man of Reason*, 229–48.

41. This point becomes one of the strongest articulations between Paine and Emerson. Paine's statement in "The Author's Profession of Faith," which opens *The Age of Reason*, that "my own mind is my own church" (*AR*, 50) has its counterpart, for example, in Emerson's claim that "every man makes his own religion, his own God" (*J*, 3: 179).

42. For a discussion of the way in which Emerson and the Romantics shifted the source of inspiration from the Bible to Nature, see Bercovitch, "Emerson the Prophet."

43. Emerson's sensitivity to Paine's point may have been accentuated by Coleridge's similar suggestion in his *On the Constitution of the Church and State*. There, Coleridge writes: "the idea of an ever-originating social contract, this is so certain and so indispensable, that it constitutes the whole ground of the difference between subject and serf, between a commonwealth and a slave-plantation. And this, again, is evolved out of the yet higher idea of person, in contra-distinction from thing—all social law and justice being grounded on the principle, that a person can never, but by his own fault, become a thing, or, without grievous wrong, be treated as such" (15). For Coleridge's response to Paine, see his *Lectures on Revealed Religion*.

44. As Fliegelman has suggested, the American Revolution was a

"revolution against patriarchal authority—a revolution in the understanding of the nature of authority that affected all aspects of eighteenth-
century culture" and that "was not confined to America" (*Prodigals and
Pilgrims*, 5).

45. Franklin, *The New England Courant*, n.p.

46. Paine, *Rights of Man*, 41–42.

47. If Emerson's strategy is to appropriate and then mobilize against
Webster the critical potential of texts such as Paine's and Franklin's, he
does not leave these texts untouched either. He may claim, in a journal
entry from September 1836 (the month of *Nature*'s appearance), that
"Paine and the infidels began with good intentions" (*J*, 5: 202), but he
nevertheless sees their reliance on principles of reason as the beginning
of their end. Although these writers question the reliability and authority
of scriptural revelation, they fail to question their own belief in reason as
"the most formidable weapon against errors of any kind" (*AR*, 49). They
fail to recognize that reason itself grounds the religious or patriarchal
forms they so decidedly wish to undo. As Tannenbaum argues, although
the higher criticism regarded the Bible as poetic, deists were "in essential
agreement about the authority of reason" (*Biblical Tradition in Blake's
Early Prophecies*, 14).

48. See Porte, *Representative Man*, 76.

49. Ibid., 78.

50. In his book *Ralph Waldo Emerson*, Oliver Wendell Holmes refers
to *Nature* as "the Book of Revelation of our Saint Radulphus" (103).

51. Daniel Webster, "The Bunker Hill Monument," in *Works*, 1: 70.

52. Ford, "Body Politics and the Nation's Insinuations," unpublished ms.

53. Douglass, *Life and Writings*, 2: 188.

54. I am indebted here to Homer O. Brown's discussion of similar
issues in his "Tristram to the Hebrews."

55. Emerson could have drawn this point from a number of different
sources, including his readings in the German biblical criticism. But two
specific passages come to mind, with which he would have been very
familiar. The first is from Coleridge's *On the Constitution of Church and
State*. In the section "The Idea of the Christian Church," Coleridge
writes: "as the mistaking of symbols and analogies for metaphors . . . has
been a main occasion and support of the worst errors in Protestantism;
so the understanding the same symbols in a literal *i.e. phaenomenal* sense,
notwithstanding the most earnest warnings against it, the most express
declarations of the folly and danger of interpreting *sensually* what was
delivered of objects *super*-sensual—this was the rank wilding, on which

'the prince of this world,' the lust of power and worldly aggrandizement, was enabled to graft, one by one, the whole branchery of papal superstition and imposture" (120). The second is from Shelley's "A Philosophical View of Reform": "From the dissolution of the Roman Empire, that vast and successful scheme for the enslaving of the most civilized portion of mankind, to the epoch of the present year, have succeeded a series of schemes, on a smaller scale, operating to the same effect. Names borrowed from the life; and opinions of Jesus Christ were employed as symbols of domination and imposture; and a system of liberty and equality (for such was the system preached by that great Reformer) was perverted to support oppression.—Not his doctrines, for they are too simple and direct to be susceptible of such perversion—but the mere names" (*Complete Works*, 7: 5).

56. As Emerson suggests in "Quotation and Originality," this alterity—always present in one form or another—can never be overcome: "it is as difficult to appropriate the thoughts of others, as it is to invent. Always some steep transition, some sudden alteration of temperature, or of point of view, betrays the foreign interpolation" (*W*, 8: 183).

57. Allen, *Waldo Emerson*, 186.

58. I am indebted in the reading that follows to Hamacher's essay on Hegel's reading of the Lord's Supper, "The Reader's Supper."

59. On this point see ibid., 59.

60. Cited in Richardson, *Emerson*, 17.

61. Cf. *J*, 3: 318, and 4: 380.

62. Andrews Norton, "On the Divinity School Address," 9.

63. Andrews Norton, *A Statement of Reasons for Not Believing the Doctrines of Trinitarians*, 162. For a discussion of Norton's various attacks of Emerson, see Gura, *The Wisdom of Words*, esp. chaps. 1 and 3.

64. Porte, *Representative Man*, 119.

65. Although not directly interested in the issue of Emerson's political dimension, Kronick's discussion of the relationship among nature, language, and history in his *American Poetics of History* is helpful here.

66. Theodore Parker, "The Writings of Ralph Waldo Emerson," 34.

67. Whitman, "Emerson's Books (The Shadows of Them)," in *Complete Poetry and Collected Prose*, 1053.

68. In Emerson, *The Correspondence of Emerson and Carlyle*, 371.

69. Ibid., 373.

70. Nietzsche, *Human, All Too Human*, 290.

71. Nietzsche—still, today, one of Emerson's best readers—lends credence to this point in a fragment from his notebooks, written during the composition of his *Gay Science*, a book which takes its title from a

phrase in Emerson's essay "Poetry and Imagination" (see *W*, 8: 37). Speaking of Emerson, he writes, "the author who has been richest in ideas [*gedankenreichste*] in this century so far has been an American (unfortunately clouded over by German philosophy—frosted glass)." See *Nachgelassene Fragmente: 1880–1882*, 602. There would be much to say about this passage in relation to the metaphorics of frost that have traversed this reading, especially as that metaphor reappears within, say, Norton's attacks against Emerson for his alignment with various German forms of philosophical "infidelity."

72. See Porte, *Representative Man*, 116–17; and Ellison, *Emerson's Romantic Style*, 110.

73. Porte, *Representative Man*, 117.

74. For a discussion of the relation between Frost and Emerson, see Conrad Wright, "Emerson, Barzillai Frost, and the Divinity School Address," in his *The Liberal Christians*, 41–61.

75. Firkins, *Ralph Waldo Emerson*, 163. Wright suggests that the viciousness of the attack on Frost may be due to Emerson's viewing him as the lifeless and "benighted preacher" he himself might have become had he not left the ministry in 1832. "Part of the extraordinary vehemence of his reaction to Frost's theology," he writes, "may well have stemmed from the fact that he was condemning a part of his earlier self" (*The Liberal Christians*, 47).

Chapter 3

1. Cf. Timothy Sweet, *Traces of War*, esp. 1–10.

2. See ibid., 165.

3. Lincoln, *Collected Works*, 6: 408.

4. My summary of the debates over emancipation is throughout indebted to McPherson, *The Struggle for Equality*, esp. chaps. 3–5.

5. *Douglass' Monthly*, September 1861.

6. The Washington Lecture Association was one of the most effective of these organizations, perhaps because of its location in the nation's capital. The association sponsored more than twenty lectures in the hall of the Smithsonian Institution during the winter. Emerson's speech "American Civilization" was delivered within this series.

7. *The Liberator*, September 26, 1862; cited in McPherson, *The Struggle for Equality*, 119. Although always for total and immediate abolition, Garrison as late as the fall of 1861 had written a widely circulated petition in which he urged Congress to decree abolition under the war power but also recommended giving fair compensation to *loyal* masters

"as a conciliatory measure, and to facilitate an amicable adjustment of difficulties" (McPherson, *The Struggle for Equality*, 93). The petition, although resisted by some because of the inclusion of compensation, was nevertheless signed by most abolitionists. This is another indication of the difficult contradictions so pervasive within the rhetoric of abolition, as well as within any of the efforts to confront the incalculability of the war's outcome.

8. Emerson had been arguing for emancipation as early as the fall of 1861. In January 1862, in "American Civilization," a lecture he delivered before the Smithsonian Institution in Washington, D.C., he proclaimed its immediate necessity: "If the American people hesitate, it is not for want of warning or advice. The telegraph has been swift enough to announce our disasters. The journals have not suppressed the extent of the calamity. . . . We cannot but remember that there have been days in American history, when, if the free states had done their duty, slavery had been blocked by an immovable barrier, and our recent calamities forever precluded. The free states yielded, and every compromise was surrender and invited new demands. Here again is a new occasion which heaven offers to sense and virtue. It looks as if we held the fate of the fairest possession of mankind in our hands, to be saved by our firmness or to be lost by hesitation. Emancipation is the demand of civilization. That is a principle; everything else is an intrigue. . . . Congress can, by edict, as a part of the military defense which it is the duty of Congress to provide, abolish slavery" (*W*, 11: 300, 303–5). With Lincoln's pronouncement of his preliminary Proclamation, however, Emerson, along with other abolitionists who had criticized Lincoln for hesitating to support such an act, chooses to praise the act in order to help see it through. Given the exigencies of the moment, he temporarily puts aside his doubts for the sake of winning support for the Proclamation. Finding himself in a similar position as he speaks on the "Emancipation of the British West Indies," he explains that although "there are other comparisons and other imperative duties which come sadly to mind . . . I do not wish to darken the hours of this day by crimination; I turn gladly to the rightful theme, to the bright aspects of the occasion" (*AS*, 26).

9. See Davis, *Slavery and Human Progress*, 268–70; and Litwack, *Been in the Storm So Long*, 64–103, 169.

10. For a summary of the reactions to Emerson's reading, see the January 8, 1863, issue of *The Liberator* and the February 1863 issue of *Douglass' Monthly*.

11. For an account of the role and place of the jeremiad sermon form within black rhetoric, see Howard-Pitney, *The Afro-American Jeremiad*.

12. See: Bercovitch, *The American Jeremiad* and *The Puritan Origins of the American Self*; Hatch, *The Sacred Cause of Liberty*; and Elliott, *Power and the Pulpit in Puritan New England*.

13. See Gura, *A Glimpse of Sion's Glory*, 215–16.

14. On this point, see ibid., esp. part 2. I am indebted in what follows to Gura's discussion of the evolution of this myth during the first two decades of the settlement.

15. In late summer 1860, Emerson cites a passage from a letter of Humboldt to Varnhagen von Ense in his journal. The passage is already a citation, and I cite it here because it serves as a source for the first line that God speaks to the Pilgrims: "God getting tired of Kings. Antonio Perez quotes a wise counsellor of Philip II, who said to him, 'Should God once get tired of monarchies, he will give another form to the political world'" (*J*, 14: 356). It is rather unusual for God to be speaking in the form of a jeremiad, but, as this citation makes clear, God is not speaking in his own voice. In fact, one of the main questions within the "Hymn" is precisely what gets said in the name of God.

16. Gura, *A Glimpse of Sion's Glory*, 7.

17. On the heterogeneity that characterized the colony's religious life, see: Gura, *A Glimpse of Sion's Glory*, esp. chaps. 6 and 8; Rutman, *American Puritanism* and *Winthrop's Boston*; and Stoever, *"A Faire and Easie Way to Heaven."* Each of these writers in one way or another challenges Perry Miller's conclusions about the existence of a unified body of thought called "American Puritanism." As Gura suggests, "A full understanding of seventeenth-century New England Puritanism depends on an acknowledgement that many of those who migrated to America did not share a fixed ideology or commitment to an agreed-upon ecclesiastical program as much as a common spiritual hunger and a disenchantment with the Church of England's refusal to address the nation's spiritual famine" (*A Glimpse of Sion's Glory*, 8).

18. Although in his speech "The President's Proclamation" Emerson links the Proclamation to the Declaration of Independence, his omission here is perhaps not without significance. More than once Emerson points to the ambiguities within a declaration that pretends to speak for everyone but in truth speaks only for a limited few. Neither the South's declaration of independence by secession nor the revolutionaries' declaration of independence from British rule made provisions for the independence of the black man.

19. As Davis explains, "Early expansionists like William Gilmore Simms had hailed black slavery as 'the medium & great agent for rescuing and recovering to freedom & civilization all the vast tracts of Texas, Mexico, & c.'" (*Slavery and Human Progress*, 271).

20. To use the motion of the planets as a metaphor for one's fidelity to the Law was pervasive during the seventeenth and eighteenth centuries in both England and America and corresponds to the attempt to join the tenets of theology with those emerging from Newtonian and Keplerian physics. As Emerson notes in his sermon "Astronomy": "the science of astronomy has had an irresistible effect in modifying and enlarging the doctrines of theology. . . . Cheered by these results we come to feel that planet gravitates to planet and star attracts star, each fulfilling the last mile of its orbit as surely in the round of space as the bee which launches forth for the first time from its dark cell into light, and wandering amidst flowers all day, comes back at eve with unerring wing to the hive. It is the same invisible guide that pilots the bee and pilots the planet, that established the whole and perfected the parts, that giveth to all beauty, and order, and life, and usefulness. And thus I say, my friends, that to the human race the discoveries have reconciled the greatness to the greatness of the mind" (*Young Emerson Speaks*, 173, 176). The planetary metaphor goes back at least to Milton, who, in *The Reason of Church Government*, in a discussion of the freedom consequent upon reading the Gospels, claims that man may therefore become "as it were an invariable Planet of joy and felicity" (186). See also Breitwieser, *Cotton Mather and Benjamin Franklin*, 33–34; and Lowance, *The Language of Canaan*.

21. For example, stanzas 13 and 16 come directly from the opening of "American Civilization." There, Emerson writes: "Use, labor of each for all, is the health and virtue of all beings. *Ich dien*, I serve, is a truly royal motto. And it is the mark of nobleness to volunteer the lowest service, the greatest spirit only attaining to humility. Nay, God is God because he is the servant of all . . . now here comes this conspiracy of slavery,—they call it an institution, I call it a destitution . . . standing on this doleful experience, these people have endeavored to reverse the natural sentiments of mankind, and to pronounce labor disgraceful, and the well-being of a man to consist in eating the fruit of other men's labor. Labor: a man coins himself into his labor; turns his day, his strength, his thought, his affection into some product which remains as the visible sign of his power; and to protect that . . . is the object of all government" (*W*, 11: 297). Stanzas 16–18 are indebted to "The Emancipation of the British West Indies" and "American Slavery" (*W*, 11: 125–26, 145, 469). For stanza 18, see also "American Civilization" (*W*, 11: 310–11). Stanza 22 is indebted to "The Celebration of the Intellect" (*W*, 12: 119, 121). Other references are perhaps less direct, although one can hear echoes of "Self-Reliance," "The American Scholar," and "Over-Soul" in stanzas 14–15 and 17.

22. Cf. the following passage from Emerson's "Over-Soul": "When

we have broken our god of tradition, and ceased from our god of rhetoric, then may God fire the heart with his presence" (*W*, 2: 292).

23. Cited in McPherson, *The Struggle for Equality*, 65.

24. Conway, *The Rejected Stone*, 23–24.

25. Ibid., 110. No doubt the situation was more complex and difficult than Conway wished it to be. As Anne Norton notes: "When the South seceded, declaring its independence of the Union, those who disputed the legality of the act, Lincoln among them, named their independence mere rebellion. But Lincoln knew, as much as any other man, that there could no longer be mere rebellion in America. The nation's revolutionary origins had granted all such popular upheavals a kinship with creative authority. The Rebellion had at least a family resemblance to the Revolution. . . . Confederates engaged in the active emulation of that enterprise recognized that this aspect of reenactment brought not merely legitimacy, but grandeur and sanctity to their cause" (*Alternative Americas*, 240). Nevertheless, the necessity of emancipation compelled many abolitionists to overlook their own earlier attacks on the North's support of slavery. Not wishing to detract from the administration's movements toward emancipation, these freedom fighters, Emerson included, threw their weight in support of the northern cause.

26. Cf. the following from Emerson's essay "The Poet": "With what joy I begin to read a poem which I confide in as an inspiration! And now my chains are to be broken: I shall mount above these clouds and opaque airs in which I live,—opaque, though they seem transparent,—and from the heaven of truth I shall see and comprehend my relations. . . . Poets are thus liberating gods" (*W*, 3: 12, 30).

27. See esp. Sumner, *The Landmark of Freedom*.

28. Phillips, *Speeches, Lectures, and Letters*, 2d series (1900), 5.

29. Cf. the following, even earlier argument in Emerson's essay "Politics": "Whenever I find my dominion over myself not sufficient for me, and undertake the direction of his also, I overstep the truth, and come into false relations to him. . . . it is a lie, and hurts like a lie to both him and me" (*W*, 3: 214).

30. This passage appears in this form only in the Riverside Centenary Edition of Emerson's writings. In Gougeon's and Myerson's edition of Emerson's antislavery writings, it is included not in his 1851 address but in his 1855 "Lecture on Slavery" (*AS*, 105–6). In any case, Emerson expands this argument in a remarkable passage from the end of this later lecture. "We shall one day bring the states shoulder to shoulder, and the citizens man to man, to exterminate slavery. It is said, it will cost two thousand millions of dollars. Was there ever any contribution levied that

was so enthusiastically paid as this will be? The United States shall give every inch of the public lands. The states shall give their surplus revenues, their unsold lands. The citizen his private contribution. We will have a chimney tax. We will give up our coaches, and wine, and watches. The churches will melt their plate. The Father of his country shall wait well-pleased a little longer for his monument: Franklin for his; the Pilgrim Fathers for theirs. We will call on those rich benefactors who found Asylums, Hospitals, Athenaeums, Lowell Institutes, Peabody Institutes, Bates and Astor City Libraries. On wealthy bachelors and wealthy maidens to make the State their heir as they were wont in Rome. The merchant will give his best voyage. The mechanic will give his fabric. The needlewomen will give. Children will have cent societies. If really the matter could come to negotiation and a price were named, I do not think that any price founded on an estimate that figures could tell would be unmanageable. Every man in the land would give a week's work to dig away this accursed mountain of sorrow once and forever out of the world" (*AS*, 106).

31. That these lines may have had particular resonance for the former slaves in Emerson's Music Hall audience can be gathered from a letter of January 1864 by Thomas Wentworth Higginson to Emerson. In the letter Higginson, a leader of a regiment of black troops, tells Emerson that his surgeon, Doctor Rogers, had recently read the "Boston Hymn" to his black soldiers and that "they understood every word of it. . . . I recall vividly the thrill that went through me as he read the grand verse beginning 'Pay ransom to the owner,' and thought that these were the owners before us" (cited in Gougeon, *Virtue's Hero*, 305–6).

32. It should be noted, however, that even when Emerson was arguing for compensation to slaveowners he had already registered the importance of the question of property to slavery. In his 1837 essay "Politics," for example, he writes: "In a theory of government, this principle lies at the foundation, that property should make law for property, and persons the law for persons. But to embody this theory in the form of a government is not easy. For persons and property mix themselves in every transaction. The violences upon persons are oftenest for the sake of property as in . . . slavery. . . . No distinction seems to be so fundamental in politics as this of persons and property. Out of an inattention to it arises the whole sophism of slavery" (*EL*, 1: 72–73). Or, as he puts it in a journal entry in 1846, "Slavery and Anti-Slavery is the question of property and anti-property" (*J*, 11: 430).

33. See Pierce, *Memoir and Letters of Charles Sumner*, 4: 49.

34. *The Liberator*, January 17, 1862.

35. Cited in McPherson, *The Struggle for Equality*, 93.

36. At the end of "American Civilization," Emerson makes clear that he supports immediate rather than gradual emancipation. He writes: "If Congress accords with the President, it is not yet too late to begin the emancipation; but we think it will always be too late to make it gradual. All experience agrees that it should be immediate" (*W*, 11: 310–11).

37. See Beecher, "Teachings of Snow," 53.

38. "Snow," *Atlantic Monthly* (February 1862), 188.

39. See "Meteorology," *Atlantic Monthly* (July 1860), 7.

40. Lincoln, *Collected Works*, 2: 276.

41. See Hughes, *Emerson's Demanding Optimism*, 121–22.

42. This figure also reappears in Wigglesworth, *The Day of Doom*. See Messerole, ed., *Seventeenth-Century American Poetry*, 46, 56.

43. See Breitwieser, *Cotton Mather and Benjamin Franklin*, 210.

44. See Mather, *Magnalia Christi Americana*, 2: 368; and Edwards, *Personal Narrative*, 1: 62.

45. This participation is the subject of Emerson's poem "Voluntaries," written in celebration of the Massachusetts 54th Regiment, one of the first black regiments in the Union army.

46. See, for example, Gossett, *Race*, 5; Davis, *The Problem of Slavery in Western Culture*, 63–64, 316–17; *Slavery and Human Progress*, 21–22, 42–43, 86–87; *The Problem of Slavery in the Age of Revolution*, 539–41; and Jordan, *White over Black*, 18–19, 35–37, 41–42, 54–56.

47. Davis, *Slavery and Human Progress*, 39.

48. Locke, *An Essay Concerning Human Understanding*, 2: 129.

49. Cf. this statement from his speech on the emancipation of the British West Indies: "a man is added to the human family" (*AS*, 29). Emerson suggests the necessity of this inclusion in a journal entry from 1846 and does so within the context of the Cain story. Indicating his awareness of the association between the curse of Cain and the black man, he writes: "Nature loves to cross her stocks. A pure blood, Bramin on Bramin, marrying in & in, soon becomes puny & wears out. Some strong Cain son, some black blood must renew & refresh the paler veins of Seth" (*J*, 9: 365).

50. On this point, see Anne Norton, *Alternative Americas*, 299.

51. Or, as he puts it in his essay "Art," "in eloquence, the great triumphs of the art are when the orator is lifted above himself; when consciously he makes himself the mere tongue of the occasion and the hour, and says what cannot be said. Hence the term *abandonment*, to describe the self-surrender of the orator. Not his will, but the principle on which he is horsed, the great connection and crisis of events, thunder in the ear of the crowd" (*W*, 7: 49).

52. McPherson, *The Struggle for Equality*, 192. For other accounts of the history of black troops during the war, see McPherson, *The Negro's Civil War*. This book is an invaluable source of primary materials on this issue. See also: Williams, *A History of the Negro Troops in the War of the Rebellion*; Quarles, *The Negro in the Civil War*; and Litwack, *Been in the Storm So Long*.

53. *Douglass' Monthly*, 5 (August 1863): 852.

54. Ibid., 4 (September 1861): 516; Speech at Cooper Union, February 12, 1862, reported in the *New York Tribune*, February 13, 1862.

55. McPherson, *The Struggle for Equality*, 197.

56. In his notes to Emerson's *Complete Works*, Edward Emerson cites Mrs. Ednah Cheney's description of a meeting of the friends of the 54th. The description includes the following anecdote of Emerson's response to the third of these reasons: "Mr. Emerson came in from the ante-room with his face on fire with indignation, as I never saw it on any other occasion, and announced to the audience that he had just learned that South Carolina had given out the threat that colored soldiers, if captured, should not be treated as prisoners, but be put to death. 'What answer does Massachusetts send back to South Carolina?' he said. 'Two for one!' shouted voices in the audience. 'Is that the answer that Massachusetts sends?' he asked; and the audience responded with applause. He retired from the platform, it seemed to me a little appalled at the spirit he had raised" (*W*, 9: 470).

57. *Douglass' Monthly*, 5 (March 1863): 802.

58. McPherson, *The Negro's Civil War*, 191.

59. *National Anti-Slavery Standard*, August 8, 1863; *New York Tribune*, September 8, 1865; both cited in McPherson, *The Struggle for Equality*, 211–12. Weld is cited in McPherson, *The Negro Civil War*, 191.

60. For the publication history of the poem, see Emerson, *Poetry Notebooks*, 959. For Emerson's letter to Francis Shaw, see *L*, 5: 336.

61. This is especially evident in his essay "Fate," which, I would argue, is Emerson's reading of Manifest Destiny in terms of the question of race. His discussion of race during the 1850s belongs not only to the political implications of his antislavery discourse but also, as Robinson has noted, to his "attempt to measure, and ultimately to limit, a determinist explanation for human achievement" (*Emerson and the Conduct of Life*, 115). In "Fate," for example, suggesting that "a good deal of our politics is physiological," Emerson ventriloquizes nearly every scientific explanation for racial difference available to him, from the racial theories of Tacitus and Linnaeus to Robert Chamber's theory of ameliorative evolution, from the phrenology of Spurzheim to the statistics of Quetelet, from climatic explanations of racial difference to evolutionary theo-

ries of the development and ruin of races. The entire essay can be read as an analysis of the various discourses that have throughout history—but especially throughout the eighteenth and nineteenth centuries—worked to enable one race to live, as Emerson puts it, at the expense of another race. This is particularly evident when, soon after citing Robert Knox's discussion of race as a natural category in *The Races of Men* (a gesture that has been read by others as a signal of Emerson's own latent racism), he writes: "See the shades of the picture. The German and Irish millions, like the Negro, have a great deal of guano in their destiny. They are ferried over the Atlantic, and carted over America, to ditch and to drudge, to make corn cheap, and then to lie down prematurely to make a spot of green grass on the prairie" (*W*, 6: 16–17). Emerson here claims that the American landscape—even America herself—is flourishing over the guano that the ethnic minorities have become. Far from endorsing Knox's evolutionary theories, he suggests that Knox's book is not only "rash and unsatisfactory" but also a piece of guano. (He introduces his citations from the book by stating that it is charged with "pungent" truths.) I trace Emerson's political and rhetorical strategies in this essay in relation to the prevailing scientific attitudes toward race in his day and in relation to the debates in the 1840s and 50s over the importation of guano into the United States in my forthcoming "Emerson and the Guano of History."

62. Emerson is quite specific about what the climate can influence. As he states in a related journal passage: "Manners seem to be more closely under the influence of climate. They belong more to the body than the soul, & so come under the influence of the sun" (*J*, 3: 59).

63. "Snow," *Atlantic Monthly* (February 1862), 189 and 200–1.

64. On the history of the United States flag, see Quaife et al., *The History of the United States Flag*; and Edward W. Richardson, *Standards and Colors of the American Revolution*.

65. What follows is to some degree indebted to de Man's discussion of the aesthetic as "a principle of articulation between various known faculties, activities, and modes of cognition" ("Aesthetic Formalization," 263–90, 313–14).

66. See Crevecoeur, *Sketches of Eighteenth Century America*, esp. the chap. entitled "A Snow Storm as it Affects the American Farmer." See also Noah Webster, "On the Supposed Change in the Temperature of Winter." The Webster article engages a debate between Jefferson and others about whether or not the globe was warming. Jefferson claimed that it indeed was warming and that this had everything to do with the sunny prospects of America. Webster, on the other hand, claimed that

we should not argue that the world was warming, because such an event would draw us away from what makes us Americans. When we crossed the ocean to settle the wilderness, he argues, one of the things we had to do was undergo the trial of the winter: being American therefore includes the experience of the winter. In an important passage that anticipates many debates now taking place over global warming, over the ways in which we ourselves create the weather, Webster writes: "It appears that all the alterations in a country, in consequence of clearing and cultivation, result only in making a different distribution of heat and cold, moisture and dry weather, among the several seasons. The clearing of lands opens them to the sun, their moisture is exhaled, they are more heated in summer, but more cold in winter near the surface; the temperature becomes unsteady, and the seasons irregular. This is the fact. . . . Every forest in America exhibits this phenomenon . . . it appears that the weather, in modern winters, is more inconstant, than when the earth was covered with wood, at the first settlement of Europeans in the country; that the warm weather of autumn extends further into the winter months, and the cold weather of winter and spring encroaches upon the summer; that the wind being more variable, snow is less permanent, and perhaps the same remark may be applicable to the ice of the rivers. These effects seem to result necessarily from the greater quantity of heat accumulated in the earth in summer, since the ground has been cleared of wood, and exposed to the rays of the sun; and to the greater depth of frost in the earth in winter, by the exposure of its uncovered surface to the cold atmosphere" (148 and 161).

67. See also *J*, 7: 209 and 314–15, for more extended comments on the painting. For discussions of Emerson's interest in the figure of the auroras, see Porte, *Representative Man*, 50–54; and Ellison, *Emerson's Romantic Style*, 117–18.

68. See Franklin, *Writings*, 7: 209–15.

69. Cited in William Petrie, *Keoeeit*, 121. The cause of the auroras is believed to be the injection of electrically charged particles, especially of solar origin, into the earth's magnetic field. It is tempting to associate these charged elements to the drive of the 54th's black troops. Of solar origin, they are charged with the moral responsibility around which Emerson wishes the nation to be magnetized.

70. See ibid., esp. chap. 1.

71. "The Northern Lights and the Stars," *Atlantic Monthly* (December 1859), 689.

72. Whittier, *Legends of New England*, 132.

73. Cited in the notes to Melville's "Aurora-Borealis," in his *Battle-*

Pieces and Aspects of the War, 272. Melville's poem is an interesting supplement to Emerson's use of the auroras, especially since Melville's was written in May 1865, in "Commemoration of the Dissolution of Armies at the Peace."

74. Ibid., 272.

75. Williams, *A History of the Negro Troops in the War of the Rebellion*, 193. The same account is cited in McPherson, *The Negro's Civil War*, 189. Williams had distinguished himself by being one of the first black officers in the Massachusetts Volunteer Militia.

76. Williams, *A History of Negro Troops in the War of the Rebellion*, 195–96.

77. Ibid., 199.

78. Quarles, *The Negro in the Civil War*, 6–7.

79. Ibid., 16–17.

80. Ibid., 20–21.

81. Sweet makes a similar point in relation to Melville's Civil War poetry in *Traces of War*, 180.

🐛 Bibliography

Adams, John. *The Earliest Diary of John Adams*. Ed. L. H. Butterfield et al. Cambridge: Harvard Univ. Press, 1966.

———. *The Political Writings of John Adams*. Ed. George A. Peek. Indianapolis: Bobbs-Merrill, 1954.

Adams, John Quincy. *Answer to Pain's Rights of Man*. London: Glasgow, Brash and Reid, Booksellers, 1793.

———. *Lectures on Rhetoric and Oratory*. Cambridge, Mass.: Hilliard and Metcalf, 1810.

Aldridge, Alfred Owen. *Benjamin Franklin and Nature's God*. Durham: Duke Univ. Press, 1967.

———. *Man of Reason: The Life of Thomas Paine*. Philadelphia: J. B. Lippincott Co., 1959.

Allen, Gay Wilson. *Waldo Emerson*. New York: Penguin, 1981.

Anderson, Quentin. *The Imperial Self: An Essay in American Literary and Cultural History*. New York: Alfred A. Knopf, 1971.

Aristotle. *Politics*. Trans. Carnes Lord. Chicago: Univ. of Chicago Press, 1984.

Bailyn, Bernard. *The Ideological Origins of the American Revolution*. Cambridge: Harvard Univ. Press, 1967.

———. Introduction to *Pamphlets of the American Revolution*. Cambridge: Harvard Univ. Press, 1965.

Baxter, Maurice G. *One and Inseparable: Daniel Webster and the Union*. Cambridge: Harvard Univ. Press, 1984.

Beecher, H. W. "Teachings of Snow." *Cloud Crystals: A Snowflake Album, Collected and Edited by a Lady*. New York: D. Appleton & Co., 1864.

Bell, Ian F. A. "The Hard Currency of Words: Emerson's Fiscal Metaphor in *Nature*." *ELH* 52.3 (Fall 1985): 733–53.

Bercovitch, Sacvan. *The American Jeremiad.* Madison: Univ. of Wisconsin Press, 1978.

———. "The Biblical Basis of the American Myth." In Giles Gunn, ed., *The Bible and American Arts and Letters.* Philadelphia: Fortress Press, 1983. 219–29.

———. "Emerson the Prophet: Romanticism, Puritanism, and Auto-American Biography." In David Levin, ed., *Emerson: Prophecy, Metamorphosis, and Influence.* New York: Columbia Univ. Press, 1975. 1–27.

———. *The Puritan Origins of the American Self.* New Haven: Yale Univ. Press, 1975.

———. *The Rites of Assent: Transformations in the Symbolic Construction of America.* New York: Routledge, 1993.

Bishop, Jonathan. *Emerson on the Soul.* Cambridge: Harvard Univ. Press, 1964.

Breitwieser, Mitchell. *Cotton Mather and Benjamin Franklin: The Price of Representative Personality.* Cambridge: Cambridge Univ. Press, 1984.

Brigance, William Norman, ed. *A History and Criticism of American Public Address.* New York: McGraw-Hill, 1943.

Brown, Homer O. "Tristram to the Hebrews: Some Notes on the Institution of a Canonic Text." *MLN* 99.4 (Sept. 1984): 743–44.

Brown, Jerry Wayne. *The Rise of Biblical Criticism in America, 1800–1870: The New England Scholars.* Middletown, Conn.: Wesleyan Univ. Press, 1969.

Browne, Sir Thomas. *The Major Works.* Ed. C. A. Patrides. New York: Penguin, 1977.

Brownson, Orestes. *Works of Orestes Brownson.* Ed. Henry F. Brownson. Detroit: T. Nourse, 1882–98.

Buchanan, James. *Mr. Buchanan's Administration on the Eve of the Rebellion.* Freeport, N. Y.: Books for Libraries Press, 1970.

Buell, Lawrence. *New England Literary Culture: From Revolution Through Renaissance.* Cambridge: Cambridge Univ. Press, 1986.

Cabot, James Elliot. *A Memoir of Ralph Waldo Emerson.* Boston: Houghton Mifflin, 1887.

Cavell, Stanley. "Emerson's Constitutional Amending: Reading 'Fate.' " In *Philosophical Passages: Wittgenstein, Emerson, Austin, Derrida.* Oxford: Blackwell, 1995. 12–41.

Chapman, John Jay. *The Selected Writings of John Jay Chapman.* Ed. Jacques Barzun. Garden City, N.Y.: Doubleday, 1959.

Cheyfitz, Eric. Foreword to Maurice Gonnaud, *An Uneasy Solitude: Individual and Society in the Work of Ralph Waldo Emerson.* Princeton: Princeton Univ. Press, 1987. vii–xviii.

————. *The Trans-Parent: Sexual Politics in the Language of Emerson*. Baltimore: Johns Hopkins Univ. Press, 1981.

Cmiel, Kenneth. *Democratic Eloquence*. New York: Morrow, 1990.

Cohen, Henning, ed. *Battle-Pieces and Aspects of the War*. New York: Thomas Yoseloff, 1963.

Coleridge, Samuel Taylor. *Coleridge: Poetical Works*. Ed. Ernest Hartley Coleridge. Oxford: Oxford Univ. Press, 1978.

————. *Lectures on Revealed Religion*. In *Lectures 1795: On Politics and Religion*, ed. Lewis Patton and Peter Mann. *The Collected Works of Samuel Taylor Coleridge*, ed. Kathleen Coburn. Princeton: Princeton Univ. Press, 1971. 1: 75–229.

————. *On the Constitution of Church and State*. Ed. John Colmer. Vol. 10 of *The Collected Works of Samuel Taylor Coleridge*, ed. Kathleen Coburn. Princeton: Princeton Univ. Press, 1976.

Conway, Moncure. *The Life of Thomas Paine: With a History of His Literary, Political and Religious Career in America, France, and England*. 2 vols. New York: G. P. Putnam's Sons, 1892.

————. *The Rejected Stone: or Insurrection vs. Resurrection in America*. Boston: Walker, Wise and Co., 1861.

Cover, Robert M. *Justice Accused: Antislavery and the Judicial Process*. New Haven: Yale Univ. Press, 1975.

Crevecoeur, St. John. *Sketches of Eighteenth Century America*. Ed. Henri L. Bourdin et al. New York: Benjamin Blom, 1972.

Davis, David Brion. *The Problem of Slavery in the Age of Revolution: 1770–1823*. Ithaca: Cornell Univ. Press, 1975.

————. *The Problem of Slavery in Western Culture*. Ithaca: Cornell Univ. Press, 1966.

————. *The Slave Power Conspiracy and the Paranoid Style*. Baton Rouge: Louisiana State Univ. Press, 1969.

————. *Slavery and Human Progress*. New York: Oxford Univ. Press, 1984.

de Man, Paul. "Aesthetic Formalization: Kleist's *Über das Marionettentheater*." In *The Rhetoric of Romanticism*. New York: Columbia Univ. Press, 1984. 263–90, 313–14.

————. "Intentional Structure of the Romantic Image." In *The Rhetoric of Romanticism*. New York: Columbia Univ. Press, 1984. 1–18, 291.

Derrida, Jacques. "Déclarations d'Indépendance." In *Otobiographies: L'enseignement de Nietzsche et la politique du nom propre*. Paris: Galilée, 1984. 11–32.

————. *Limited Inc*. Trans. Samuel Weber. Evanston, Ill.: Northwestern Univ. Press, 1988.

———. *Of Spirit: Heidegger and the Question.* Trans. Geoffrey Bennington and Rachel Bowlby. Chicago: Univ. of Chicago Press, 1989.

———. *Specters of Marx: The State of the Debt, the Work of Mourning, and the New International.* Trans. Peggy Kamuf. New York: Routledge, 1994.

Douglass, Frederick. *The Life and Writings of Frederick Douglass.* Ed. Philip S. Foner. 4 vols. New York: International Publishers, 1975. (Rpt. of 1950 ed.)

Edwards, Jonathan. *Personal Narrative. The Works of Jonathan Edwards.* New York: G. & C. & H. Carvill, 1830.

Elliot, Emory. *Power and the Pulpit in Puritan New England.* Princeton: Princeton Univ. Press, 1975.

Ellison, Julie. *Emerson's Romantic Style.* Princeton: Princeton Univ. Press, 1984.

Emerson, Ralph Waldo. *The Complete Works of Ralph Waldo Emerson.* Ed. Edward Waldo Emerson. 12 vols. Centenary Edition. Boston: Houghton Mifflin, 1903–4.

———. *The Correspondence of Emerson and Carlyle.* Ed. Joseph Slater. New York: Columbia Univ. Press, 1964.

———. *The Early Lectures of Ralph Waldo Emerson.* Ed. Stephen Whicher, Robert E. Spiller, and Wallace E. Williams. 3 vols. Cambridge: Harvard Univ. Press, 1961.

———. *Emerson in His Journals.* Ed. Joel Porte. Cambridge: Harvard Univ. Press, 1982.

———. *Emerson's Antislavery Writings.* Ed. Len Gougeon and Joel Myerson. New Haven: Yale Univ. Press, 1995.

———. *The Journals and Miscellaneous Notebooks of Ralph Waldo Emerson.* Ed. William H. Gilman, et al. 16 vols. to date. Cambridge: Harvard Univ. Press, 1960–.

———. *The Letters of Ralph Waldo Emerson.* Ed. Ralph L. Rusk. 6 vols. New York: Columbia Univ. Press, 1939.

———. *The Poetry Notebooks of Ralph Waldo Emerson.* Ed. Ralph H. Orth, Albert J. Von Frank, Linda Allardt, and David W. Hill. Columbia: Univ. of Missouri Press, 1986.

———. *Selected Writings of Ralph Waldo Emerson.* Ed. William H. Gilman. New York: New American Library, 1965.

———. *Young Emerson Speaks: Unpublished Discourses on Many Subjects.* Ed. Arthur Cushman McGiffert, Jr. Port Washington, N.Y.: Kennikat Press, Inc., 1968.

Espy, James Pollard. *The Philosophy of Storms.* Boston: Little & Brown, 1841.

Faust, Drew Gilpin. *The Ideology of Slavery: Proslavery Thought in the Antebellum South, 1830–1860*. Baton Rouge: Louisiana State Univ. Press, 1981.

———. *A Sacred Circle: The Dilemma of the Intellectual in the Old South*. Baltimore: Johns Hopkins Univ. Press, 1977.

Fehrenbacher, Don E. *Prelude to Greatness: Lincoln in the 1850s*. Stanford: Stanford Univ. Press, 1962.

Firkins, O. W. *Ralph Waldo Emerson*. Boston: Houghton Mifflin, 1915.

Fliegelman, Jay. *Prodigals and Pilgrims: The American Revolution Against Patriarchal Authority, 1750–1800*. Cambridge: Cambridge Univ. Press, 1982.

Foner, Eric. *Free Soil, Free Labor, Free Men: The Ideology of the Republican Party Before the Civil War*. New York: Oxford Univ. Press, 1970.

———. *Tom Paine and Revolutionary America*. New York: Oxford Univ. Press, 1976.

Franklin, Benjamin. *The New England Courant: A Selection of Certain Issues Containing Writings of Benjamin Franklin*. Boston: American Academy of Arts and Sciences, 1956.

———. *The Writings of Benjamin Franklin*. Ed. Albert Henry Smith. New York: Haskell House Publishers, Ltd., 1970.

Frederickson, George M. *The Black Image in the White Mind: The Debate on Afro-American Character and Destiny, 1817–1914*. Middletown, Conn.: Wesleyan Univ. Press, 1971.

———. *The Inner Civil War: Northern Intellectuals and the Crisis of the Union*. New York: Harper and Row, 1968.

Fuller, Margaret. "Emerson's Essays." In *Margaret Fuller: American Romantic*, ed. Perry Miller. Garden City, N.Y.: Doubleday, 1963. 191–200.

Garrison, William Lloyd. *Selections from the Writings and Speeches of William Lloyd Garrison*. Boston: R. F. Wallcut, 1852.

Gienapp, William E. "The Republican Party and the Slave Power." In Robert H. Abzug and Stephen E. Maizlish, eds., *New Perspectives on Race and Slavery in America: Essays in Honor of Kenneth M. Stampp*. Lexington: Univ. Press of Kentucky, 1986. 51–78.

Gilmore, Michael. *American Romanticism and the Marketplace*. Chicago: Univ. of Chicago Press, 1985.

———. "Eulogy as Symbolic Biography: The Iconography of Revolutionary Leadership, 1776–1826." In Daniel Aaron, ed., *Studies in Biography*, Harvard English Studies 8. Cambridge: Harvard Univ. Press, 1978. 131–57.

Gonnaud, Maurice. *An Uneasy Solitude: Individual and Society in the*

Work of Ralph Waldo Emerson. Trans. Lawrence Rosenwald. Princeton: Princeton Univ. Press, 1987.

Gossett, Thomas F. *Race: The History of an Idea in America.* Dallas: Southern Methodist Univ. Press, 1963.

Gougeon, Len. *Virtue's Hero.* Athens: Univ. of Georgia Press, 1990.

Grusin, Richard A. *Transcendentalist Hermeneutics: Institutional Authority and the Higher Criticism of the Bible.* Durham: Duke Univ. Press, 1991.

Gura, Philip. *A Glimpse of Sion's Glory: Puritan Radicalism in New England, 1620–1660.* Middletown, Conn.: Wesleyan Univ. Press, 1984.

———. *The Wisdom of Words: Language, Theology, and Literature in the New England Renaissance.* Middletown, Conn.: Wesleyan Univ. Press, 1981.

Gustafson, Thomas. *Representative Words: Politics, Literature, and the American Language, 1776–1865.* Cambridge: Cambridge Univ. Press, 1992.

Hamacher, Werner. "The Reader's Supper: A Piece of Hegel." Trans. Timothy Bahti. *Diacritics* 11.2 (Summer 1981): 52–67.

Harding, Walter. *Emerson's Library.* Charlottesville: Univ. Press of Virginia, 1967.

Hatch, Nathan. *The Sacred Cause of Liberty: Republican Thought and the Millennium in Revolutionary New England.* New Haven: Yale Univ. Press, 1977.

Heeren, Arnold. *Reflections on the Politics of Ancient Greece.* Trans. George Bancroft. Boston: Cummings, Hilliard, 1824.

Hegel, Georg Wilhelm Friedrich. *Aesthetics.* Trans. T. M. Knox. Oxford: Oxford Univ. Press, 1975.

Hildebrandsson, H., and T. L. Teisserene de Bort. *Les bases de la météorologie dynamique.* 2 vols. Paris: 1898, 1900.

Holland, Laurence B. "Authority, Power, and Form: Some American Texts." *The Yearbook of English Studies: American Literature Special Number* 8 (1978): 3–28.

Holmes, Oliver Wendell. *Ralph Waldo Emerson.* Boston: Houghton, Mifflin, 1885.

Horsman, Reginald. *Race and Manifest Destiny: The Origins of American Radical Anglo-Saxonism.* Cambridge: Harvard Univ. Press, 1981.

Howard-Pitney, David. *The Afro-American Jeremiad: Appeals for Justice in America.* Philadelphia: Temple Univ. Press, 1990.

Howe, Daniel Walker. *The Political Culture of the American Whigs.* Chicago: Univ. of Chicago Press, 1979.

Howe, Irving. *The American Newness: Culture and Politics in the Age of Emerson.* Cambridge: Harvard Univ. Press, 1986.

Hughes, Gertrude Reif. *Emerson's Demanding Optimism*. Baton Rouge: Louisiana State Univ. Press, 1984.

Hume, David. *A Treatise of Human Nature*. Ed. L. A. Selby-Bigge. Oxford: Oxford Univ. Press, 1978.

Irving, Washington. *Salmagundi*. In *History, Tales, and Sketches*, ed. James Tuttleton. New York: Library of America, 1983. 45–361.

Jay, Gregory. "Hegel and the Dialectics of American Literary Historiography: From Parrington to Trilling and Beyond." In Joseph Kronick and Bainard Cowan, eds., *Theorizing American Literature: Hegel, the Sign, and History*. Baton Rouge: Louisiana State Univ. Press, 1991. 83–122.

Jefferson, Thomas. *Jefferson's Extracts from the Gospels*. Ed. Dickinson W. Adams. Princeton: Princeton Univ. Press, 1983.

Johnson, J. W. "Of Differing Ages and Climes." *Journal of the History of Ideas* 21.4 (Oct.–Dec. 1960): 465–80.

Jordan, Winthrop. *White Over Black: American Attitudes Toward the Negro, 1550–1812*. Chapel Hill: Univ. of North Carolina Press, 1968.

Kalinevitch, Karen. "Turning from the Orthodox: Emerson's Gospel Lectures." In Joel Myerson, ed., *Studies in the American Renaissance*. Charlottesville: Univ. Press of Virginia, 1986. 69–112.

Kateb, George. *Emerson and Self-Reliance*. Modernity and Political Thought 8. Thousand Oaks, Calif.: Sage Publications, 1995.

Kramer, Michael P. *Imagining Language in America: From the Revolution to the Civil War*. Princeton: Princeton Univ. Press, 1992.

Kronick, Joseph G. *American Poetics of History: From Emerson to the Moderns*. Baton Rouge: Louisiana State Univ. Press, 1984.

Kupperman, Karen O. "Fear of Hot Climates in the Anglo-American Colonial Experience." *William and Mary Quarterly* 41.2 (1984): 213–40.

Leiber, Francis, ed. *Encyclopedia Americana*. Philadelphia: Carey, Lea and Carey, 1829–33.

Lewis, R. W. B. *The American Adam*. Chicago: Univ. of Chicago Press, 1955.

Lincoln, Abraham. *The Collected Works of Abraham Lincoln*. Ed. Roy P. Basler. New Brunswick, N.J.: Rutgers Univ. Press, 1953.

Litwack, Leon F. *Been in the Storm So Long: The Aftermath of Slavery*. New York: Alfred A. Knopf, 1979.

Locke, John. *An Essay Concerning Human Understanding*. Ed. Alexander C. Fraser. 2 vols. New York: Dover, 1959.

———. *Two Treatises of Government*. Ed. Thomas I. Cook. New York: Hafner Press, 1947.

Lopez, Michael. "Emerson's Rhetoric of War." *Prospects: An Annual of American Cultural Studies* 12 (1987): 293–320.

Lowance, Mason I. *The Language of Canaan: Metaphor and Symbol in New England from the Puritans to the Transcendentalists.* Cambridge: Harvard Univ. Press, 1980.

Macleod, Duncan. *Slavery, Race, and the American Revolution.* Cambridge: Cambridge Univ. Press, 1974.

McPherson, James. *The Negro's Civil War: How American Negroes Felt and Acted During the War for the Union.* New York: Pantheon, 1965.

———. *The Struggle for Equality: Abolitionists and the Negro in the Civil War and Reconstruction.* Princeton: Princeton Univ. Press, 1964.

Madison, James, et al. *The Federalist Papers.* Ed. Clinton Rossiter. New York: New American Library, 1961.

———. *Letters and Other Writings of James Madison.* 4 vols. New York: R. Worthington, 1884.

Maizlish, Stephen E. "Race and Politics in the Northern Democracy, 1854–1860." In Robert H. Abzug and Stephen E. Maizlish, eds., *New Perspectives on Race and Slavery in America: Essays in Honor of Kenneth M. Stampp.* Lexington: Univ. Press of Kentucky, 1986. 79–90.

Mann, Horace. *Slavery: Letters and Speeches.* Boston: B. B. Mussey & Co., 1851.

Marx, Karl, and Frederick Engels. *The Eighteenth Brumaire of Louis Bonaparte.* Vol. 11 of Karl Marx and Frederick Engels, *Collected Works.* New York: International Publishers, 1979. 99–197.

Mather, Cotton. *Magnalia Christi Americana.* New York: Russell and Russell, 1967.

Matthiessen, F. O. *American Renaissance: Art and Expression in the Age of Emerson and Whitman.* New York: Oxford Univ. Press, 1968.

May, Henry F. *The Enlightenment in America.* New York: Oxford Univ. Press, 1976.

Melville, Herman. *Battle-Pieces and Aspects of the War.* Ed. Henning Cohen. New York: Thomas Yoseloff, 1963.

———. *Great Short Works of Herman Melville.* Ed. Warner Berthoff. New York: Harper and Row, 1969.

Mergen, Bernard. "Winter Landscape in the Early Republic: Survival and Sentimentality." In Mick Gidley and Robert Lawson-Peebles, eds., *Views of American Landscapes.* Cambridge: Cambridge Univ. Press, 1989. 167–82.

Messerole, Harrison T., ed. *Seventeenth-Century American Poetry.* New York: New York Univ. Press, 1968.

Michael, John. *Emerson and Skepticism: The Cipher of the World.* Baltimore: Johns Hopkins Univ. Press, 1988.

————. "Emerson's Chagrin: Benediction and Exhortation in 'Nature' and 'Tintern Abbey.' " *MLN* 101.5 (Dec. 1986): 1067–85.

Middlekauf, Robert. *The Mathers: Three Generations of Puritan Intellectuals, 1596–1728.* New York: Oxford Univ. Press, 1971.

Middleton, William Edgar Knowles. *A History of the Theories of Rain and Other Forms of Precipitation.* New York: Franklin Watts, Inc., 1966.

Miller, Perry. *Errand into the Wilderness.* Cambridge: Harvard Univ. Press, 1956.

————. *Nature's Nation.* Cambridge: Harvard Univ. Press, 1962.

————. *The New England Mind: From Colony to Province.* Cambridge: Harvard Univ. Press, 1953.

Milton, John. *The Reason of Church Government.* Vol. 3 of *Works of John Milton,* ed. Frank Allen Patterson. New York: Columbia Univ. Press, 1931. 181–279.

Moody, Marjory M. "The Evolution of Emerson as an Abolitionist." *American Literature* 17 (Dec. 1945): 1–21.

Morais, Herbert M. *Deism in Eighteenth-Century America.* New York: Russell and Russell, 1934.

Morgan, Edmund S. *American Slavery, American Freedom: The Ordeal of Colonial Virginia.* New York: W. W. Norton, 1975.

————. *The Puritan Dilemma: The Story of John Winthrop.* Boston: Little, Brown, 1958.

————. *Visible Saints: The History of a Puritan Idea.* Ithaca: Cornell Univ. Press, 1965.

Mullett, Charles F. *Fundamental Law and the American Revolution: 1760–1776.* New York: Octagon Books, Inc., 1966.

Newmark, Kevin. *Beyond Symbolism: Textual History and the Future of Reading.* Ithaca: Cornell Univ. Press, 1991.

Nicoloff, Philip. *Emerson on Race and History.* New York: Columbia Univ. Press, 1961.

Nietzsche, Friedrich. *Human, All Too Human: A Book for Free Spirits.* Trans. R. J. Hollingdale. Cambridge: Cambridge Univ. Press, 1986.

————. *Nachgelassene Fragmente: 1880–1882.* Vol. 9 of *Sämtliche Werke: Kritische Studienausgabe,* ed. Giorgio Colli and Mazzino Montinari. Berlin: de Gruyter, 1967–1977.

————. "On Truth and Lie in an Extra-Moral Sense." In *Philosophy and Truth: Selections from Nietzsche's Notebooks of the Early 1870s,* trans. and ed. Daniel Breazeale. Atlantic Highlands, N.J.: Humanities Press, Inc., 1979. 77–97.

Norton, Andrews. "On the Divinity School Address." In Milton R. Konvitz, ed., *The Recognition of Ralph Waldo Emerson: Selected Criticism Since 1837.* Ann Arbor: Univ. of Michigan Press, 1972. 7–9.

———. *A Statement of Reasons for Not Believing the Doctrines of Trinitarians, Concerning the Nature of God and the Person of Christ*. 7th ed. Boston: American Unitarian Association, 1859.

Norton, Anne. *Alternative Americas: A Reading of Antebellum Political Culture*. Chicago: Univ. of Chicago Press, 1986.

Packer, B. L. *Emerson's Fall: A New Interpretation of the Major Essays*. New York: Continuum, 1982.

———. "Origin and Authority: Emerson and the Higher Criticism." In Sacvan Bercovitch, ed., *Reconstructing American Literary History*. Cambridge: Harvard Univ. Press, 1986. 67–92.

Paine, Thomas. *The Age of Reason*. Ed. Eric Foner. Secaucus, N.J.: Citadel Press, 1974.

———. *Common Sense*. Ed. Isaac Kramnick. New York: Penguin, 1983.

———. *The Complete Writings of Thomas Paine*. Ed. Philip S. Foner. New York: Citadel Press, 1969.

———. *Rights of Man*. Ed. Eric Foner. New York: Penguin, 1984.

Parker, Edward G. *The Golden Age of American Oratory*. Boston: Whittmore, Niles, and Hall, 1854.

Parker, Theodore. *The Slave Power*. New York: Arno Press, 1969.

———. "The Writings of Ralph Waldo Emerson." In Milton R. Konvitz, ed., *The Recognition of Ralph Waldo Emerson: Selected Criticism Since 1837*. Ann Arbor: Univ. of Michigan Press, 1972. 26–42.

Parrington, Vernon L. *The Romantic Revolution in America, 1800–1860*. Vol. 2 of *Main Currents in American Thought*. New York: Harcourt, Brace, 1954.

Pease, Donald. *Visionary Compacts: American Renaissance Writings in Cultural Context*. Madison: Univ. of Wisconsin Press, 1987.

Perkins, Howard Cecil, ed. *Northern Editorials on Secession*. New York: D. Appleton-Century Co., 1942.

Petrie, William. *Keoeeit: The Story of the Aurora Borealis*. New York: Pergamon, 1963.

Phillips, Wendell. *The Constitution, a Proslavery Compact; or, Selections from the Madison Papers*. New York: Negro Universities Press, 1969.

———. *A Review of Lysander Spooner's Unconstitutionality of Slavery*. Boston: Andrews & Prentiss, 1847.

———. *Speeches, Lectures, and Letters*. Boston: Walker, Wise, and Co., 1864.

———. *Speeches, Lectures, and Letters*. 2d series. Vol. 5. Ed. Rev. Theodore C. Pease. Boston: Walker, Wise, and Co., 1900.

Pierce, Edward L. *Memoir and Letters of Charles Sumner*. 4 vols. Boston: Roberts Brothers, 1877–93.

Playfair, John. *Illustrations of the Huttonian Theory of the Earth*. Edinburgh: Cadell and Davies, 1802.

Poirier, Richard. *Poetry and Pragmatism*. Cambridge: Harvard Univ. Press, 1992.

Porte, Joel. *Representative Man: Ralph Waldo Emerson in His Time*. New York: Oxford Univ. Press, 1979.

Porter, Carolyn. *Seeing and Being: The Plight of the Participant Observer in Emerson, James, Adams, and Faulkner*. Middletown, Conn.: Wesleyan Univ. Press, 1981.

Potter, David. *The Impending Crisis: 1848–1861*. New York: Harper and Row, 1976.

Quaife, Milo M., Melvin J. Weif, and Roy E. Appleman. *The History of the United States Flag: From the Revolution to the Present, Including a Guide to Its Use and Display*. New York: Harper and Row, 1961.

Quarles, Benjamin. *The Negro in the Civil War*. Boston: Little, Brown, 1953.

Reed, Arden. "The Mariner Rimed." In Arden Reed, ed., *Romanticism and Language*. Ithaca: Cornell Univ. Press, 1984. 168–201.

———. *Romantic Weather: The Climates of Coleridge and Baudelaire*. Hanover: Univ. Press of New England, 1983.

Reventlow, Henning Graf. *The Authority of the Bible and the Rise of the Modern World*. Trans. John Bowden. London: SCM Press Ltd., 1984.

Richardson, Edward W. *Standards and Colors of the American Revolution*. Philadelphia: Univ. of Pennsylvania Press and the Pennsylvania Society of Sons of the Revolution and Its Color Guard, 1982.

Richardson, Robert D., Jr. *Emerson: The Mind on Fire*. Berkeley: Univ. of California Press, 1995.

Riddel, Joseph. "Emerson and the 'American' Signature." In Mark Bauerlein, ed., *Purloined Letters: Originality and Repetition in American Literature*. Baton Rouge: Louisiana State Univ. Press, 1995. 42–71.

Robinson, David. *Emerson and the Conduct of Life: Pragmatism and Ethical Purpose in the Later Work*. Cambridge: Cambridge Univ. Press, 1993.

Rogin, Michael. *Fathers and Children: Andrew Jackson and the Subjugation of the American Indian*. New York: Alfred A. Knopf, 1975.

———. *Ronald Reagan, the Movie, and Other Episodes in Political Demonology*. Berkeley: Univ. of California Press, 1987.

———. *Subversive Genealogy: The Politics and Art of Herman Melville*. New York: Alfred A. Knopf, 1983.

Rose, Anne C. *Transcendentalism as a Social Movement, 1830–1850*. New Haven: Yale Univ. Press, 1981.

Ross, Andrew. "Forecasting Ideology and the Weather: The Work of

Nature in the Age of Electronic Emission." *Social Text: Theory/Culture/Ideology* 6.3 (Winter 1987–88): 116–28.

Rothman, David J. *The Discovery of the Asylum: Social Order and Disorder in the New Republic*. Boston: Little, Brown, 1971.

Rousseau, Jean-Jacques. *The Social Contract and Discourse on the Origin of Inequality*. Ed. Lester G. Crocker. New York: Simon and Schuster, 1967.

Rutman, Darrett. *American Puritanism: Faith and Practice*. Philadelphia: Lippincott, 1970.

———. *Winthrop's Boston: A Portrait of a Puritan Town: 1630–1649*. New York: W. W. Norton, 1972. Orig. pub. 1965.

Scobey, David. "Revising the Errand: New England's Ways and the Puritan Sense of the Past." *William and Mary Quarterly* 41.1 (Jan. 1984): 3–31.

Shaffer, E. A. *Coleridge, "Kubla Khan," and the Fall of Jerusalem: The Mythological School in Biblical Criticism and Secular Literature, 1770–1880*. Cambridge: Cambridge Univ. Press, 1975.

Shaw, Warren Choate. *History of American Oratory*. Indianapolis: Bobbs-Merrill, 1928.

Shelley, Percy Bysshe. *The Complete Works of Percy Bysshe Shelley*. Ed. Roger Ingpen and Walter E. Peck. New York: Gordian Press, 1965.

———. *Shelley's Poetry and Prose*. Ed. Donald H. Reiman and Sharon B. Powers. New York: W. W. Norton, 1977.

Sheridan, Eugene R. Introduction to Thomas Jefferson, *Jefferson's Extracts from the Gospel's*. Ed. Dickinson W. Adams. Princeton: Princeton Univ. Press, 1983. 3–42.

Simpson, David. *The Politics of American English, 1776–1850*. New York: Oxford Univ. Press, 1986.

Slotkin, Richard. *Regeneration Through Violence: The Mythology of the American Frontier, 1600–1860*. Middletown, Conn.: Wesleyan Univ. Press, 1973.

Smith, Henry Nash. *Virgin Land: The American West as Symbol and Myth*. Cambridge: Harvard Univ. Press, 1950.

Smith, Olivia. *The Politics of Language: 1791–1819*. New York: Oxford Univ. Press, 1986.

Stampp, Kenneth M. *And the War Came: The North and the Secession Crisis: 1860–1861*. Baton Rouge: Louisiana State Univ. Press, 1950.

Stanton, William. *The Leopard's Spots: Scientific Attitudes Toward Race in America, 1815–1859*. Chicago: Univ. of Chicago Press, 1960.

Stoever, William K. B. *"A Faire and Easie Way to Heaven": Covenant Theology and Antinomianism in Early Massachusetts*. Middletown, Conn.: Wesleyan Univ. Press, 1978.

Sumner, Charles. *Charles Sumner: His Complete Works*. New York: Negro Universities Press, 1969.

———. *The Landmark of Freedom: Speech of Hon. Charles Sumner, Against the Repeal of the Missouri Prohibition of Slavery*. Boston: J. P. Jewett and Co., 1854.

Sundquist, Eric. *Faulkner: The House Divided*. Baltimore: John Hopkins Univ. Press, 1983.

———. "Slavery, Revolution, and the American Renaissance." In Walter Benn Michaels and Donald E. Pease, eds., *The American Renaissance Reconsidered*. Baltimore: John Hopkins Univ. Press, 1985. 1–33.

Sweet, Timothy. *Traces of War: Poetry, Photography, and the Crisis of the Union*. Baltimore: Johns Hopkins Univ. Press, 1990.

Tannenbaum, Leslie. *Biblical Tradition in Blake's Early Prophecies*. Princeton: Princeton Univ. Press, 1982.

Thomas, Brook. *Cross-Examinations of Law and Literature: Cooper, Hawthorne, Stowe, and Melville*. New York: Columbia Univ. Press, 1987.

Thompson, E. P. *The Making of the English Working Class*. New York: Vintage Books, 1966.

Walters, Ronald. *The Antislavery Appeal: American Abolitionism After 1830*. New York: W. W. Norton, 1984.

Warner, Michael. *The Letters of the Republic: Publication and the Public Sphere in Eighteenth-Century America*. Cambridge: Harvard Univ. Press, 1990.

Wasserman, Earl. *Shelley: A Critical Reading*. Baltimore: Johns Hopkins Univ. Press, 1971.

Webster, Daniel. "Rev. of *Account of the Battle of Bunker Hill*, by Henry Dearborn." *North American Review* 20 (July 1818): 225–58.

———. *The Works of Daniel Webster*. Boston: Charles C. Little and James Brown, 1851.

Webster, Noah. "Government: The Practice of Instructing Representatives Absurd and Contrary to the True Principles of Liberty." *American Magazine* 1 (1787–88): 132–47.

———. "On the Supposed Change in the Temperature of Winter." In *A Collection of Papers on Political, Literary and Moral Subjects*. New York: Burt Franklin, 1968. 118–62.

———. *Selected Works of Noah Webster*. Boston: Little, Brown, 1824.

West, Cornel. *The American Evasion of Philosophy: A Genealogy of Pragmatism*. Madison: Univ. of Wisconsin Press, 1989.

Whicher, Stephen E. *Freedom and Fate: An Inner Life*. Philadelphia: Univ. of Pennsylvania Press, 1971.

White, Morton. *The Philosophy of the American Revolution*. New York: Oxford Univ. Press, 1978.

Whitman, Walt. *Complete Poetry and Collected Prose*. Ed. Justin Kaplan. New York: Library of America, 1982.

Whittier, John Greenleaf. *Legends of New England*. Gainesville, Fla.: Scholars' Facsimiles and Reprints, 1965.

Wigglesworth, Michael. *The Day of Doom*. In Harrison T. Messerole, ed., *Seventeenth-Century American Poetry*. New York: New York Univ. Press, 1968. 46–56.

———. "God's Controversy with New-England." In Jane Donahue Eberwein. ed., *Early American Poetry*. Madison: Univ. of Wisconsin Press, 1978.

Williams, George Washington. *A History of the Negro Troops in the War of the Rebellion: 1861–65*. New York: Bergman Publishers, 1968. Orig. pub. 1888.

Wood, Gordon S. *The Creation of the American Republic, 1776–1787*. Chapel Hill: Univ. of North Carolina Press, 1969.

———. *Representation in the American Revolution*. Charlottesville: Univ. Press of Virginia, 1969.

Wordsworth, William. *The Poetical Works of William Wordsworth*. Ed. E. de Selincourt. 5 vols. Oxford: Oxford Univ. Press, 1952.

Wright, Benjamin Fletcher, Jr. *American Interpretations of Natural Law: A Study in the History of Political Thought*. New York: Russell and Russell, Inc., 1962.

Wright, Conrad. *The Liberal Christians: Essays on American Unitarian History*. Boston: Beacon, 1970.

❧ Index

In this index an "f" after a number indicates a separate reference on the next page, and an "ff" indicates separate references on the next two pages. A continuous discussion over two or more pages is indicated by a span of page numbers, e.g., "57–59." *Passim* is used for a cluster of references in close but not consecutive sequence.

Library of Congress Cataloging-in-Publication Data

Cadava, Eduardo.
    Emerson and the climates of history / Eduardo Cadava.
      p.   cm.
    Includes bibliographical references.
    ISBN 0-8047-2813-5 (cloth : alk. paper). — ISBN 0-8047-2814-3
(pbk. : alk. paper)
    1. Emerson, Ralph Waldo, 1803–1882 — Knowledge — History.
    2. Literature and history — United States — History — 19th century.
    3. Emerson, Ralph Waldo, 1803–1882 — Political and social views.
    4. Politics and literature — United States — History — 19th century.
I. Title.
PS1642.H5C33   1997
814'.3 — dc20   96-31974
                                                         CIP

♾ This book is printed on acid-free paper
Original printing 1997
Last figure below indicates year of this printing
06 05 04 03 02 01 00 99 98 97

1015